Taxcafe.co.uk Tax Guides

# Using a Property Company to Save Tax

## By Carl Bayley BSc ACA

# Important Legal Notices:

Taxcafe®
TAX GUIDE - 'Using a Property Company to Save Tax'

**Published by:**
Taxcafe UK Limited
67 Milton Road
Kirkcaldy
KY1 1TL
Tel: (01592) 560081
Email address: team@taxcafe.co.uk

Thirteenth Edition, May 2017
ISBN 978-1-911020-18-9

**Disclaimer**
Before reading or relying on the content of this Tax Guide please read the disclaimer.

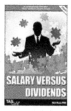

# Disclaimer

1. Please note that this publication is intended as **general guidance** only and does NOT constitute accountancy, tax, financial or other professional advice. The author and Taxcafe UK Limited make no representations or warranties with respect to the accuracy or completeness of the contents of this publication and cannot accept any responsibility for any liability, loss or risk, personal or otherwise, which may arise, directly or indirectly, from reliance on information contained in this publication.

2. Please note that tax legislation, the law and practices of government and regulatory authorities (e.g. HM Revenue and Customs) are constantly changing. Furthermore, your personal circumstances may vary from the general information contained in this tax guide which may not be suitable for your situation. We therefore recommend that for accountancy, tax, financial or other professional advice, you consult a suitably qualified accountant, tax specialist, independent financial adviser, or other professional adviser who will be able to provide specific advice based on your personal circumstances.

3. This guide covers UK taxation only and any references to 'tax' or 'taxation', unless the contrary is expressly stated, refer to UK taxation only. Please note that references to the 'UK' do not include the Channel Islands or the Isle of Man. Foreign tax implications are beyond the scope of this guide.

4. Whilst in an effort to be helpful this tax guide may refer to general guidance on matters other than UK taxation, Taxcafe UK Limited and the author are not expert in these matters and do not accept any responsibility or liability for loss which may arise from reliance on such information contained in this guide.

5. Please note that Taxcafe UK Limited has relied wholly on the expertise of the author in the preparation of the content of this tax guide. The author is not an employee of Taxcafe UK Limited but has been selected by Taxcafe UK Limited using reasonable care and skill.

6. The views expressed in this publication are the author's own personal views and do not necessarily reflect the views of any organisation which he may represent.

## About the Author

Carl Bayley is the author of a series of 'Plain English' tax guides designed specifically for the layman and the non-specialist. Carl's particular speciality is his ability to take the weird, complex and inexplicable world of taxation and set it out in the kind of clear, straightforward language that taxpayers themselves can understand. As he often says himself, "my job is to translate 'tax' into English".

Carl enjoys his role as a tax author, as he explains: "Writing these guides gives me the opportunity to use the skills and knowledge learned over more than thirty years in the tax profession for the benefit of a wider audience. The most satisfying part of my success as an author is the chance to give the average person the same standard of advice as the 'big guys' at a price which everyone can afford."

Carl takes the same approach when speaking on taxation, a role he frequently undertakes with great enthusiasm, including his highly acclaimed annual 'Budget Breakfast' for the Institute of Chartered Accountants.

In addition to being a recognised author and speaker on the subject, Carl has often spoken on property taxation on radio and television, including the BBC's 'It's Your Money' programme and BBC Radio 2's Jeremy Vine Show.

Carl began his career as a Chartered Accountant in 1983 with one of the 'Big 4' accountancy firms. After qualifying as a double prize-winner, he immediately began specialising in taxation.

Having honed his skills with several major international firms, Carl began the new millennium by launching his own tax and accounting practice, Bayley Miller Limited, through which he provides advice on a wide variety of taxation issues; especially property taxation and tax planning for small and medium-sized businesses.

Carl is the Chairman of the Tax Faculty at the Institute of Chartered Accountants in England and Wales, a member of the Institute's governing Council, and a former President of ICAEW Scotland. He has co-organised the annual Practical Tax Conference for the last 15 years.

When he isn't working, Carl takes on the equally taxing challenges of hill walking and creative writing – his Munro tally is now 98 and he has just completed his first novel.

Carl lives in the Scottish Borders and has four children.

# Dedication

## *For the Past,*

Firstly, I dedicate this book to the memory of those I have loved and lost:

First of all, to my beloved mother Diana – what would you think if you could see me now? The memory of your love warms me still. Thank you for bringing me into the light and making it all possible;

To my dear grandfather, Arthur - your wise words still come back to guide me; and to my loving grandmothers, Doris and Winifred;

Between you, you left me with nothing I could spend, but everything I need.

Also to my beloved friends: Mac, William, Edward, Rusty, Dawson, and the grand old lady, Morgan. Thank you for all those happy miles; I still miss you all.

## *For the Future,*

I also dedicate this book to some very special young people:

Robert – the 'chip off the old block', who is both cursed and blessed to have inherited a lot of my own character; luckily for him, there is a lot of his mother in him too!

James – the intellectual of the family, a true twenty-first century gentleman and one of the nicest guys I have ever met;

And lastly, and furthest from least:

Michelle – my truly wonderful daughter, I told her when she was just sixteen that she was one of the most interesting people I had ever met: since then she has grown more interesting, and more amazing, with every passing year!

I am so very proud of every one of you and I can only hope that I, in turn, will also be able to leave each of you with everything you need.

# Thanks

First and foremost, I must say an enormous thank you to Isabel: for all her help researching everything from obscure points of tax legislation to popular girls' names in Asia; for reading countless drafts; and, most of all, for putting up with me when I'm under pressure. She is truly the other half of 'Carl Bayley Author and Presenter'. I simply cannot ever thank her enough for everything she has done for me!

Thanks to the Taxcafe team, past and present, for their help in making these books far more successful than I could ever have dreamed.

I would like to thank my old friend and mentor, Peter Rayney, for his inspiration and for showing me that tax and humour can mix.

Thanks to Rebecca, Paul and David for taking me into the 'fold' at the Tax Faculty and for their fantastic support at our Peebles conference over many years.

Thanks are also due to Gregor for giving me a chance to see theory put into practice.

And last, but far from least, thanks to Nick for giving me the push!

**C.B., Roxburghshire, May 2017**

# Contents

# Contents cont...

# Contents cont...

# Contents cont...

# Contents cont...

# Contents cont...

# Foreword

*By the author*

People in the UK have invested in property for centuries. Substantial increases in personal wealth and disposable income over the last few decades, together with problems in other areas of investment and in the pensions industry, have, however, combined to make this an important new area of personal financial planning.

Despite recent economic difficulties in the UK and elsewhere, I personally believe that the property investment sector as we know it today is here to stay. Naturally, the sector will have its ups and downs, as any other sector does, but the philosophy of property investment as a 'career move', or a 'pension plan', is now so well entrenched that it is impossible to imagine that it could ever disappear altogether.

In 2002, in response to the huge demand for advice on property taxation issues which we had been experiencing at Taxcafe.co.uk, we published the first edition of *How to Save Property Tax*, the sister publication to this guide. In the following years, the demand for property taxation advice continued to grow at a phenomenal pace and this is responsible for the fact that our first guide is now in its twentieth edition and this guide is in its thirteenth.

But it isn't just the **quantity** of advice being demanded that we have seen increase, it is also the level or, if you like, the **quality** of advice being demanded that we have seen increase significantly.

We have also seen a huge broadening in the type of activities undertaken by the typical property 'investor', many of whom will now, at least partly, be classed as property developers, dealers or managers. This guide, along with its sister publication, has evolved in line with our readership and now caters for the whole range of property businesses which our readers undertake.

As I have already suggested above, a strong trend has emerged for people to enter the property investment business as a profession or as a means to save for retirement.

This 'new breed' of property investor is entering the market with a much higher degree of sophistication and is prepared to devote substantial time and resources to the business.

Almost every one of these 'professional investors' asks me the same question: "Should I use a company?" Very often, they are hoping for a nice, simple, single-word answer and, being the helpful chap that I am, I give them one: "Maybe!"

1

Being an accountant, you may think that my slightly evasive response is merely a ploy to enable me to earn more fees from consultancy work. However, you would be quite wrong, as "maybe" is the only answer I could possibly give. This question is not an easy one to answer. There are a huge number of factors to be taken into account, not all of which relate to taxation, and it is therefore impossible (not to mention inadvisable) to simply give a straightforward "yes" or "no" answer. (And, in any case, I have plenty of consultancy work already, thank you!)

The first aim of this guide, though, *is* to answer that question, not in a single word, but in the many thousands of words which, in reality, the answer to this highly complex question actually requires. So, to provide you with a truly thorough answer to this crucial question, we will begin, in Chapters 1 and 2, by looking at the basic tax (and non-tax) implications of using a company.

The UK tax regime for companies is quite different from that applying to individuals, or indeed to partnerships, trusts or other potential investment vehicles. The company tax regime has quite a few quirks, which can prove to be costly traps for the unwary. It is therefore extremely important that any property investor considering the company route understands what they are getting themselves into!

In Chapters 3 to 10, we will move on to a more detailed look at the taxation of UK property companies. Here we will discover that there are several different types of property company and that each gives rise to a different set of tax implications which need to be considered carefully by the prospective corporate property investor.

Chapter 11 then provides a summarised comparison of the tax position of companies and individuals.

Following that, in Chapter 12, we will take a detailed look at all the factors involved in making the decision whether to use a company and their implications for the property investor. This is illustrated throughout by several examples designed to highlight the key issues.

In Chapter 13 we will begin to apply what we have learned so far by focussing on one of the most important benefits of using a property company: interest relief.

As most readers will know, individual residential property investors are now subject to restrictions on the rate of relief available for their interest and finance costs. These restrictions are covered in detail in the Taxcafe.co.uk guides *'How to Save Property Tax'* and *'Landlord Interest'*, although we will also take a brief look at them in Chapter 13 of this guide.

Companies are not subject to these new restrictions: providing a major benefit to investors running a residential property letting business through a company. (A separate set of restrictions do apply to companies: but these only apply to annual interest costs in excess of £2m.)

Furthermore, on top of this, individual landlords can only set interest and finance costs against their rental income: often leading to rental losses or surplus unrelieved interest which can generally only be carried forward and cannot usually be set off against other income or even capital gains on the same property.

A further benefit for a property investor using a company is the ability to set interest on funds borrowed for a company's property investments against other income or capital gains within the company or even the investor's own salary or other income.

In Chapter 13 we will see the difference that this different treatment of interest costs can make to a property investor over many years as the economic cycle produces both short-term losses and long-term gains.


## Reaching a Conclusion

In the end, only **you** can really decide whether a property company is appropriate for you - by undertaking a detailed examination of your own individual position and weighing up all of the factors involved.

My aim in this guide is to enable you to reach that unique individual conclusion and make a well-informed decision armed with a strong understanding of the many issues involved.

Whether you're one of those 'professional investors' whom I referred to earlier, or one of the many 'gifted amateurs' whom I also frequently meet; whether you see your property business as your pension plan or just a good way to supplement your income; whether you're developing, dealing, managing or just renting out your properties; whether you've always had a master plan or you stumbled into property investment by accident; in fact, whatever your circumstances may be, this guide will help you understand the questions you need to ask yourself before you can make a truly informed decision whether to use a property company or not.

And you may also find that "yes" or "no" are not the only answers to the property company question that you come up with. Many of my clients, with my guidance, decide that the answer for them is "partly" or "later".

There is absolutely nothing to stop an investor from running two property businesses in parallel – one as an individual and one through a company. Many investors also find that the best route for them is to start with a small property business owned personally and then to start up a second property business in a company later on.

## Operating Your Property Company

Once you've made the decision to operate some or all of your property business through a company, whether with the help of this guide or not, you will then want to run your company in the most beneficial way possible.

The second function of this guide is therefore to provide the tax-planning advice and the warnings of potential pitfalls that you will need to know in order to minimise your tax burden as a property company owner.

Hence, as well as providing the overall summary of the property company tax regime in the early chapters of this guide, many more potential planning opportunities and possible pitfalls are covered in Chapters 14 to 16.

Chapter 17 then introduces some more specialised property company structures before lastly, in Chapter 18, at the end of the guide, our detailed findings are neatly summarised, giving you a final opportunity to weigh the whole thing up.

## Tips and Warnings

Sprinkled throughout this guide, you will also find many **'Tax Tips'** and **'Wealth Warnings'** designed to highlight key points where there are extra savings to be made or traps to catch the unwary! Watch out for both of these as you read the guide.

## Predicting the Future

In order to reinforce the issues discussed in this guide, I will demonstrate the tax implications of corporate property investment through the use of several worked examples.

In my examples, I have naturally had to make various assumptions about external factors beyond the control of the property investor, including:

- The growth of property values
- The future rate of inflation
- Interest rates
- The rates of return on property investment (i.e. market rental levels)
- Future changes to the UK tax system

I have made my assumptions as reasonable as possible, based on my experience of the property investment sector and the UK taxation regime.

However, if I can predict one thing with any certainty it is that the future will not be exactly as any of us may predict. Hence, whilst I believe that the conclusions I have been able to draw in this guide are validly based on sound principles, the reader must nevertheless bear in mind that those conclusions are, to some extent, dependent on uncertain predictions about the future.

In preparing the examples in this guide, I have assumed that the UK tax regime will remain unchanged in the future except to the extent of any announcements already made at the time of publication and some minor changes to personal tax bands, exemptions and allowances (as explained in Section 11.2).

The personal tax rates and allowances for 2017/18 are included in Appendix A. Estimated rates and allowances for 2018/19 are included in the same appendix. For later years, please remember that all of my assumptions are made simply for illustrative purposes and are only my 'best guess'; so some variation from my figures can be expected. The further we look into the future, the greater that variation is likely to be.

In reality, we are bound to see more significant changes to the UK tax system at some point in the future, especially following any change of Government. Whilst we have no idea when such changes will take place, they will almost certainly occur within the timescale that most long-term property investors are considering.

In Section 18.2, at the end of the guide, I have therefore attempted to analyse the potential impact of any further changes to small company taxation that we may see over the next few years.

Nevertheless, despite the ever-present possibility of changes to the tax regime, I remain firmly of the opinion that there will always still be a great many property investors for whom the use of a company vehicle to hold their investments will continue to be highly beneficial.

As with any other tax planning, my advice is this:

Hope for the best,
Plan for the worst,
Review your position constantly, and
Expect the unexpected!

**About the Examples**

In addition to the points made above regarding the future of the UK tax regime, please note that, unless specifically stated to the contrary, all persons described in the examples in this guide are:

i)   UK resident and domiciled for tax purposes
ii)  Not subject to the High Income Child Benefit Charge
iii) Not Scottish taxpayers (and will thus pay Income Tax at normal UK rates)

See Section 16.9 regarding the rates applying to Scottish taxpayers from 2017/18 onwards and the impact this has on the issues discussed in this guide.

All persons described in the examples in this guide are entirely fictional characters created specifically for the purposes of this guide. Any similarities to actual persons, living or dead, or to fictional characters created by any other author, are entirely coincidental.

Likewise, the companies described in the examples in this guide are similarly fictional corporations created specifically for the purposes of this guide and any similarities to actual companies, past or present, are again entirely coincidental.

**Scope of this Guide**

This guide is aimed primarily at UK resident property investors considering or using a UK resident company to run their property business (although issues facing non-resident investors or non-resident companies are covered briefly in Section 16.6).

The reader must bear in mind the general nature of this guide. Individual circumstances vary and the tax implications of an individual's actions will vary with them. For this reason, it is always vital to get professional advice before undertaking any tax planning or other transactions that may have tax implications. The author and Taxcafe UK Ltd cannot accept any responsibility for any loss that may arise as a consequence of any action taken, or any decision to refrain from action taken, as a result of reading this guide.

**Married Couples & Registered Civil Partnerships**

Throughout this guide, you will see me refer many times to 'married couples', spouses, or husbands and wives.

In each case, the tax treatment being outlined applies equally to:

- Married couples of opposite sexes,
- Married couples of the same sex, and
- Registered civil partners

Hence, any references to 'married couples' throughout this guide should be taken to also include registered civil partnerships; any reference to the taxpayer's 'spouse' will also include their civil partner where relevant; and any reference to 'husbands' or 'wives' will include spouses of the same gender and civil partners.

However, it remains important to remember that, unless specified to the contrary, the tax treatment being outlined applies to legally married couples and legally registered civil partners only. Unmarried couples are subject to entirely different rules.

Remember also that marriage, or civil partnership, is not always advantageous for tax purposes. It really is a case of 'for better or worse'!

**Abbreviations**

Generally, at Taxcafe, we don't like using abbreviations or jargon because we want to keep our guides as simple as possible. To save some space in this guide, however, we have allowed ourselves a few abbreviations. We think they are fairly obvious ones, so they should not cause any confusion. We will explain what each abbreviation means the first time we use it and they are also set out again in Appendix H for your ease of reference.

Large numbers, such as £1,000,000 or more, are also abbreviated by use of the letter 'm'. For example:

£2,500,000 will be written as £2.5m

**The Last Word**

Finally, to close this foreword, may I just say that whatever type of property investor you are, and whatever decision you reach about the possible benefits of using a company, I would like to thank you for reading this guide and wish you every success with your investments.

# Chapter 1

# Why Use a Company?

## 1.1    INTRODUCTION

Many UK property investors are drawn towards the idea of holding their property investments through a limited company. Why is this?

Unlike most other types of business, it does not generally appear to be due to the protection afforded by a company's limited liability status.

No, this decision appears to be almost entirely tax-driven and is a direct result of the comparatively favourable Corporation Tax ('CT') regime.

In 2010, the Coalition (later Conservative) Chancellor, George Osborne, announced a series of reductions in CT rates. These were later improved upon with further reductions announced in subsequent Budgets. We will take a detailed look at Osborne's CT reductions in Section 2.5, but the main point to note is that the current rate is just 19%.

Whilst CT rates have fallen over the last few years, Governments of all persuasions have put in place a series of personal taxation increases for individuals, including:

- Unprecedented restrictions on interest relief for residential landlords
- Reducing the basic rate tax band for five years in succession from 2010/11 to 2015/16: thus pushing a great many more people into the higher rate Income Tax bracket (for English, Welsh and Northern Irish taxpayers, the higher rate tax threshold only finally clawed its way back above its 2009/10 level after eight years, in April 2017; for Scottish taxpayers, it still hasn't!)
- Introducing the High Income Child Benefit Charge to claw back Child Benefit claimed by households where any individual has income over £50,000
- Withdrawing personal allowances from individuals with income over £100,000
- Introducing the 'additional rate' on income over £150,000
- Increasing all of the main National Insurance ('NI') rates (which was set to get even worse before Philip Hammond was forced into an embarrassing U-turn in March 2017)

- Increasing the Capital Gains Tax ('CGT') rate to 28% for higher rate taxpayers (later reduced to 20%: but **not** for residential property!)

Hence, with CT rates falling and personal tax rates looking set to remain high for the foreseeable future, the apparent attraction of running any type of business through a company has been significantly increased.

For property investors, the relatively beneficial CT regime looks extremely tempting. With CT rates considerably lower than higher rate Income Tax at 40% or additional rate tax at 45%, many investors feel that using a company must surely be the easiest way to save tax on their investments.

Furthermore, the more beneficial interest relief regime enjoyed by investors using a property investment company (see Chapter 13) is often also an important factor.

With lower tax on profits and better relief for both interest and losses; using a property company does initially seem pretty attractive.

But is it really that simple? Clearly, the fact that we have published a whole guide dedicated to this question indicates that it is not!

Yes, at first glance, the CT rates do look very attractive compared with higher or additional rate Income Tax. However, as we shall see, basing the decision to use a company on this one factor alone would be extremely short-sighted.

As we proceed to examine this issue in greater depth, we will see that the CT benefits will not always be as great as they may, at first, appear to be. The advantage gained through the lower CT rate is reduced or sometimes even eliminated by the problems surrounding the extraction of profits from the company.

Furthermore, with the wide range of CGT reliefs available to individual property investors, there is sometimes a danger that the long-term position, taking capital growth and the eventual disposal of investment properties into account, may be significantly and detrimentally affected by the use of a company.

Nevertheless, despite these drawbacks, there are still some situations where using a company can prove advantageous to the long-term property investor acquiring a portfolio of properties over time. Where the property portfolio is effectively regarded as a 'pension plan', for example, there may be substantial long-term benefits to be derived from using a company as an investment vehicle.

Furthermore, for those involved in property development, dealing or management, the way that these businesses are treated for Income Tax and NI purposes means that a company can be even more attractive in these cases.

## 1.2    NON-TAX REASONS FOR USING A COMPANY

Before we go on to examine all of the taxation considerations behind the use of a company for property businesses, it is first worth having a brief look at some of the non-taxation factors involved.

There are many non-taxation issues involved in the decision whether to use a company or not. Some of these are covered briefly below, although this list is far from exhaustive.

### Limited Liability Protection

Although this does not appear to be the major reason behind most property investors' decision to incorporate, it is still, nevertheless, a factor to be considered. A company is a separate legal entity and, as such, is responsible for its own debts and other liabilities.

The usefulness of this, however, is often limited. Banks will often insist on personal guarantees from the directors or shareholders before they will lend money to the company.

Furthermore, modern insolvency law passes a large part of the company's financial responsibilities to its directors, who may find themselves personally liable where the company has been used in an attempt to avoid the payment of liabilities arising in the normal course of its business.

Nevertheless, limited liability is useful when the business faces unexpected losses or legal liabilities. This can be particularly important when the economy takes a turn for the worse!

Note that limited liability status can also be obtained by using a Limited Liability Partnership ('LLP'). For property investors, however, LLPs suffer the major drawback that interest relief is not available for funds invested in an LLP engaged in property investment.

## Status

A business that is run through a company is generally perceived as having greater status than a business owned by an individual. For some reason, most people think that 'John Smith Investments Limited' sounds a lot more reliable than plain 'John Smith'.

This perception is, of course, complete rubbish, as is evidenced by the many corporate collapses we have seen.

Nevertheless, the perception of companies as steady and reliable still remains and corporate property investors may find that they can use this to their advantage.

## Flexibility of Ownership

Without the use of a company, it is difficult to involve many other people in the ownership of your property business. Joint ownership with your spouse or partner is easy enough to achieve, but later, as the business hopefully grows, you may wish to involve adult children or key employees.

It is far easier to spread small parcels of ownership of the business through the medium of company shares.

## Separation of Ownership and Management

A company structure will also enable you to separate ownership and management. As your business grows and the years go by, you may eventually wish either to retire or to move on to other ventures. However, you may still have a highly profitable business that you do not yet wish to sell.

Using a company will enable you to retain ownership (as a shareholder) while passing management responsibility on to others (the directors). A company structure also enables this business succession process to take place at a more controlled and steady pace.

**Tax Tip**

Taking the succession planning idea a step further, a company is often a good vehicle for passing wealth on to your children (or other intended beneficiaries).

The problem with a property investment or letting business is that it does not qualify for business property relief for Inheritance Tax ('IHT') purposes. Hence, on the owner's death, the whole portfolio is exposed to IHT.

What a company can provide in this situation is a means to allow the owner to pass on small parcels of ownership over a number of years, thus making use of the CGT and IHT annual exemptions and avoiding both taxes.

A sophisticated share structure may also enable you to keep control of your company while passing on a significant proportion of the underlying value to your children.


**Finance**

Many investors wishing to hold properties through the medium of a company find it difficult to obtain the level of finance that they require. This problem seems to most affect those who are just starting their property business, or who only have one or two existing investment properties.

A 'Deed of Trust' arrangement can often be used to get around this problem. We will look at how this type of arrangement works in Section 13.6.

Conversely, for the larger portfolio, corporate status seems to become a positive factor in the eyes of many lenders, probably for the reasons explained under 'Status' above.

Additionally, where the investor is non-UK resident, but looking to invest in the UK property market, the UK's lending institutions have been known to favour the use of a UK-registered company, as this gives the investor a presence in the UK.

## Legal Rights

If you run your business through a company, you personally will no longer own property. Instead, you will own company shares. Legally, these are an entirely different kind of asset, giving rise to different legal rights.

What kind of difference this will make to your affairs will depend on your personal circumstances, as well as in what part of the UK (or other country) you and your properties are located.

As I am not a lawyer, I will not attempt to advise property investors on these issues, but the advice I **will** give is that you should get legal advice on the implications of owning your properties through a company.

## Company Law

If you use a UK-registered company, you will be subject to the requirements of UK company law. This, for example, may restrict your ability to utilise funds from your business for private purposes.

## Audit and Other Statutory Requirements

Larger companies require a statutory annual audit of their accounts. Even the smallest companies must file annual accounts, an annual return and certain other documentation with Companies House.

We will take a closer look at these statutory requirements in Chapter 14.

## Costs

Inevitably, the additional statutory requirements involved in running a company will lead to increases in accountancy and other professional costs. These additional costs must be weighed against the tax and other benefits that incorporation brings.

## Time

Running a company will take up more of your time. There is more bureaucracy, more paperwork and more administration to think about. Whatever you do, there are only 24 hours in a day, so the time eaten up by bureaucracy means less time to concentrate on your investments.

Hence, you have to ask yourself if the financial savings that the company brings are sufficient to compensate you for the time that the company takes up.

It's a question of how you value your time. If the company is saving you a large amount of money then obviously it is worth investing your time. But, in borderline cases, this could actually be the factor that decides against the company. Naturally, if the company saves you enough money, it will be worth employing someone else to do all that tedious paperwork. Then you can save money and time!

## 1.3    OVERVIEW OF COMPANY TAX PROS AND CONS

We now turn to the tax implications of running a property business through a company. As a broad overview, in general terms, it is reasonable to say that:

**A company often produces a better taxation result on <u>income</u> BUT**
**Personal ownership can sometimes produce a better result on <u>capital</u> growth**

To illustrate this further, let's take a look at some of the taxation pros and cons of investing through a limited company.

### Using a Company: The Pros

- From 1st April 2017, almost all UK companies pay CT at just 19% on any level of annual profits

- From 1st April 2020, the CT rate will fall to just 17%

- Companies are not subject to the horrendous new restrictions on relief for interest and finance costs relating to residential lettings which apply to individuals and partnerships from 6th April 2017. (Some restrictions do apply to interest relief for companies: but only to amounts in excess of £2m per year)

- Companies still get indexation relief for capital gains purposes. This exempts the portion of any capital gain that arises purely due to inflation

- The same CT rates that apply to income also apply to capital gains made by companies. Hence, most companies will now pay tax at just 19% on their capital gains (17% from 2020)

- Stamp Duty is payable at a rate of only 0.5% on the purchase of company shares

- You may choose any year-end accounting date for your company that you wish (an individual's property letting business is taxed on a tax year basis)

- Company shares may be passed on in small quantities at regular intervals, thus utilising the donor's CGT and IHT annual exemptions

- A company may claim relief for interest and finance costs incurred for property investment purposes against any income or capital gains arising in the same period or, in many cases, against any income or capital gains of future periods. (But see Section 4.7 regarding furnished holiday lettings)

- A company may also claim relief for other losses arising from a UK property letting business (excluding interest and finance costs) against any other income or capital gains which it has for the same period or, in most cases, a later one. (Note, however, that this does not apply to losses on furnished holiday lettings)

- A company is not subject to the limits on relief for trading losses which apply to individuals (see Section 13.9). Some limits do apply: but only to amounts in excess of £5m

- An investor may claim relief for interest costs on funds borrowed to invest in a property company against any other income, including salary, self-employment income or their own personal rental income. (Although this relief is subject to some limitations – see Section 13.9 for details)

- Only companies are eligible for up to 150% tax relief for the costs of cleaning up and preparing contaminated land for development

- Companies will not be subject to mandatory digital record keeping and quarterly reporting (under the 'Making Tax Digital', or 'MTD', proposals) until 1st April 2020

## Using a Company: The Cons

- Companies do not get a personal allowance

- Companies do not get an annual exemption for capital gains purposes

- Companies are not eligible for entrepreneurs' relief for capital gains purposes. (Individuals may claim entrepreneurs' relief on qualifying business disposals, reducing the rate of CGT to just 10% on up to £10m of capital gains. This relief will seldom apply to property investors, however, except in the case of furnished holiday lettings)

- Any personal use of properties owned by the company by the investor or their family may have severe tax consequences. This should be contrasted with the CGT benefits of personal use when investing in property directly

- Personal tax liabilities will usually arise when extracting trading or rental profits or property sale proceeds from the company

- It can sometimes be more difficult to obtain relief for certain administrative expenses, such as 'use of home as office' and motor expenses, when investing via a company

- The Stamp Duty exemption for lower value company share purchases only applies to purchase consideration not exceeding £1,000 (compared with the Stamp Duty Land Tax ('SDLT') exemption for property purchases under £40,000)

- Companies cannot have a principal private residence, and hence are unable to claim the principal private residence exemption, private letting relief, or rent-a-room relief

- UK resident companies may face an 'exit charge' on emigration

- Companies are not eligible to calculate taxable profits on a 'cash basis'

- Many other personal tax planning techniques, such as investing in Enterprise Investment Scheme shares, are simply not available to companies

When it comes to the important issue of capital gains, we can readily see that there are more cons than pros here. This, however, is set off by the fact that companies are still entitled to indexation relief and will pay tax at just 17% on most capital gains in the future (after April 2020).

Furthermore, the benefits of the lower CT rates are highly significant, especially when combined with the more generous regime for relieving interest costs and other rental losses when using a company. As we shall see later in the guide, these benefits will sometimes be large enough to ensure that the company route does remain preferable overall.

The biggest 'con', however, is the potential additional tax arising when rental profits or property sales proceeds are extracted from the company. What this, and all the other 'cons' set out above, mean is that using a company is an extremely complex decision requiring some very careful consideration.

# Chapter 2

# A Plain English Guide to Corporation Tax

## 2.1　WHAT TAXES DO COMPANIES PAY?

In this chapter, we will take a detailed look at how CT is calculated: sticking, as far as possible, to plain English!

First, however, it is worth summarising the different taxes that companies pay.

### Income and Capital Gains

A UK resident company pays CT on its total profits, made up of its worldwide income, profits and capital gains. It does not pay Income Tax, nor will it usually have to pay CGT (but see Section 16.7 for details of some important exceptions).

Occasionally, a company may suffer a deduction of Income Tax at source on part of its income, but this can be deducted from its CT liability for the same period.

### Stamp Duty and Stamp Duty Land Tax

Companies generally pay Stamp Duty and SDLT on their purchases at exactly the same rates as an individual does; with the exception of some purchases of residential property for a consideration in excess of £500,000. These taxes are covered further in Chapter 8.

### Inheritance Tax

Companies are only liable for IHT in the most exceptional of circumstances and, even then, the tax only arises as a result of external factors involving the company's shareholders.

A company does not die, so IHT does not arise. Instead, companies are wound up and we will come to the implications of this later in the guide.

None of this, however, alters the fact that, when a shareholder dies, the value of his or her property company shares must be taken into account as part of their estate for IHT purposes.

## VAT

Broadly speaking, a company is liable for VAT in the same way as an individual. This subject is covered in detail in Chapter 9.

### National Insurance

If you employ anyone to help you in your corporate property business, the company will be liable for secondary Class 1 NI, at the rate of 13.8%, in its capacity as an employer (subject to the £3,000 employment allowance – see Section 10.2).

The company is also liable for Class 1A NI on any benefits in kind provided to employees and Class 1B NI on any voluntary settlements negotiated with HM Revenue and Customs ('HMRC') (e.g. on the cost of sandwiches provided at lunchtime business meetings).

Furthermore, like any other employer, the company has to deduct primary Class 1 NI from its employees' pay and account for this through the PAYE system.

All of this is exactly the same as the situation where you employ someone to help you in your sole trader or partnership business.

The key difference, however, comes from the fact that NI will also be due if you pay yourself a salary out of the company's profits, or provide yourself with any benefits in kind (such as a company car). We will look further at the implications of this in Section 10.2.

Apart from Class 1, Class 1A and Class 1B, however, a company cannot be liable for any other Class of NI.

Unlike a sole trader or partnership, this remains the case regardless of what type of property business you have and there can never be any question of Class 2 or Class 4 NI being payable.

**The Annual Tax on Enveloped Dwellings ('ATED')**

ATED applies to companies and certain other entities owning UK residential properties which are not in 'business use'. Fortunately, the definition of 'business use' includes property letting businesses, so most property investment companies should escape the charge.

Nonetheless, any company owning any individual UK residential property worth in excess of £500,000 may potentially be subject to the charge. Even when the company is exempt from the charge, the exemption must be claimed.

It is therefore essential for property investors using, or considering using, a company to be aware of ATED and we will look at the charge in more detail in Section 16.7.


## 2.2    INTRODUCTION TO CORPORATION TAX

All of a company's income and capital gains for an accounting period are simply added together and then treated as a single total sum of profits chargeable to CT (apart from any amounts subject to CGT, as detailed in Section 16.7).

The starting point for establishing the company's profits is its statutory accounts for the relevant accounting period (see Section 14.6). Further, more detailed, accounts may also need to be prepared where the company has more than one type of income for CT purposes.

Fundamentally, capital gains, rental profits and trading profits within a company are all calculated in much the same way as for individuals.

In the case of rental profits, however, there is a key difference arising due to the treatment of interest and finance costs as general company overheads. We will deal with the implications of this in more detail in Section 4.7.

Further differences arise in the way the income and gains are taxed, the reliefs and exemptions available and the rates of tax applying.

For capital gains, the biggest difference lies in the fact that companies continue to be eligible for indexation relief on their capital assets.

We will return to the differences between the corporate and personal tax regimes again in Chapters 11 to 13, where we will be taking a detailed look at their impact on the property investor.

## Financial Years

CT operates by reference to 'Financial Years'. Just to make life even more confusing than it already undoubtedly is, the Financial Year is slightly different to the tax year ending on 5th April, which applies to income received by individuals.

A Financial Year is the year ending on 31st March in any calendar year but is officially described by reference to the calendar year in which it began. Hence, for example, the 2017 Financial Year is the year commencing on 1st April 2017 and ending on 31st March 2018.

It is important to be aware of this official terminology, as this is what is used on the CT Return.

## Periods Spanning Two Financial Years

Where your company's accounting period does not end on 31st March, it will generally span two Financial Years.

The profits of the accounting period are then split across the two Financial Years on a pro rata basis. For example, a profit of £100,000 for a twelve month accounting period ending on 31st December 2017 would be split as follows:

2016 Financial Year: £100,000 x 90/365 =     £24,658
2017 Financial Year: £100,000 x 275/365 =     £75,342

Where the CT rates applying in both Financial Years are the same, this allocation is completely academic and can effectively be ignored.

However, where there is a change in the CT rate, the allocation will produce a 'hybrid' tax rate. This will be relevant to all companies with accounting periods spanning 1st April 2017. An example is included in Section 2.4.

## 2.3    CORPORATION TAX RATES

Since 1st April 2015, there has been just one CT rate applying to companies of all sizes and all profit levels (except for some companies operating in the oil and gas sector).

The past, current, and proposed future levels of this single CT rate are as follows:

1st April 2015 to 31st March 2017:      20%
1st April 2017 to 31st March 2020:      19%
1st April 2020 onwards:                 17%

Different rates are to apply to companies trading in Northern Ireland at some point in the future. The rate is likely to be 12.5% (to match the rate used in the Irish Republic) but the date of introduction is uncertain. We will look at the potential impact on investors operating in Northern Ireland in Section 16.10.


## 2.4    SPLIT YEAR TREATMENT

The CT rates given in Section 2.3 are fine if your company happens to have a 31st March year end. In other cases, however, we may have to look at the 'split year' treatment. In other words, the company's profits may need to be split across two Financial Years with different CT rates applying in each.

This will apply to all companies with accounting periods spanning 1st April 2017.

Where 'split year' treatment applies, the element of profit falling into each Financial Year is taxed separately using the applicable rates for each of the two relevant Financial Years.


### *Example*

*St Etienne Limited draws up accounts to 30th June each year. For the year ending 30th June 2017, the company's taxable profits are £480,000.*

*The first part of this accounting period, from 1st July 2016 to 31st March 2017, falls into the 2016 Financial Year (i.e. the year ending 31st March 2017). This part of the accounting period is 274 days in duration, so the portion of St Etienne Limited's 2017 taxable profits falling into the 2016 Financial Year is therefore 274/365 x £480,000 = £360,329. This part of the company's profit is subject to CT at 20%.*

*The remaining £119,671 of the company's profit falls into the 2017 Financial Year and is taxed at 19%.*

*St Etienne Limited's CT bill for the year ending 30th June 2017 is therefore as follows:*

| | | |
|---|---|---|
| *2016 Financial Year:* | *£360,329 @ 20% =* | *£72,066* |
| *2017 Financial Year:* | *£119,671 @ 19% =* | *£22,737* |
| *Total:* | | *£94,803* |

*This equates to an overall effective CT rate of just over 19.75%.*

Using similar principles, we can derive the effective CT rates for any accounting period. These work out as detailed in Appendix C. (For rates applying to accounting periods commencing before 1st April 2015, see the previous edition of this guide.)

## 2.5 FUTURE CORPORATION TAX RATES

Before being ousted from office in 2016, former Chancellor George Osborne had suggested that there might be further reductions in the UK CT rate after 2020. Conversely, of course, a future change of Government could lead to increases in CT rates.

At present, however, there are no firm proposals for any further changes beyond April 2020.

Hence, the CT rate of 17% currently proposed for accounting periods commencing after 31st March 2020 remains our best forecast for the long term and we will therefore be basing our calculations on this rate when we come to make our long-term predictions regarding the benefits of a property company later in the guide.

## 2.6 PAYING CORPORATION TAX

For most companies, payment of CT is due in one single lump sum payable within nine months and one day after the end of the accounting period.

For example, the CT for the year ending 31st December 2017 will be due by 1st October 2018.

As usual, interest is charged on late payments. Unlike Income Tax, however, interest on overdue CT is a deductible expense.

Larger companies with annual profits in excess of £1.5m must pay their tax in quarterly instalments. Very large companies or groups with profits in excess of £20m will be subject to even earlier payment dates for accounting periods commencing after 31st March 2019. Such companies will then be required to pay all their CT 'in-year'.

All CT liabilities must now be paid online.

## 2.7    CASHFLOW BENEFITS OF USING A COMPANY

It is worth noting that the timing of a company's CT payment is totally dependent on its accounting year-end date. This is quite different to individuals and partnerships, where tax is always due on the same dates under the Self Assessment system (i.e. instalments on 31st January during the tax year and 31st July following the tax year, with a balancing payment, or repayment, the following 31st January).

For stable and profitable property businesses, there is a huge cashflow advantage to using a company. This is quite independent of any tax savings that might be involved. Let's look at an example by way of explanation:

### *Example*

*Gordon has a thriving property letting business. His Income Tax liability has remained at the same level for a number of years (pretty rare in practice, but this is just an example, after all) and hence he has to pay half his tax on 31st January within the tax year and half on the following 31st July. If we 'averaged out' these two payments, this would be equivalent, for cashflow purposes, to a single payment on 1st May.*

*Remember that, like any other individual with property letting income, Gordon MUST pay tax based on his profits for the year ending 5th April. Hence, on average, he effectively has to pay his tax just **26 days** after the end of his accounting period!*

If we contrast this 26-day 'average' payment period with the nine months and a day available to companies, we can see what a large cashflow advantage the companies have – over eight months!

Wouldn't you rather keep your money for an extra eight months? Think what you could do with it in that time, especially in the rapidly moving property investment sector!

### What if Profit isn't Stable?

The example above is perhaps not entirely typical, as it is based on a stable annual profit. In practice, profits tend to fluctuate, which can sometimes mean that the company cashflow advantage is not quite so great. Nevertheless, in the vast majority of cases, the 'average' payment date for an individual investor (or a partnership) would still fall somewhere within three months of the end of the accounting period, meaning that a company would usually produce at least six months of cashflow advantage.

#### Wealth Warning

Note, however, that if the company is making large enough profits to be under the quarterly instalment system (see Section 2.6 above), its 'average' payment date is actually about a month **before** the end of its accounting period. In this case, the company actually produces a cashflow *disadvantage* (although, by the time profits have reached this kind of level, other considerations are likely to be far more important).

#### Tax Tip

As already explained, a company may choose any accounting year-end date that it wishes, whereas an individual property investor is effectively forced to stick with 5th April (accounts can be drawn up for any period but the tax liability will always be based on profits for the year to 5th April).

In the corporate regime this can sometimes provide scope to delay the tax on profits that do not arise regularly over the year. This is particularly relevant to those letting holiday accommodation or student accommodation.

## *Example*

*Laura lets out a number of student flats through a company, Laura's Lettings Limited. Generally, they are let from October to June, but are often vacant during the summer months. Hence, all of Laura's profit arises during the nine months to June.*

*If the company were to draw up its accounts to 30th June each year, its CT liability would be due on 1st April the following year. Instead of this, however, Laura arranges for Laura's Lettings Limited's accounting year-end to be 30th September. The company's CT is therefore not due until 1st July the following year.*

*This one simple step has given Laura an additional three-month cashflow saving every year!*

## 2.8    COMPANY TAX RETURNS

Companies fall under a Self-Assessment system referred to as Corporation Tax Self Assessment or 'CTSA' for short. Under CTSA, the company is generally required to submit a Tax Return within twelve months of its accounting date.

The CTSA Return document is called a CT600. At four pages, the basic CT600 (Short) Return used by most companies is actually shorter than the Tax Return for individuals.

However, with its CTSA Return, the company is also required to submit:

- Its statutory accounts (small and medium-sized companies who are permitted to file abbreviated accounts with Companies House must nevertheless still submit a full set of accounts to HMRC with their Tax Return)

- A CT computation (i.e. a calculation of the amount of profits and gains chargeable to CT for the accounting period)

- A CT Self-Assessment (i.e. a calculation of the amount of CT due)

These last two items can generally be prepared as a single combined calculation and there is plenty of accountancy software available to produce this.

**Compulsory Online Filing**

Online filing of CT Returns and supporting documentation is now compulsory. Electronic versions of the supporting documents outlined above need to be submitted in 'iXBRL' format.

## 2.9　PENALTIES

Until recently, the penalties arising under the corporate regime were a little stricter than those applying to individual taxpayers. Sadly, the reason this is no longer true is the fact that a harsher penalty regime has now been implemented for individual taxpayers!

New legislation has, in fact, been enacted to create a new penalty regime for all taxpayers – companies and individuals alike. However, whilst the new regime has already been fully implemented for individuals, it has only been partly implemented for companies at present.

The system of penalties for late Tax Returns under CTSA therefore currently remains as follows:

    i)   Returns filed up to three months late incur a penalty of £100
    ii)  Returns filed more than three months late incur a penalty of £200
    iii) The above amounts are generally increased to £500 and £1,000 respectively in the case of a third, or subsequent, late submission
    iv) The company is also liable for a 'tax-geared' penalty of 10% of unpaid tax if it files its return between 18 and 24 months after the end of the accounting period
    v)  The 'Tax-Geared' penalty increases to 20% if the Tax Return is filed more than two years after the end of the relevant period

### Wealth Warning

It is important to note that the flat-rate penalties described under (i) to (iii) above are applied regardless of whether or not the company has any CT liability for the period.

### Changes Ahead

It had been planned that, at some future date, the new penalty regime discussed above would be brought fully into force for CT purposes. However, HMRC has now proposed an alternative 'points based' system instead. As usual, the future remains uncertain!

# Chapter 3

# Different Types of Property Company

## 3.1 INTRODUCTION

In Chapter 2 we looked at the basic mechanics of how a company is taxed in the UK. We will now begin looking in more detail at the UK taxation issues relating specifically to *property* companies.

Whilst it would be possible to come up with a very long list of different 'types' of property companies, I would tend to regard the following four categories as the definitive list as far as UK taxation treatment is concerned:

a) Property investment (or letting) companies
b) Property development companies
c) Property trading (or dealing) companies
d) Property management companies

Before we go on to look at the detailed tax treatment of these different types of property companies, it is perhaps worth spending a little time to explain exactly what these different terms mean in a taxation context.

I should probably also point out at this stage that there is nothing different about the way in which these different types of companies are formed, nor usually in their constitutions (see Section 14.2). No, it is the nature of the property business itself that determines what type of company we are looking at.

It is also important to understand that these different types of property business are not exclusive to companies and that these different categorisations may also be applied to an individual property investor, a partnership, or any other kind of property investment vehicle.

Over the course of the next five chapters, we will examine the CT consequences of having a company which falls into each of the four categories that I have outlined above, as well as the implications for the owner of the company.

SDLT and VAT will then be considered in Chapters 8 and 9 respectively. NI payable by companies was covered in Section 2.1 and will be unaffected by the type of property business involved.

A company can, of course, carry on more than one type of property business, which would result in a mixture of tax treatments. I will spend a little time on the possible consequences of this in Section 3.6.

**Why Does It Matter?**

As we will discover over the next few chapters, the type of property business carried on by the company has only a relatively minor effect on the way in which the company itself is taxed.

The impact on the owner of the company is more significant, however, as there are several important CGT and IHT reliefs which are dependent on the type of property company which you have.

Even more important is the fact that individuals who are not using a company are taxed very differently on different types of property businesses.

This means that the contrast between an individual investor's tax position and a company investor's tax position is significantly affected by the type of property business involved.

Hence, it is absolutely crucial to understand what type of property business you have in order to be able to determine whether a company is appropriate for you.

We will return to take a detailed look at the contrast between individual and company investors with different types of property business in Chapters 11 to 13 when we have finished looking at how the various types of property companies and their owners are taxed.

## 3.2  PROPERTY INVESTMENT COMPANIES (AKA PROPERTY LETTING COMPANIES)

These are companies that predominantly hold properties as long-term investments. The properties are the company's fixed assets, which are held to produce income in the form of rental profit.

Whilst capital growth will be anticipated and will form part of the company's business plan, short-term property disposals should usually only take place where there is a strong commercial reason, such as an anticipated decline in value in that particular geographical location or a need to realise funds for other investments.

### Example

*All Blacks Limited purchases three properties 'off-plan'. On completion of the properties, the company sells one of them in order to provide funds for continued expansion. The other two properties are then rented out for a number of years.*

*Although All Blacks Limited sold one of the properties very quickly, there was a good commercial reason for doing so. Hence, the company may still be regarded as a property investment company.*

In general, therefore, most properties will usually be held for a long period and rapid sales for short-term gain will be exceptional.

Having said that, however, where exceptional opportunities for short-term gains do arise, it would be unreasonable to suggest that the company, like any other investor, should not take advantage of those opportunities.

In some cases, the investors themselves will have a minimal level of involvement in the day-to-day running of the business, but there are also many other property letting businesses which are much more 'hands on'.

As long as the company meets the overall long-term investment criterion outlined above, it remains a property investment company for all tax purposes, regardless of the level of the investor's own personal involvement on a day-to-day basis.

Managing your company's own properties would not, in itself, mean that you had a property management company.

## Tax Treatment

A property investment company is **not** regarded as a trading company for tax purposes. This has some unfortunate consequences for the owner of the company, including:

- The shares in the company are not eligible for entrepreneurs' relief or holdover relief for CGT purposes (see further in Chapter 7)

- The shares in the company are not eligible for business property relief for IHT purposes, meaning that the full value of the company would be included in the investor's estate on his or her death when calculating the IHT due

**Tax Tip**

Furnished holiday lettings (see Section 4.6) enjoy a special status for tax purposes.

While companies whose income is derived predominantly from these lettings continue to be regarded as property investment companies for a number of purposes, shares in such companies will remain eligible for entrepreneurs' relief and holdover relief. Shares in such companies may sometimes also be eligible for business property relief for IHT purposes.

### How Are Property Investment Companies Taxed?

A property investment company must account for its rental profits under the specific rules applying to property income (see Chapter 4).

Interest and finance costs are not treated as part of the company's rental business but are regarded as a general overhead of the company with some very generous rules applying to the way in which these costs are relieved for CT purposes. We will cover those rules in Section 4.7.

Note, however, that different rules apply to interest costs relating to furnished holiday lettings. We will again examine these in Section 4.7.

Property disposals are dealt with as capital gains (see Chapter 6).

### Is there any advantage to having a property investment company rather than any other type of property company?

Very little!

For a company, the only advantage in having a property investment business rather than any other type of property business is the availability of indexation relief against capital gains arising on the company's investment properties.

Individuals (as well as partnerships, trusts, etc.), however, **do** enjoy a number of advantages if regarded as having a property investment business, rather than one of the other types of property business.

It is therefore essential to understand what type of property business you have, or will have, before deciding whether you want to operate it within a company.

### Wealth Warning

Although there is little advantage to this type of tax treatment for a company, it is nevertheless important to appreciate that it is the way in which you carry on your business that determines the tax treatment: you are not allowed to choose how your company is taxed!

The vast majority of landlords and 'buy-to-let' investors are carrying on a property investment business and hence, if they form a company, they will therefore have a property investment company.

This is, perhaps, unfortunate, since it is in the case of property investment businesses that we see the most uncertainty over whether the use of a company is beneficial or not. The subject therefore warrants a great deal of further detailed examination and we will return to this issue in Chapters 11 and 12.

For other types of property business, it is often far more clear-cut that a company would be beneficial.

## 3.3    PROPERTY DEVELOPMENT COMPANIES

These are companies that predominantly acquire properties or land and carry out building or renovation work with a view to selling developed properties for profit.

The term covers quite a broad spectrum of activities, from major building companies that acquire vacant land and construct vast new property developments, to small owner-managed companies that acquire the occasional 'run-down' property to 'do up' for onward sale at a profit. No one would doubt that the former are correctly categorised as property development companies, but not everyone realises that the latter type of activity may also lead to the company being regarded as a property development company.

Generally speaking, a property will be disposed of as soon as possible after building or renovation work has been completed.

It is the profit derived from this work which produces the company's income and it does not usually look to rent properties out other than as a matter of short-term expediency.

### *Example*

*All Whites Limited purchases three old barns in February 2017 and converts them into residential property. The work is completed in August 2017 and the company sells two of the former barns immediately.*

*The third property, unfortunately, proves difficult to sell. In order to generate some income from the property, All Whites Limited lets it out on a short six-month lease. The property is never taken off the market during the period of the lease and a buyer is found in January 2018, with completion taking place in March.*

*Although All Whites Limited let one of the properties out for a short period, its main business activity remained property development. This was reinforced by the fact that the property remained on the market throughout the lease. All Whites Limited is therefore a property development company.*

### Tax Treatment

A property development company is regarded as a *trading company*. Shares in the company are eligible for both entrepreneurs' relief and holdover relief for CGT purposes (see Chapter 7).

It is important to stress that we are talking here about the <u>shares</u> in the company rather than the <u>properties</u> owned by the company. Companies cannot qualify for entrepreneurs' relief or holdover relief on the properties that they own (nor, indeed, on any other assets).

Shares in a property development company are also eligible for business property relief for IHT purposes.

The company's profits from its property development activities, i.e. the profits arising from development property sales, are taxed as trading profits. We will look at the taxation of trading profits in more detail in Chapter 5.

Interest and finance costs relating to the company's property development activities are simply treated as part of its normal trading expenses and do not require the special treatment set out in Section 4.7.

Capital gains treatment will continue to apply to any disposals of the company's long-term fixed assets, such as its own offices, for example.

Where, as in the example above, there is some incidental short-term rental income it should, strictly speaking, still be dealt with under the specific rules applying to property income. In practice, however, it has sometimes been known for this to be accepted as incidental trading income. This is very important, since this treatment ensures that the company's trading status is not affected.

Property developers who utilise the services of subcontractors for any building work, including plumbing, decorating and electrical work, are required to operate the Construction Industry Scheme for tax purposes. This may involve having to deduct tax, at a special rate particular to the Construction Industry Scheme, from payments made to subcontractors and then account for it to HMRC, rather like PAYE.

The current rate for the mandatory deductions under the Construction Industry Scheme is either 20% or 30%, depending on whether the subcontractor is registered under the scheme.

## 3.4    PROPERTY TRADING COMPANIES

This type of company used to be fairly rare, but has become more common in recent years.

Property trading companies are companies that generally only hold properties for short-term gain. Properties are bought and sold frequently and are held as trading stock. Properties will not usually be rented out, except in the interests of short-term financial expediency.

Such companies may sometimes also be known as property dealing companies.

The company's income is derived from making a profit on the properties it sells. These companies differ from property development companies in that no actual development takes place on the properties. Profits are made simply by ensuring a good margin between buying and selling price.

### Example

*All Greys Limited has bought 20 different properties 'off-plan' over the last few years. In each case, it has sold the properties immediately on completion of the development.*

*Since All Greys Limited has neither developed the properties, nor held on to them as investments for any length of time, it is clearly a property trading company.*

### Tax Treatment

A property trading company's profits should be taxed as trading income (see Chapter 5). Interest and finance costs relating to the company's property trading activities will represent trading expenses.

Any incidental letting income that does arise should be dealt with under the specific rules applying to property income.

Shares in such a company are specifically not eligible for business property relief for IHT purposes.

As for CGT, the theory is that a property trading company is still a 'trading company' and hence the shares in such a company should be eligible for both entrepreneurs' relief and holdover relief (see Chapter 7).

In practice, however, I feel there is a strong danger that some resistance will be encountered, with HMRC contending that the company is, in fact, a property investment company, so that its shares do not qualify for these reliefs.

**Wealth Warning**

The major difference between property investment and property trading lies in the treatment of the profit arising on property disposals. In essence, the question is whether such 'profits' are capital gains or trading profits.

This is very much a 'grey area' and HMRC can be expected to examine borderline cases very carefully and to argue for the treatment that produces the most tax.

As explained above, HMRC may be inclined to deny the existence of a trading activity where entrepreneurs' relief or holdover relief is at stake.

Conversely, where an investor is potentially exempt from tax on capital gains (e.g. a non-resident individual or company investing in UK commercial property), HMRC may argue that there is a trading activity in order to be able to levy tax on that investor. We will look at the potential benefits of using a company in this situation in Section 16.6.

New legislation applying from 5th July 2016 also enables HMRC to **deem** the profit arising on the disposal of UK land and property to be a trading profit under certain circumstances. We will take a closer look at that new legislation in Section 3.7.

## 3.5    PROPERTY MANAGEMENT COMPANIES

These companies do not generally own properties at all. Instead, they provide management services to property owners.

If you have a property letting agent taking care of the day-to-day running of your properties, the chances are that your agent is probably a property management company.

A property management company's income is derived from the management or service charges that it charges to the actual owners of the property.

**Tax Treatment**

A property management company is a trading company for all tax purposes. Hence, shares in such a company are usually eligible for entrepreneurs' relief and holdover relief for CGT purposes (see Chapter 7) and business property relief for IHT purposes.

The company's profits from its property management activities will be treated as trading profits. Interest and finance costs incurred in relation to property management activities will be treated as trading expenses.

Capital gains treatment will apply to any disposals of the company's long-term fixed assets, such as its own offices, for example.

Any incidental letting income should, as usual, be dealt with under the specific rules applying to property income.

The interesting point is that, under the right circumstances, you may be able to set up your own property management company. The possible use of such a company for tax-planning purposes is considered in Section 17.1.

## 3.6   COMPANIES WITH A 'MIXED' PROPERTY BUSINESS

"What if my company doesn't happen to fit neatly into one of these four categories?" you may be asking.

If the company has a 'mixed' property business, involving more than one of the four types of business described above, then each of the business types will need to be dealt with separately. It may even be necessary to draw up separate accounts for the different elements of the business.

The impact on the owner of the company will depend on which types of property business are involved in the mixed business and in what proportions.

### Capital Gains Tax

For CGT purposes, the company will only be considered to be a trading company, with its shares eligible for both entrepreneurs' relief and holdover relief (see Chapter 7), if its activities do not include any 'substantial' element of non-trading. For this purpose, property investment and property letting are deemed to be non-trading activities (except furnished holiday lettings).

HMRC have very helpfully told us that they regard 'substantial' as meaning 'more than 20%'. "More than 20% of what?" you ask. Here, they have attempted to retain a little more control over the situation since, depending on the facts of the case, they may apply this '20% rule' to any of the following:

- Turnover (i.e. gross income)
- Profit
- Expenditure
- Time spent by directors and employees
- Asset values

HMRC's view of the meaning of 'substantial' is not, however, the law; it is merely their interpretation of the law.

In particular, most experts suggest that it should only be necessary to keep non-trading activities under the 20% level according to some of the measures set out above, rather than all of them; and that the position should be decided by looking at the overall picture formed by the company's activities.

Nevertheless, the only absolutely certain way to ensure that both entrepreneurs' relief and holdover relief are available on the shares of a company carrying on a mixed property business is to keep the company's non-trading activities down to a level which does not exceed 20% of any of the measures set out above.

### Tax Tip

As we shall see in Chapter 7, whether your company qualifies as a trading company for CGT purposes can make an enormous difference to the amount of tax you will eventually pay on a sale of your shares or a winding up of your company. For a couple owning a company together, the potential tax saving generated by preserving the company's trading status could be up to £2m!

To preserve the trading status of the company, it will often be worth keeping any 'non-trading' activities, such as property letting, separate from those activities that are accepted by HMRC as having trading status. This can be done either by keeping the 'non-trading' activities out of the company, or by putting them into a different company.

**Impact on Business Property Relief for Inheritance Tax**

The test for whether shares in a company with a 'mixed' property business qualify for business property relief is considerably less stringent than the CGT test set out above.

It is only necessary to ensure that the company's business does not consist wholly or mainly of property investment, property letting or dealing in property.

'Mainly' is defined as over 50%, meaning that a property company's shares will generally remain eligible for business property relief as long as over half of its business comes from property development or property management.

To maximise the available business property relief, it is also important to ensure that all of the company's activities are an integral part of the same business and not run separately.

For further details on the benefits of business property relief, see the Taxcafe.co.uk guide *'How to Save Inheritance Tax'*.


### 3.7 INVESTMENT OR TRADING?

As explained earlier in this chapter, it makes little difference to a UK company's CT liabilities whether its property disposals are treated as trading profits or capital gains. However, this issue is hugely important to:

i)     The CGT and IHT treatment of the owner's shares in the company,
ii)    Non-resident companies (see Section 16.6), and
iii)   Individual property investors

Point (iii), in turn, impacts on the question of whether using a company will be beneficial for those investors. All three points make it important for us to examine this critical issue in detail.

In general terms, it is usually beneficial for individuals and non-resident companies if their property disposals are treated as capital gains.

It generally makes little difference to UK resident companies themselves, but it is usually beneficial for their owners if the company's activities give rise to trading profits.

So, in very broad terms, trading works better in a company; long-term investment is better for individuals. However, as we shall see in later chapters, none of that means that a company will not be beneficial for long-term investments in some cases.

In the meantime, let's take a closer look at the 'investment or trading' issue.

## The Boundary Between Investment and Trading

Until recently, a property disposal was generally treated as a capital gain unless the *sole or main purpose* behind the acquisition of the property was to realise a profit on its disposal.

New legislation applying from 5th July 2016, however, states that the profit on disposal of UK property will be *treated* as a trading profit whenever the main purpose, or *one of the main purposes*, behind its acquisition was to realise a profit on its disposal.

This broadens the scope of what might be considered to be a trading profit quite considerably. It does not, however, alter the basic principles which determine when a trade actually exists. In other words, a middle ground has been created where there is no actual trade, but where profits are simply treated as trading profits.

The situation applying for property disposals made after 4th July 2016 can therefore be summarised as follows:

1. **Where the sole or main purpose behind the acquisition was to make a profit on disposal:** a property trade exists and the profit on disposal is trading income.

2. **Where one of the main purposes behind the acquisition (but not the only, or dominant, purpose) was to make a profit on disposal:** the profit on disposal will be treated as trading income but, for all other purposes, the business will be treated as a property investment business.

3. **Where making a profit on disposal was not a main purpose behind the acquisition:** the profit on disposal will be a capital gain and, if a business does exist, it will be a property investment business.

The principles used in determining whether a business falls under Category 1 above are well established and have been discussed earlier in this chapter, but the dividing line between Categories 2 and 3 is perhaps less clear. The problem lies in understanding what '**a** main purpose' is. It is far easier to identify '**the** main purpose'!

When the legislation was first published, many commentators feared that almost all property disposals would be treated as giving rise to a trading profit since almost every time anyone buys a property they hope to realise a gain on its disposal.

However, in contrast to the rather broad scope of the legislation, HMRC guidance issued in December 2016 suggests that very few disposals will fall into Category 2. The guidance states that the new legislation should not apply to:

> "Transactions such as buying or repairing a property for the purpose of earning rental income or as an investment to generate rental income and enjoy capital appreciation", or

> "Straightforward long-term investment where the economic benefit arising to the owner is the result of market movement from holding that asset ...."

The guidance also states that long-term capital appreciation may be a reasonable expectation without it necessarily forming a main purpose of the acquisition.

The general thrust of the guidance seems to suggest that it is only where a profit can already be anticipated due to the property's current value, or where a profit is anticipated due to some action to be carried out by the owner (typically developing the property), that the new deemed trading provisions can apply. Even then, the profit on disposal will need to be a 'main purpose' behind the acquisition.

The mere hope of a long-term gain does not make this a main purpose behind the acquisition. There would need to be a more concrete strategy involving the realisation of a gain before this can be regarded as one of the main purposes behind the acquisition. Nonetheless, it is clear that the 'goalposts' have been moved and investors now need to be very careful about documenting their intentions when acquiring property.

It is almost impossible to give a definitive answer to explain exactly when investment becomes trading, but some useful guidelines are set out below. (Those marked * are included within the HMRC guidance on the issue.)

## Renovation and Conversion Work*

Activity such as building, conversion or renovation work may sometimes be indicative that there is a trading motive behind the purchase of land or property. However, the mere fact that this work takes place does not, in itself, necessarily make it a property development trade.

If the property is held for several years after completion of the building work, it is likely that it is still an investment property.

On the other hand, however, if the property is sold immediately after completing the work, a trade is likely to exist unless the investor's original intention had been to keep the property and rent it out, but some change in circumstances led them to change their mind.

## Frequency of Transactions

If an investor only sells a property once every few years, they are likely to be carrying on a property investment business. If they make several sales every year, representing a high proportion of their portfolio, they may be a property trader or developer.

## Number of Transactions

As well as their frequency, the number of property transactions which the investor has carried out can be a factor in deciding whether they are trading.

## Finance Arrangements*

Long-term finance arrangements, such as mortgages or longer term loans are generally indicative of an investment activity.

Financing a purchase through short-term arrangements, such as bank overdrafts will be more indicative of a development or dealing trade. Short-term finance tends to indicate short-term assets.

## Length of Ownership*

There is no definitive rule as to how long a property must be held for it to be an investment rather than trading stock. Like everything else, length of ownership is just one factor to consider. For example, many property developers hold land stocks for many years before commencing development (known as a 'land bank') but this does not alter the trading nature of their activities.

Where there is no obvious trading activity, I have heard it suggested that an ownership period of three years or more is generally regarded as being indicative of a property investment business: although there is no legal basis for this. This is not to say that ownership for any lesser period cannot represent an investment where the facts of the case otherwise support it.

In practice, the longer the period properties are held for, the more likely they are to be accepted as investments.

### Renting the Properties Out*

Renting properties out provides a pretty good indication that they are being held as investments and not part of a property trade. Like everything else on this list though, it may not be conclusive on its own.

### Living in a Property*

Living in the property is another useful way to evidence an intention to hold it as a long-term asset. Once again though, this may not be enough if the other facts of the case prove to be contrary to this idea.

This will generally only be relevant to properties held by individuals: see Section 16.2 regarding the dangers of making personal use of a property held by your own company.

### 'Hands On' Involvement

Being actively involved in the renovation or development of a property makes the owner look like a property developer. Contracting all of the work out looks more like property investment.

### Existing Trade*

Where an investor already has an existing property trade, such as property development or property dealing, then it is more likely that other property investments will also be trading assets.

### In Summary

Remember that each of the points examined above is just one factor in determining what kind of property business an investor has.

Ultimately, it is the overall picture formed by the investor's intentions, their behaviour and their investment pattern which will eventually decide whether they have a property investment business, a property trade, or both.

In many cases, this 'overall picture' will point to a fairly clear answer and the correct treatment of the business will be obvious.

In some cases, however, the position may be more borderline and the correct treatment will not be clear. This could create a risk that the investor might fall into the middle one of the three categories described at the beginning of this section.

In these cases, it may sometimes be beneficial to adapt your behaviour a little, bearing the guidelines set out above in mind, in order to produce a clearer picture of the nature of the business.

## Changes of Intention

An existing investment property may become a trading asset where there is a change of intention. In this case, the profit arising after the change will be a trading profit, but any increase in value arising prior to that point will remain a capital gain.

### Example

*BOD Limited buys a block of ten flats for £1m in 2017. It rents out the flats until 2022, at which time the property is worth £1.2m. The company then redevelops the property into four luxury apartments at a cost of £250,000 and sells all of the apartments for £500,000 each.*

*As usual, the treatment of the development gain will depend on a number of factors: the most important being BOD Limited's intentions at the time the redevelopment work commenced.*

*However, if it is clear that the redevelopment was carried out with a main purpose of realising an additional profit on the disposal of the property then the development gain of £550,000 will be a trading profit. (4 x £500,000 = £2m – £1.2m – £250,000 = £550,000)*

*The gain of £200,000 (£1.2m – £1m) arising prior to the start of the development work will continue to be a capital gain and the company will be able to claim indexation relief as appropriate.*

# Property Rental Income and Expenses

## 4.1 CORPORATION TAX ON RENTAL PROFITS

In this chapter, we will look at how rental income and other property investment income received by a company are taxed. In the next chapter, we will move on to the tax treatment of companies with property businesses that are classed as trades.

The first point to note is that interest and finance costs incurred by the company in connection with most investment or letting properties are not treated as expenses of the letting business, but as general overheads instead. We will look at the treatment of these costs, and how the company obtains CT relief for them, in Section 4.7.

Subject to this rather peculiar quirk, property letting is treated like any other business from a purely accounting point of view. The company has to draw up accounts, usually once a year, which detail all of its rental income, as well as all relevant expenses.

If the company is letting a number of UK properties on a commercial basis, these will usually be treated as a single UK property business. Landlords operating through companies may, of course, draw up separate sets of management accounts for any individual property, or group of properties, if they wish.

Some types of letting must, however, be accounted for separately for CT purposes, as they are subject to different tax rules. In these cases, a separate set of accounts will be required in support of the company's CT calculations.

Separate letting accounts are required in the following cases:

- Furnished holiday lettings in the UK
- Furnished holiday lettings elsewhere in the European Economic Area
- Other overseas lettings
- Non-commercial lettings

Special rules apply to furnished holiday lettings in the UK or elsewhere in the European Economic Area (see Appendix G).

The qualifying criteria for furnished holiday lettings are set out in Section 4.6 and their different treatment for CT purposes is covered as appropriate throughout this chapter.

'Non-commercial lettings' refers to cases where less than full market rent is charged for a property due to some special relationship between the landlord and the tenant. Generally, as we will see later in the guide, I would advise strongly against holding such properties through a company.

Company accounts must be drawn up in accordance with either UK 'Generally Accepted Accounting Principles' ('GAAP') or International Financial Reporting Standards ('IFRS'). Most UK companies draw accounts up under GAAP, as IFRS is only mandatory for large companies (but see Section 14.6 regarding current developments in this area).

The most important aspect of GAAP is that accounts must be drawn up on an 'accruals' basis. This means that income and expenditure is recognised when it arises, or is incurred, rather than when it is received or paid (the latter being the 'cash basis', which is not permitted for CT purposes).

### *Example*

*Jake, Sandy and Tilly own a small property company, JST Properties Limited, which draws up accounts to 30th November each year. JST Properties Limited acquires a new property on Kirkcaldy High Street in October 2017 and rents it out for the first time on 29th November at a monthly rent of £1,000 payable in advance.*

*At 30th November 2017, JST Properties Limited will have received one monthly rental of £1,000. However, under the 'accruals' concept, the company is only required to account for two days' rent. This amounts to just £66, calculated as follows: £1,000 x 12 x 2/365 = £66.*

*This simple (and correct) adjustment will reduce JST Properties Limited's CT bill on 1st September 2018 by £181.*

### Tax Tip

Expenses should similarly be recognised as they are incurred. The timing of allowable expenditure is therefore critical in planning your CT affairs and it is the date expenses are *incurred* (i.e. when work takes place, or goods are purchased) that is important, not when they are invoiced or paid for.

***Example***

*MYB Ltd has an accounting date of 31st March, and has some roof repairs carried out on one of its rented properties in March 2018. The roofer does not get around to invoicing the company until May and it pays the invoice in July.*

*Despite the fact that MYB Ltd does not pay for the repairs until July, it may nevertheless still deduct the cost in its accounts for the year ending 31st March 2018.*


## 4.2 CALCULATING RENT RECEIVABLE

A company is subject to CT on its rental **profits**, rather than its gross rental **income**.

It is tempting to think, therefore, that it does not matter whether rental expenses are shown separately in the accounts, or just deducted from rental income, as long as the net rental profit is correct.

This is not the case, however, as the correct calculation of gross rental income is important for a number of reasons, including:

- The wear and tear allowance (see Section 4.5)
- Accounting disclosure requirements (see Section 14.6)
- The VAT registration threshold (see Section 9.2)
- The audit threshold (see Section 14.7)

Gross rental income is derived from rent receivable and therefore includes any amounts of rent due but unpaid (i.e. bad debts). Any agent's commission deducted from rents received must also be added back for these purposes and shown separately as an expense.

Tenant's deposits should not be included within rental income unless and until the landlord has cause to retain them (or part of them) – usually at the end of a lease.


## 4.3 EXPENSES YOU CAN CLAIM

The rules on what types of expenditure may be claimed by the company as deductions are generally much the same as for property-letting businesses run by individuals or partnerships.

Some of the main deductions include:

- Property maintenance and repair costs
- Heating and lighting costs, if borne by the landlord company
- Insurance costs
- Letting agent's fees
- Advertising for tenants
- Accountancy fees
- Legal and professional fees (see further below)
- The cost of cleaners, gardeners, etc, where relevant
- Ground rent, service charges, etc.
- Bad debts
- Pre-trading expenditure (see further below)
- Administrative expenditure (see further below)
- Salaries paid to staff or directors (the latter is covered in more detail in Section 10.2)

All expenses must be incurred wholly and exclusively for the purposes of the company's business and, naturally, must actually be borne by the company itself (i.e. the company cannot claim any expenses if the tenant is paying them directly).

Interest and finance costs are not deducted from letting income received by a company, but are treated as general company overheads instead. We will look at how CT relief is obtained for these costs in Section 4.7.

**Legal and Professional Fees**

Most legal fees and other professional costs incurred for the purposes of the business may be claimed as a deduction against rental income. Typically, this will include items such as the costs of preparing tenants' leases and, perhaps, debt collection expenses.

Legal fees and other costs incurred on the purchase or sale of properties, however, may not be claimed against rental income. All is not lost though, as these items may usually be claimed as allowable deductions for capital gains purposes (see Chapter 6).

**Wealth Warning**

There remains the problem of abortive expenditure, such as the cost of building surveys on properties that you do not, in fact, actually purchase. HMRC tends to regard these as capital items, which therefore cannot be claimed against rental income. But, since the property is never actually purchased, they cannot be claimed against any capital gain either.

In my view, there is an argument that such expenses are part of the general administrative cost of running a property investment company and should therefore still be claimed against rental income. Some resistance to this approach may, however, be encountered from HMRC.

**Tax Tip**

A more persuasive argument is that expenditure of this type only becomes capital if it is incurred after the decision to acquire the property has been taken. The best approach, therefore, is to ensure that, wherever possible, you record the fact that such expenditure is being incurred 'with a view to deciding whether or not the property should be purchased by the company' – i.e. that no such decision has yet been made.

This can be done by way of directors' board minutes or within a letter instructing the surveyor (or other professional, as the case may be) to carry out the work.

**Another Tax Tip**

Part of the professional fees arising on the purchase of a property will often relate to the raising of finance.

It may therefore be worth arranging to have this element of the fees invoiced separately, so that they can be claimed as a finance cost within general overheads, as detailed in Section 4.7.

This will provide CT relief for these costs without having to wait until the property is sold.

## Pre-trading Expenditure

You may incur some expenses for the purposes of your property business before you form your company or start to let out any properties.

In general, deductible expenses incurred within seven years before the commencement of a business may still be allowable if they would otherwise qualify under normal principles. In such cases, the expenses can be claimed as if they were incurred on the first day of the business.

### Tax Tip

In the case of a new company, a number of 'pre-trading' expenses will often have been paid for by the investor personally before the company has been formed.

The best thing to do in these circumstances is to:

i) Keep track of the relevant expenditure, retaining receipts, etc, as usual.

ii) Once the company has been formed, 'recharge' the expenses to the company. What this means in practice is that a 'director's loan account' is set up in the company recording the expenditure previously incurred by the director.

iii) The expenses recharged by the director may (subject to the normal principles of deductibility) be claimed in the company's first accounting period.

iv) The director may be repaid the 'loan account' as soon as the company has available funds.

## Administrative Expenditure

This heading is perhaps the broadest, and can extend to the cost of running an office, motor and travel costs.

In the case of a company, it will also cover costs associated with running the company itself (as opposed to running its business). This would include filing fees payable to Companies House and audit fees, if applicable. Costs of the company formation (see Section 14.1) are not allowable as these are deemed to be a capital item.

As usual, the general rule is that any expenditure must be incurred wholly and exclusively for the purposes of the business. Unfortunately, however, business entertaining expenditure is specifically excluded. (Staff entertaining is allowed though – and will not even give rise to Income Tax charges for the staff in some cases, unless HMRC's prescribed limits are exceeded.)

## 4.4 CAPITAL EXPENDITURE YOU CAN CLAIM

The main type of disallowable expenditure in a property-letting or property-investment business is capital expenditure on property improvements and on furniture, fixtures and fittings.

Some relief is, however, given for certain types of capital expenditure in the form of capital allowances.

Apart from the fact that any rule changes generally apply from 1st April for companies, instead of 6th April for individuals or partnerships, the rules explained in this section are pretty much the same as for individuals or partnerships with rental property.

### Plant and Machinery Allowances

The main type of capital allowances currently available is 'plant and machinery allowances'. These allowances are available on qualifying plant, machinery, furniture, fixtures, fittings, computers and other equipment used in a business.

Since April 2008, 'plant and machinery allowances' have also been available on 'integral features' within qualifying property. This term is explained further below.

More details on the type of expenditure qualifying for 'plant and machinery allowances' are given in the Taxcafe.co.uk guides *'How to Save Property Tax'* and *'Capital Allowances: Your Emergency Tax Planning Guide'*.

### Capital Allowances on Rental Properties

Capital allowances are available on qualifying expenditure within rented commercial property (shops, offices, etc) and furnished holiday lettings (see Section 4.6).

**Wealth Warning**

Landlords may lose the right to capital allowances on fixtures and fittings within a commercial property if they grant a long lease (two years or more) to a tenant and charge a lease premium. As such a premium is wholly or partly regarded as a capital sum for tax purposes, the landlord will be treated as having made a partial disposal of the property and may therefore lose the right to claim any capital allowances on assets within it.

A landlord may also lose the right to claim capital allowances on any items not qualifying as 'background' plant and machinery when a property is leased for more than five years. However, this should not generally apply to assets on which the landlord had been able to claim capital allowances previously, before the commencement of the new lease.

Finally, landlords may also lose the right to capital allowances on any fixtures or fittings which they lease to the tenant separately under a different agreement to the lease of the property itself. However, this particular problem can often be avoided by making a joint election with the tenant. Furthermore, this can also be a useful method to enable the landlord to retain the right to capital allowances on assets within the property where a long lease has been granted at a premium as described above.

## Residential Property

Sadly, any expenditure on assets for use within a rented 'dwelling-house' is ineligible for capital allowances. Hence, capital allowances cannot generally be claimed on expenditure within a residential rental property. There are some important exceptions to be aware of, however, including:

- Furnished holiday lets (see Section 4.6)
- Expenditure within communal areas (e.g. lift machinery or a utility room in a block of flats)

A company which rents out residential property may also claim 'plant and machinery allowances' on equipment purchased for its own business use outside its rental properties, such as computers and office furniture.

Like other landlords, before April 2016 companies were able to claim a 'wear and tear allowance' on furnished residential lettings. This allowance was not part of the capital allowances regime and has now been abolished. Companies may, however, claim the cost of replacement furniture, furnishings and equipment within rented residential property. See Section 4.5 for further details.

## The Amount of Allowances Available

We will now look at how 'plant and machinery allowances' are calculated. As these are the only type of capital allowances which we will be concerned with for the rest of this section, I will simply refer to them as 'capital allowances' from now on.

The precise amount of capital allowances available depends on the date on which the qualifying expenditure is incurred. At present, the most important allowance for the majority of businesses is the annual investment allowance.

## The Annual Investment Allowance

Qualifying companies are currently entitled to an annual investment allowance of up to £200,000.

(The allowance is also available to sole traders and most partnerships. Note, however, that where a company is a member of a partnership, the allowance will not be available to that partnership.)

The annual investment allowance provides 100% tax relief for qualifying expenditure on plant and machinery up to a specified limit in each accounting period.

The specified limits for recent and current periods are as follows:

1st April 2014 to 31st December 2015:   £500,000
From 1st January 2016:                  £200,000

Transitional rules apply where a company's accounting period spans a change in the specified limit. These rules mean that the company's annual investment allowance is subject to an overall maximum for the period as a whole; with additional restrictions applying to expenditure during certain parts of that period.

## Periods Straddling 1st January 2016

A company with accounting periods ending on 31st March each year was entitled to a maximum annual investment allowance for the year ended 31st March 2016 of:

£500,000 x 275/366 =   £375,683
£200,000 x 91/366 =     £49,727
Total:                 £425,410

Within this overall maximum for the year as a whole, the company's claim in respect of expenditure incurred during the latter part of its accounting period, from 1st January to 31st March 2016, will also be restricted to a maximum of just £49,727. (Any amount up to the full maximum of £425,410 for the year can be claimed in respect of expenditure incurred between 1st April and 31st December 2015.)

The maximum annual investment allowance applying for some popular accounting periods straddling 1st January 2016 is as follows:

| Year end in 2016: | 31-Mar | 30-Apr | 30-Jun | 30-Sep |
|---|---|---|---|---|
| For the year as a whole | £425,410 | £400,820 | £350,820 | £275,410 |
| After 31/12/2015 | £49,727 | £66,120 | £99,454 | £149,727 |

Another set of transitional rules applied to accounting periods which straddled 1st April 2014. See the previous edition of this guide for further details.

### Restrictions on the Annual Investment Allowance

The annual investment allowance is restricted where a company has an accounting period of less than twelve months' duration. This will often apply to a new company's first accounting period.

For example, a company drawing up accounts for the six month period ending 31st December 2017 will be entitled to a maximum annual investment allowance of:

£200,000 x 184/365 = £100,822

The annual investment allowance must also be shared between companies which are members of the same group, or which are otherwise closely related to each other.

The annual investment allowance is not available for expenditure on cars.

### Enhanced Capital Allowances

Various qualifying energy-saving or environmentally beneficial equipment is eligible for 100% enhanced capital allowances. These allowances are available in addition to the annual investment allowance. Further details can be found at www.etl.decc.gov.uk and www.envirowise.wrap.org.uk

## Writing Down Allowances

Apart from expenditure qualifying for enhanced capital allowances, other qualifying expenditure in excess of the annual investment allowance is eligible for 'writing down allowances'.

Writing down allowances also apply to any expenditure on qualifying plant and machinery which is not eligible for either the annual investment allowance or enhanced capital allowances.

The rate of writing down allowances on most plant and machinery is currently 18%.

Qualifying expenditure in excess of the annual investment allowance is pooled together with the unrelieved balance of qualifying expenditure brought forward from the previous accounting period. This pool of expenditure is known as the 'main pool'.

The writing down allowance is then calculated at the appropriate rate on the total balance in the main pool.

The remaining balance of expenditure is then carried forward and the appropriate percentage of that balance may be claimed in the next accounting period. And so on.

However, where the balance in the main pool reduces to £1,000 or less, the full balance may then be claimed immediately.

## The Special Rate Pool

Certain expenditure must be allocated to a 'special rate pool' instead of the main pool. This includes:

- Expenditure of £100,000 or more on plant and machinery with an anticipated working life of 25 years or more.

- Certain defined categories of 'integral features' (see below).

- Expenditure on thermal insulation of an existing building used in a qualifying trade.

Expenditure in the special rate pool is eligible for a writing down allowance of just 8% instead of the usual 18%.

It is worth noting, however, that the annual investment allowance may be allocated to any such expenditure in preference to expenditure qualifying for the normal rate of writing down allowance.

Where the balance on the special rate pool reduces to £1,000 or less, the full balance may then be claimed immediately in the same way as for the main pool.

## Integral Features

Expenditure on assets included in a defined list of 'integral features' within commercial property, qualifying furnished holiday accommodation, or communal areas within rented residential property, falls into the special rate pool.

However, as explained above, these assets remain eligible for the annual investment allowance, so up to £200,000 per year of qualifying expenditure on assets in this category could currently attract immediate 100% relief.

The following items are classed as integral features:

- Electrical lighting and power systems
- Cold water systems
- Space or water heating systems, air conditioning, ventilation and air purification systems and floors or ceilings comprised in such systems
- Lifts, escalators and moving walkways
- External solar shading

The integral features regime applies to expenditure incurred by companies after 31st March 2008, including fixtures within second-hand buildings purchased after that date (but see further below regarding second-hand buildings).

It is worth noting that some of the items within the list of 'integral features' were not previously eligible for plant and machinery allowances, particularly cold water systems (i.e. basic plumbing) and most electrical lighting and power systems.

In other words, for expenditure incurred from April 2008 onwards, these items represent significant additions to the categories of expenditure within commercial property, qualifying furnished holiday accommodation, and communal areas within rented residential property which attract capital allowances.

Combining this with the annual investment allowance, many property investment companies are able to benefit quite significantly.

### *Example*

*Hook Limited draws up its accounts to 31st March each year. In June 2017, the company buys an old property and then converts it into office units to rent out.*

*Although the office units are really just basic 'shells' with the absolute minimum of fixtures and fittings, Hook Limited's surveyors nevertheless calculate that the company has spent £200,000 on 'integral features' and other fixtures qualifying as plant and machinery.*

*Hook Limited can therefore claim an annual investment allowance of £200,000 for the year ending 31st March 2018.*


## Thermal Insulation of Commercial Property

Expenditure on thermal insulation of an existing commercial building used in a qualifying business also falls into the special rate pool. The annual investment allowance is again available on this expenditure, currently providing immediate tax relief on up to £200,000 each year.


## Planning with the Annual Investment Allowance

The annual investment allowance is available to each qualifying business entity. Any individual or company with a property rental business is a qualifying business entity.

Individuals or companies who own joint shares in rental properties, but who are not operating as a partnership, are each deemed to have their own separate property business.

A couple buying property jointly (but not as a partnership) could therefore claim annual investment allowances of up to £200,000 each. Such a couple paying additional rate tax at 45% could therefore potentially benefit from a total tax saving of up to £180,000, simply by buying the right property!

A company can only claim one single annual investment allowance, regardless of how many shareholders it has. Even this is subject to the 'related company' rules.

Unincorporated businesses (i.e. not companies) under the control of the same person, or persons, are also subject to restrictions in the amount of annual investment allowance which they can claim.

However, for the purposes of the annual investment allowance, a company cannot be treated as being related to an unincorporated business.

Hence, an individual could buy property jointly with his or her own company (but not as a partnership) and both the individual and the company would be eligible for an annual investment allowance of up to £200,000 each.

Furthermore, a couple could even form a company together, buy property jointly with that company (but not as a partnership) and claim three separate annual investment allowances (one for each of the couple and one for the company), thus providing immediate 100% tax relief on up to £600,000 of qualifying expenditure.

Taking this idea one step further, each member of the couple could form their own company and all four entities (two individuals and two companies) could buy property jointly (but not as a partnership), thus providing scope to claim immediate 100% tax relief on up to £800,000 of qualifying expenditure in total!

## Late Claims

The annual investment allowance can only be claimed in the period that qualifying expenditure is incurred. However, it is worth noting that writing down allowances may be claimed at any time provided that the relevant asset is still in qualifying use (which includes a property letting business). Hence, it is often possible to claim writing down allowances on assets purchased in earlier years where a claim was not originally made: provided that the assets qualified in the first place of course. This is particularly relevant to purchases of second-hand property and there are companies which specialise in assisting property owners with this type of claim. There are, however, a few additional restrictions to be aware of.

## Second-Hand Property

Additional rules apply to capital allowances claims on integral features and other qualifying fixtures within second-hand property purchased after 31st March 2012.

In most cases, it is mandatory for the seller and the purchaser to agree a fixed value for the qualifying fixtures within the property by making a joint election (known as a 'Section 198 Election'). Without such an election, the purchaser will not be entitled to claim any capital allowances on the fixtures within the property.

The value specified by the Section 198 Election may be anywhere between nil and the original qualifying cost of the fixtures.

For properties purchased between 1st April 2012 and 31st March 2014, these additional rules generally only apply to fixtures on which the seller had themselves made a capital allowances claim. The purchaser is still free to allocate an appropriate element of the purchase price to any other qualifying fixtures within the property.

However, for properties purchased after 31st March 2014, the purchaser is generally only able to claim capital allowances on fixtures within the property where the seller had also made a capital allowances claim on those same fixtures **and** the purchaser and seller have agreed a fixed value by way of a Section 198 Election.

Nonetheless, there are still a number of exceptions to these rules: even for properties purchased after 31st March 2014.

Most notably, the additional rules do not usually apply where the seller was not entitled to claim capital allowances on the fixtures. The most common incidence of this is likely to be where the seller had acquired the property before April 2008 and was therefore not entitled to claim capital allowances on cold water plumbing or electrical lighting and power systems.

For further details of the regime for fixtures in second-hand property see the Taxcafe.co.uk guide: *'Capital Allowances: Your Emergency Tax Planning Guide'*.


**Balancing Charges**

When a property is sold, the proportion of sales proceeds relating to qualifying fixtures and fittings within the property must be deducted from the company's main and special rate pools. (The deduction applying to each pool is calculated independently.)

In most cases, this sum will now be the fixed value agreed by way of a Section 198 Election (this was already an optional procedure before April 2012).

Items of expenditure on which no capital allowances have been claimed do not need to be included.

If the sum to be deducted exceeds the balance on the relevant pool, the excess is added to the company's income for CT purposes. This is known as a 'balancing charge'.

### Example

*At 1st April 2017, Williams Limited has balances of £10,000 brought forward on its main pool and £20,000 on its special rate pool.*

*In June that year, the company sells Shane House, a commercial property, and enters into a Section 198 Election with the purchaser, Warburton Ltd. The agreed fixed values in the election are £17,000 for the items in the main pool and £15,000 for the items in the special rate pool.*

*After deducting the relevant amounts, Williams Limited will be left with a balance of £5,000 on its special rate pool and can therefore still claim a writing down allowance of £400 (8%) on this pool.*

*When we turn to the company's main pool, however, the £17,000 deduction relating to Shane House exceeds the balance by £7,000. Williams Limited will therefore be subject to a balancing charge of £7,000, will not be able to claim any writing down allowance on the main pool and will be left with a nil balance carried forward on this pool.*

*(I have assumed, for the sale of illustration, that Williams Limited does not purchase any new qualifying assets during the same accounting period.)*

Note that a remaining balance on one pool (e.g. the special rate pool in the example above) cannot be used to reduce the balancing charge arising on the other pool. This makes it especially important to ensure that the fixed values agreed in any Section 198 Election are considered very carefully.

Before 2008, balancing charges were fairly rare since they could generally only arise if the business ceased or the relevant assets were sold for a sum in excess of the balance on the main pool.

The impact of balancing charges on small property investment companies is now far more pronounced, however, due to the fact that most qualifying expenditure has already been claimed in full by way of the annual investment allowance.

### Other Equipment Used in the Business

See Section 5.5 for more details on the practical aspects of claiming capital allowances on the company's own plant and equipment, including motor cars.

## 4.5 FURNISHED LETTINGS

Furnished residential lettings need to be divided into three categories for tax purposes:

- Fully furnished lettings
- Partly furnished lettings
- Furnished holiday lettings

Although, as we will see later, the distinction between fully furnished lettings and partly furnished lettings is only relevant for periods prior to 1st April 2016, due to the abolition of the wear and tear allowance from that date onwards.

In this section, I will look at the tax relief available in respect of furnishings within fully furnished lettings and partly furnished lettings. Furnished holiday lettings are subject to an entirely different regime which I will examine in Section 4.6 (the key difference being that qualifying items within furnished holiday lettings are eligible for capital allowances).

It should also be noted that any items within 'communal areas' lying outside any individual dwelling (e.g. the common parts of a house divided into self-contained flats) will also be subject to a different regime and may be eligible for capital allowances (see Section 4.4 for details).

Before we look at the tax relief available for furnishings, it is important to stress that nothing in this section affects the landlord company's ability to claim repairs expenditure under normal principles – except that a company claiming the wear and tear allowance for a period prior to 1st April 2016 cannot also claim the cost of any furniture repairs in any of its fully furnished lettings for the same period.

In particular, it is worth noting that the following types of expenditure may usually be claimed as repairs expenditure:

- Replacement of fixtures and fittings (provided there is no element of improvement involved)
- Repairs to white goods, equipment, carpets, curtains and other furnishings which are not 'furniture'
- Repairs to furniture in partly furnished lettings
- Repairs to furniture in fully furnished lettings during a period where the wear and tear allowance is not being claimed

For further details of the principles applying to repairs expenditure, see the Taxcafe.co.uk guide *'How to Save Property Tax'*.

## What Are Furnishings?

The first, and most important, thing to understand is that fixtures, fittings, and anything else which is part of the fabric of the building, are not classed as furnishings for tax purposes.

Generally speaking, anything which is permanently fixed to the building is not classed as a 'furnishing' and replacing these items will often be claimable as a repair expense regardless of how the furnishings in the property are being dealt with.

Hence, items which are classed as 'furnishings' for tax purposes include:

- Furniture
- Electrical equipment
- Free-standing 'white goods', such as fridges, dishwashers, etc.
- Carpets and other floor coverings
- Curtains, blinds, etc.
- 'Soft furnishings', such as cushions, lampshades, etc.
- Cutlery, crockery and cooking utensils
- Bed linen

Carpets often cause a lot of confusion as many people see them as a 'fitting' rather than a 'furnishing'. For tax purposes, however, they are classed as furnishings.

Items classed as fixtures and fittings for tax purposes include:

- Baths, toilets, sinks, showers, etc.
- Fitted kitchens, including fitted (not free-standing) cookers, fridges and other items which are an integral part of a fitted kitchen
- Central heating equipment (boilers, radiators, etc.)
- Air conditioning
- Light fittings

Where these items are replaced, the expenditure will generally be dealt with as a repair – provided that there is no element of improvement involved (see the Taxcafe.co.uk guide *'How to Save Property Tax'* for further details).

## Replacement Furniture Relief

Expenditure incurred by companies after 31st March 2016 is eligible for the new 'replacement furniture relief'. This relief is available:

- To all companies with residential lettings
- On qualifying replacement expenditure within fully furnished lets, partly furnished lets and even unfurnished lets (but not in furnished holiday lets)
- To cover replacements of all moveable items (i.e. all furnishings, as detailed above)

Any sale proceeds received on the disposal of the old item being replaced must be deducted from the replacement cost being claimed.

As usual, the new relief does not cover the costs of the original furnishings when the property is first let out, or the cost of additional items.

Companies may, however, claim part of the cost of a replacement item which performs additional functions compared to the old item which it replaces. Hence, for example, where a landlord company replaces an old fridge with a fridge-freezer costing £300, but could have purchased a new fridge for £200, it will still be able to claim the £200 direct replacement cost.

**Expenditure Prior to 1st April 2016**

For expenditure incurred prior to 1st April 2016, we must consider fully furnished lettings and partly furnished lettings separately.

**Fully Furnished Lettings**

Companies with fully furnished lettings in any period prior to 1st April 2016 were able to claim the 'wear and tear allowance'. Where a company's accounting period spans 1st April 2016, a partial 'wear and tear allowance' claim is possible. This allowance is examined in detail below.

For periods falling between 1st April 2013 and 31st March 2016, companies with fully furnished lettings had the choice of claiming either the 'wear and tear allowance' or the 'renewals allowance'. This alternative treatment is also examined below.

To be classed as a 'fully furnished letting', the company must provide sufficient furnishings so that the property is capable of normal residential use without the tenant having to provide their own furnishings. Typically, this will include beds, chairs, tables, sofas, carpets or other floor coverings, curtains or blinds, and kitchen equipment.

The key phrase here is whether the property is 'capable of normal residential use' and the level of furnishings and equipment required must be considered in this context. In essence, the company must provide the tenant (or each tenant) with some privacy, somewhere to sit, somewhere to sleep, somewhere to eat, and the facilities required to feed themselves.

## Partly Furnished Lettings

Where some furniture, equipment or other furnishings are provided, but not sufficient to enable the property to be classed as 'fully furnished' (as described above), the property will be regarded as a 'partly furnished letting'.

For expenditure incurred between 1st April 2013 and 31st March 2016, the only relief available to companies with partly furnished lettings for the cost of furnishings was the 'renewals allowance' (see below).

## The Wear & Tear Allowance

For periods falling prior to 1st April 2016, a 'wear and tear allowance' equal to 10% of the 'relevant rental amount' could be claimed against the rental income from fully furnished residential lettings. This allowance was given instead of capital allowances, which are not usually available for residential property.

In calculating the allowance, we first need to establish the 'relevant rental amount' for the property in question.

As explained in Section 4.2, it is important to remember that rent receivable (and hence also the 'relevant rental amount') includes any amounts of rent due but unpaid (i.e. bad debts) and any deposits retained at the end of a lease. Any agent's commission deducted from rents received should also be added back for the purposes of this calculation.

To arrive at the 'relevant rental amount' we must then deduct any amounts borne by the company which would normally be a tenant's own responsibility (e.g. council tax, water rates or electricity charges).

### *Example*

*Carling Limited draws up accounts to 30th June each year. The company owns a large flat in central Bristol which it lets out for £2,500 per month (£30,000 per annum). The company pays the water rates for the property, which amount to £1,000 per year, but the tenant pays their own council tax.*

*For each year up to the year ended 30th June 2015, Carling Limited was able to claim a wear and tear allowance as follows:*

| | |
|---|---|
| Total Rent Receivable: | £30,000 |
| Less: | |
| Water Rates | £1,000 |
| | |
| Relevant Rental Amount: | £29,000 |
| | |
| Wear and Tear Allowance: | £2,900 (10%) |

For the year ended 30th June 2016, Carling Limited may claim a wear and tear allowance of:

£2,900 x 275/366 = £2,179

The company may also claim replacement furniture relief in respect of the cost of any qualifying replacement items purchased after 31st March 2016.

In this example, Carling Limited has claimed a wear and tear allowance for the period that spanned 1st April 2016 using a simple 'time apportionment' method. In other cases, it may be more appropriate to use a 'just and reasonable' apportionment: i.e. using a method which is more closely aligned to the way in which the company's rental income actually fell due.

### Example

At the beginning of the year ended 31st December 2016, Hogg Limited was renting out ten fully furnished flats at a monthly rental of £1,000 each. However, the company sold seven of the flats on 1st April 2016, meaning that its income from fully furnished lettings fell to just £3,000 per month for the rest of the year.

The company's total income from fully furnished lettings for the year was £57,000 (3 x £10,000 + 9 x £3,000). Using a time apportionment basis, the company's wear and tear allowance claim for the year would therefore be:

£57,000 x 10% = £5,700 x 91/366 = £1,417

However, using a just and reasonable basis would enable the company to claim:

£1,000 x 10 x 3 = £30,000 x 10% = £3,000

Clearly this is a more appropriate claim in this case and it makes no difference to the company's ability to claim the cost of replacement furnishings after 31st March 2016.

## The Effect of a Wear and Tear Allowance Claim

When a company claims the wear and tear allowance for any accounting period, it automatically applies to all fully furnished lettings made by that company in that accounting period. (Where an accounting period spans 1st April 2016, the period prior to that date is treated as a separate accounting period for this purpose.)

As a consequence, the company cannot also claim any of the following in relation to any of its fully furnished lettings during that accounting period (or during the part of the period falling prior to 1st April 2016 where relevant):

- The renewals allowance (see below)
- Repairs to furniture

Note that it is only repairs to furniture which are excluded. It would appear that repairs to equipment (e.g. 'white goods' such as cookers or fridges) and other furnishings (e.g. carpets) could still be claimed.

The above costs are also only excluded when they are attributable to a period during which the property is subject to a fully furnished letting. However, it seems likely that furniture repairs which become necessary following a fully furnished letting period will usually be properly attributable to that period.

Despite the exclusions detailed above, the uncertainty surrounding the scope of the 'renewals allowance' (see below) means that the vast majority of companies with fully furnished lettings will have been better off claiming the wear and tear allowance for periods prior to 1st April 2016.


## The 'Renewals Allowance'

For expenditure incurred between 1st April 2013 and 31st March 2016, the 'renewals allowance' was the only means by which companies with partly furnished lettings could claim the cost of qualifying replacement items. It also existed as an alternative to the 'wear and tear allowance' for companies with fully furnished lettings.

The 'renewals allowance' was based on a provision within tax legislation (Section 68 of the Corporation Tax Act 2009) which allowed companies to claim the cost of replacing 'tools' used in a qualifying business. The legislation went on to define 'tools' as being any 'implement, utensil, or article'.

The definition of 'tools' within tax legislation could potentially be interpreted very broadly. As a result, some people (myself included) argued that the 'renewals allowance' should effectively be the same as the old 'replacements basis' which was withdrawn in April 2013 and should cover the cost of all replacement furnishings (as listed above).

Sadly, the HMRC guidance on the issue suggested that, in their view, the 'renewals allowance' had to be interpreted rather more narrowly and the allowance should only apply to smaller items, or items with only a short useful life, such as:

- Low cost 'soft furnishings', such as cushions, lampshades, etc.
- Cutlery, crockery and cooking utensils
- Bed linen
- Rugs

The guidance specifically stated that HMRC did not consider the renewals allowance to cover free standing 'white goods' such as cookers, fridges or dishwashers.

It also stated that carpets would not normally be covered, although they did acknowledge that there could be some exceptions to this where the carpets had a very short useful life (e.g. a cheap hall carpet in a house let to students which was replaced annually).

It should be borne in mind here that HMRC's guidance is not the law and that there are alternative views regarding the scope of the 'renewals allowance'. Indeed, the allowance has been successfully used in the past (by different types of business) to claim the cost of replacing far larger items than fridges, cookers and carpets.

For a more detailed discussion on the scope of the 'renewals allowance' see the Taxcafe.co.uk guide *'How to Save Property Tax'*.

One thing which remains beyond doubt is that, as with the replacements basis, the renewals allowance did not cover the costs of the original furnishings when the property was first let out, or the cost of improvements or additional items.

As explained above, the renewals allowance was also not available for expenditure on a fully furnished property during an accounting period for which the company was claiming the wear and tear allowance.

## 4.6 FURNISHED HOLIDAY LETTINGS

Properties qualifying as 'furnished holiday lettings' are subject to a special tax regime, with many of the tax advantages usually only accorded to a trade.

Admittedly, those advantages have now been somewhat curtailed as a result of the changes to loss relief on furnished holiday lets which we will look at in Section 4.8. Nonetheless, several other key advantages remain, including the ability to claim capital allowances on furniture and equipment and rollover relief for capital gains purposes.

The benefits for a shareholder owning a company that is mainly engaged in furnished holiday lettings were considered in Section 3.2.

For the purposes of both loss relief and capital allowances claims, furnished holiday lettings must be treated as a separate business to any other lettings which the company has. Furthermore, furnished holiday lettings in the UK must also be treated as a separate business to furnished holiday lettings elsewhere in the European Economic Area.

It is now worth us taking a brief look at the qualification requirements for a 'furnished holiday letting':

    i)   The property must be situated in the European Economic Area (see Appendix G)

    ii)  The property must be fully furnished (see Section 4.5)

    iii) It must be let out on a commercial basis with a view to the realisation of profits

    iv) It must be available for commercial letting to the public generally for at least 210 days in a twelve-month period

    v)   It must be so let for at least 105 such days – but see further below

    vi) The property must not normally be in the same occupation for more than 31 consecutive days at any time during a period of at least seven months out of the same twelve-month period as that referred to in (iv) above

There is some debate as to whether, strictly speaking, the tenants actually have to be using the property for the purposes of a 'holiday' (as long as the tests at (i) to (vi) above are still met). HMRC's view is that, whilst the property need not be in a recognised holiday area, the lettings should strictly be to holidaymakers and tourists in order to qualify. On this occasion, I am inclined to agree with them.

Companies may elect for properties within the furnished holiday letting regime to stay within that regime for up to two further accounting periods despite failing to meet the test under (v) above. In effect, this means that properties will generally only need to meet this test once every three years. The property will still need to meet all of the other tests, however, and the company must make genuine efforts to meet the test under (v) every year.

Alternatively, a company with more than one UK furnished holiday let (or more than one furnished holiday let elsewhere in the European Economic Area, as the case may be), may use a system of averaging to determine whether its properties meet the test under (v) above.

## 4.7    INTEREST AND FINANCE COSTS

As explained previously, interest and finance costs incurred in connection with a company's property investment or property letting business are treated as general overheads of the company rather than expenses of the letting business itself (except in the case of furnished holiday lettings – see below). This provides a tremendous advantage for property investment businesses run through a company when compared with the same type of business run by an individual or a partnership.

The interest and finance costs incurred in connection with the company's property investment business may be set off against any income or capital gains received by the company during the same accounting period.

If we contrast this with the position for an individual or a partnership where these same costs:

a) Can only be set against rental income, and

b) Are subject to restrictions in the rate of tax relief available from 2017/18 onwards,

Then we can readily see what an enormous advantage this provides.

Furthermore, as an alternative, the company may instead:

a)  Carry the costs back for set off against any interest, and certain other limited categories of income, received in the previous year,

b)  Carry the costs forward for set off against any non-trading income, including rental profits, **and** capital gains in future periods, or

c)  Surrender the costs as 'group relief' (where the company is a member of a group of companies)

For costs arising after 31st March 2017, any amounts carried forward under (b) above may generally be set off against **any** income or capital gains in future periods provided that the company continues to carry on an investment business. An investment business for this purpose includes any form of property letting other than furnished holiday letting, as well as the other categories of investment business referred to in Section 4.8, although the investment business must not be 'small'. Here there is no definition of what 'small' means, although it seems safe to assume it means very small indeed.

If the company ceases to have an investment business, or it becomes 'small' then amounts carried forward under (b) above will again only be eligible for set off against non-trading income and capital gains.

Note that furnished holiday letting profits (see Section 4.6) are classed as trading income for the purposes of (b) above and are thus ineligible for the set off of brought forward interest and finance costs arising before 1st April 2017 (or later costs when the company's investment business has ceased or become 'small').

### Tax Tip

Option (b) above enables a property investment company to effectively 'roll up' its accumulated interest costs and set them off against the capital gains arising on the sale of its investment properties.

This presents a massive advantage over individual investors who cannot set rental losses, which are usually predominantly made up of interest costs, against capital gains.

We will look at the effect of this in practice in Chapter 13.

## What do we mean by 'Finance Costs'?

In addition to interest, other costs falling within this category include:
- Guarantee fees
- Loan arrangement fees
- Early redemption fees
- Reimbursement of lender's expenses
- Professional costs relating to the raising of finance

## Loans and other Facilities Provided by the Company's Owner

In general terms, interest and finance costs (as described above) may continue to be claimed for CT purposes even when paid to one of the company's directors, shareholders, or another connected person. There are two important provisos here, however:

i)      The amount paid must not exceed a normal commercial rate.

ii)     Payment must actually be made within twelve months of the end of the company's accounting period.

We will consider the issue of loans from the owner to the company in more detail in Chapter 13.

## Non-Commercial Lettings

CT relief for interest and finance costs incurred in connection with any 'non-commercial' lettings (see Section 4.1) will be restricted so that, broadly speaking, relief is only given against any income from those lettings.

## Furnished Holiday Lettings

Interest and finance costs relating to furnished holiday lettings (see Section 4.6) are treated as a direct expense of that business and NOT as general company overheads in the manner described above.

This means that these costs may only be set off against income from the company's furnished holiday lettings. Further restrictions also apply where the company has both UK furnished holiday lettings and furnished holiday lettings elsewhere in the European Economic Area (see Section 4.8).

It is also important to remember that income from furnished holiday lettings is classed as trading income for the purposes of relief for carried forward surplus interest and finance costs relating to other lettings.

## Corporate Interest Relief Restrictions

New restrictions on interest relief apply to companies from 1st April 2017: but only where the company, or group of companies, is paying annual interest in excess of £2m.

Where the UK company or group's net interest expense exceeds £2m, the maximum amount which may be claimed for UK CT purposes will generally be limited to 30% of UK earnings before interest, tax, depreciation and amortisation ('EBITDA'), although the company can elect to use the worldwide group's average rate of interest to earnings in place of the 30% limit if this is greater.

The amount claimed for UK tax purposes cannot exceed the total net interest expense for the worldwide group.

The new restriction can only affect large companies which are members of international groups. Companies paying no more than £2m of annual interest costs, or which have no overseas associated companies, cannot be affected.

## 4.8   TAX TREATMENT OF RENTAL LOSSES

Given the fact that interest and finance costs incurred in connection with a company's property rental business are not generally treated as an expense of that business (see Section 4.7 above), rental losses within a company should be a fairly rare occurrence. In this section, however, we will look at what happens when such losses do arise.

For loss relief purposes, we must divide the company's property lettings into four categories:

i)    Ordinary UK property lettings
ii)   Ordinary overseas lettings
iii)  UK furnished holiday lettings
iv)   Furnished holiday lettings elsewhere in the European Economic Area

For the purposes of (i) and (ii) above, 'ordinary' simply means not furnished holiday lettings (as defined in Section 4.6).

### Ordinary UK Property Lettings

Subject to the exception for non-commercial lettings set out below, for CT purposes, all of a company's 'ordinary' UK property lettings are treated as a single UK property business. Hence, the loss on any one such property is automatically set off against profits on other commercially let UK properties for the same period.

Any overall net losses arising from a company's 'ordinary' UK property-letting business will be set off against the company's other income and capital gains for the same period (if any).

This again represents a major advantage over individual property investors, or partnerships, who can only carry forward any net rental loss (other than losses derived from capital allowances).

Any remaining surplus rental loss incurred by the company is carried forward and set off against the company's **total** profits (including capital gains) for the next accounting period, then the next, and so on. Rental losses may be carried forward for as long as is necessary in this way, provided that the company is still carrying on an 'ordinary' UK property-letting business in the accounting period for which the claim to offset the losses is made.

If the company's 'ordinary' UK property-letting business ceases, but the company still has an 'investment business', then any unused UK rental losses are converted to 'management expenses'. 'Management expenses' may also be carried forward and set off against the company's total profits, including capital gains, for as long as the company continues to have an 'investment business'.

An 'investment business' is any business that consists of making investments. For example, the company may have an 'investment business' if:

- It owns subsidiary companies
- It has foreign investment property
- It holds a portfolio of stock market investments

It is questionable, however, whether simply holding cash on deposit constitutes an 'investment business'.

### Wealth Warning

It is also unclear whether furnished holiday lettings constitute an 'investment business' for these purposes; so it would perhaps be unwise to rely on them as a means to preserve rental losses from an 'ordinary' UK property-letting business.

Nevertheless, it is clear that there are many ways for a company to preserve the value of its 'ordinary' UK rental losses and ensure that CT relief is ultimately obtained. This contrasts with individual investors who effectively lose the value of any 'ordinary' UK rental losses if they cease to carry on an 'ordinary' UK rental business.

A company will only lose the value of its unused rental losses if it ceases to carry on both its 'ordinary' UK letting business and any other type of 'investment business'.

### Example

*Reivers RIP Limited has an 'ordinary' UK property-letting business, as well as a steady income of £10,000 each year in interest. Unfortunately, in the year ending 31st December 2017, the company incurs a loss of £50,000 in its letting business.*

*£10,000 of the loss is therefore set off against the company's interest income for the year and the remaining £40,000 is carried forward.*

*In the year ending 31st December 2018, Reivers RIP Limited makes a profit of £8,000 on its property letting business.*

*The brought forward loss of £40,000 is treated as a letting loss for the year, resulting in an overall net loss on the letting business for CT purposes this year of £32,000. As before, £10,000 of this is set off against the interest income of the period, leaving a loss of £22,000 to carry forward.*

*In the year ending 31st December 2019, the company makes a final profit of £3,000 from UK property letting before deciding to give this business up.*

*The brought forward loss of £22,000 is again treated as a letting loss for the year, resulting in an overall net loss on the letting business for CT purposes of £19,000 in 2019. Once again, £10,000 of this is set off against the interest income for the period.*

*Whether the remaining unrelieved loss of £9,000 may be carried forward in the form of management expenses will depend on whether Reivers RIP Limited has an 'investment business'.*

*If the company does not have a continuing 'investment business' after giving up its UK property letting business then the remaining loss of £9,000 will, unfortunately, effectively be 'wasted'.*

For the sake of illustration, I have ignored the impact of any capital gains made by Reivers RIP Limited at the time of cessation of its UK letting business in this example. In practice, with careful timing, it should generally be possible to set any remaining unrelieved 'ordinary' UK rental losses against the capital gains arising on the disposal of the company's investment properties.

### Tax Tip

As long as the company continues to have an 'ordinary' UK letting business or an 'investment business', it may effectively continue to set brought forward rental losses off against other income and capital gains. Hence, a company with 'ordinary' UK rental losses may often be used as a vehicle to generate what will effectively be tax-free income or capital gains.

Either an 'ordinary' UK letting business or an 'investment business' must be continued, but this could be on a much smaller scale than previously, if desired.

### Wealth Warning

It should be noted that rental losses incurred in a company can only be set off against the company's income of the same or future periods.

There is no scope for setting such losses off against any rental profits that the owner of the company may have as an individual.

### Ordinary Overseas Lettings

All of a company's 'ordinary' overseas lettings are treated as a single business for CT purposes. This is treated as a separate business to the company's UK property letting business (if any).

Any loss on this business may be carried forward and set off against future profits from the same business – i.e. against future 'ordinary' overseas rental profits received by the company.

### Furnished Holiday Lettings

All of a company's UK furnished holiday lettings are treated as a single business. All of its furnished holiday lettings elsewhere in the European Economic Area are also treated as a single business – but a different one.

Losses arising on a furnished holiday letting business may only be carried forward and set off against future profits from the same business.

## Non-Commercial Lettings

Losses arising on any non-commercial lettings (i.e. lettings made on terms which are not normal, commercial, 'arm's length' terms) may only be set against future profits from the same letting.

## Corporate Loss Relief Restrictions

For accounting periods falling wholly or partly after 31st March 2017, the total amount of relief which a company, or group of companies, may claim for brought forward losses and unrelieved interest and finance costs is restricted to a maximum of £5m plus 50% of any profits in excess of that amount.

The £5m limit applies on an annual basis (e.g. the limit will be £2.5m for a six month period). Where an accounting period straddles 31st March 2017, the part of the period falling after that date is treated as a separate accounting period for this purpose.

## 4.9    OTHER PROPERTY INVESTMENT INCOME

Any form of income, profit or gains derived from property that the company receives will generally be subject to CT.

We will look at property trading profits in the next chapter and capital gains in Chapter 6, but in this section, it is worth considering some other items that may arise.

In Section 4.2, we saw that the company's rental income will include any tenant's deposits retained at the end of a lease.

HMRC also takes the view that any dilapidation payments received should usually be treated as rental income unless the payment is put towards the cost of repairs, when they consider that it should be netted off those costs.

This view is questionable and some experts argue that dilapidation payments are a capital receipt – i.e. effectively a part disposal of the property, meaning that the sum received represents a capital gain and that part of the property's original cost is therefore properly deductible.

HMRC does agree with this view if the property is not rented out again after receipt of the payment and is subsequently sold or adopted for some other purpose (e.g. as the company's own office premises).

Some items are specifically excluded from treatment as property income, including:

- Any amounts taxable as trading income or capital gains
- Profits from farming and market gardening
- Income from mineral extraction rights

Wayleave payments received in respect of access rights (e.g. for the electric company to have access to an electricity pylon on the company's land) are, however, sometimes included as property income.

Another important source of property income is lease premiums, which we will examine in the next section.

## 4.10    LEASE PREMIUMS

Lease premiums have a particularly complex treatment for CT purposes.

### Granting a Short Lease

Premiums received for the granting of short leases of no more than 50 years' duration are treated as being partly property income and partly capital disposal proceeds, potentially giving rise to a capital gain.

The proportion of the premium treated as capital disposal proceeds is equal to 2% of the total premium received for each full year of the lease's duration in excess of one year. The capital gain arising is calculated on the basis of a part disposal of the relevant property.

The remainder of the premium is treated as rental income.

### *Example*

*Telstra Limited owns the freehold to a property. The company grants a twelve-year lease to Fiji Limited for a premium of £50,000.*

*The lease exceeds one year by eleven years and hence 22% of this sum (£11,000) falls within the capital gains regime. This will be treated as a part disposal of the property and may or may not give rise to a taxable capital gain for Telstra Limited.*

*What is certain, however, is that Telstra Limited will be subject to CT on deemed rental income of £39,000 (i.e. £50,000 less 22%).*

A tenant paying a premium for the grant of a short lease of less than 50 years' duration may claim a deduction in respect of the proportion of the premium treated as rental income in the grantor's hands (i.e. £39,000 in the above example).

This claim must be spread over the length of the lease (e.g. £3,250 per annum for twelve years in Fiji Limited's case) and is only available if the tenant has a taxable business of their own.

If the tenant subsequently assigns the lease, they must restrict their base cost for capital gains purposes (see Section 6.3) to the element of the original lease premium treated as capital disposal proceeds in the grantor's hands (e.g. £11,000 in our example above). This base cost will then be subject to further restriction as explained below.

**Granting a Long Lease**

The grant of a lease of more than 50 years' duration is treated purely as a capital disposal. The base cost (see Section 6.3) to be used has to be restricted under the 'part disposal' rules. In essence, what this means is that the base cost is divided between the part disposed of (i.e. the lease) and the part retained (the 'reversionary interest') in proportion to their relative values at the time the lease is granted.

### *Example*

*JPR Limited owns the freehold of a commercial property in Llanelli. The company grants a 60-year lease to Brian, a businessman from Belfast moving into the area. Brian pays a premium of £90,000 for the lease. The value of JPR Limited's reversionary interest is established as £10,000.*

*The base cost to be used in calculating JPR Limited's capital gain on the grant of the lease is therefore 90% of its base cost for the property as a whole.*

## Assigning a long lease with no less than 50 years' duration remaining

This is simply a straightforward capital disposal. The capital gain arising is calculated in more or less the same way as for a freehold property sale (see Chapter 6). Any applicable capital gains reliefs may be claimed in the usual way.

## Assigning a short lease with less than 50 years' duration remaining

This is treated entirely as a capital disposal. However, leases with less than 50 years remaining are treated as 'wasting assets'. The company is therefore required to reduce its base cost in accordance with the schedule set out in Appendix F.

For example, for a lease with 20 years remaining, and which had more than 50 years remaining when first acquired, the base cost must be reduced to 72.77% of the original premium paid for the lease (plus other applicable purchase costs).

Where the lease had less than 50 years remaining when originally acquired, the necessary reduction in base cost is achieved by multiplying the original cost by the factor applying at the time of sale and dividing by the factor applying at the time of purchase.

### Example

*Calcutta Cup Limited pays a premium of £10,000 for the assignment of a lease with ten years remaining. Five years later, the company assigns the lease to Murrayfield Limited at a premium of £6,000.*

*When calculating the capital gain, the amount that Calcutta Cup Limited may claim as its base cost is:*

*£10,000 x 26.722/46.695 = £5,723*

# Chapter 5

# Property Trading Income and Expenses

## 5.1   HOW PROPERTY TRADING PROFITS ARE TAXED

Some property companies are not taxed under the rules for rental profits, as set out in Chapter 4, but are, instead, taxed on the basis that the income from their property business represents trading profit.

The most important differences in being a 'trading company' are probably the implications for the owner which we looked at in Chapter 3. As far as the computation of profits is concerned, the differences are not huge and there is therefore little point in repeating all of the rules from scratch once more.

What I will do in this chapter, however, is consider the differences for a company between the taxation of trading profits and the taxation of rental profits.

Trading losses are also subject to a different set of rules to rental losses and we will look at these in Section 5.6.

## 5.2   TRADING PROFITS VERSUS RENTAL PROFITS

The major differences between the taxation of rental profits and trading profits in a company may be summarised as follows:

- In the case of property development or property trading, the disposal proceeds received on the sale of a property represent trading income. Likewise, the cost of properties acquired represents 'cost of sales' and may be deducted from sale proceeds at the time of the property's sale.

- Legal and professional fees and other costs incurred on the purchase or sale of properties may also be included within 'cost of sales'.

- Any abortive costs relating to property purchases or sales may be claimed as company overheads.

- The costs related to any unsold properties are included in the company's accounts as 'trading stock'. We will look at the implications of this in more detail in the next section.

- Interest and finance costs relating to a company's trading activities are treated as a trading expense. They are deducted from trading profits and will also form part of any trading loss, to be dealt with as explained in Section 5.6 below. (Costs in excess of £2m per year continue to be subject to the restriction explained in Section 4.7.)

- The wear and tear allowance (see Section 4.5) is not applicable in a trading profits computation.

- Capital allowances may only be claimed in respect of assets acquired as long-term fixed assets of the business. We will look at this further in Section 5.5.

- The cost of any furnishings purchased and sold with a property may be deducted as 'cost of sales' against the disposal proceeds from that property.

- All of the company's business will usually be treated as a single business, regardless of where its properties are located. This will all be treated as UK trading income if the business is all run from the UK. (Non-UK resident companies are subject to CT on trading profits derived from UK land and property.)

Notwithstanding any of the above, any costs related to a property acquired as a long-term fixed asset of the business (such as its own offices, for example) remain capital in nature and do not form part of the company's trading stock or 'cost of sales'. A disposal of the company's own trading premises would continue to be dealt with under the rules for capital gains.


## 5.3 PROPERTIES AS TRADING STOCK

Properties held for development or sale in a property development or property dealing company are not regarded as long-term capital assets. They are, instead, regarded as the company's *trading stock*.

For tax purposes, all of the company's expenditure in acquiring, improving, repairing or converting the properties becomes part of the cost of that trading stock. Many of the issues that we need to deal with in a property investment company regarding the question of whether expenditure is revenue or capital in nature therefore become completely academic. Most professional fees and repairs or improvement expenditure are treated as part of the cost of the company's trading stock.

(The term 'revenue expenditure' means expenditure deductible from income, whereas capital expenditure is subject to different rules.)

When properties are sold, the related costs become 'cost of sales' and may be deducted from the company's sale proceeds. Sometimes, however, it may be some considerable time before this occurs. In the meantime, the property will have to be dealt with as 'trading stock'. In this section, we will take a detailed look at what this means in practice.

The way in which trading stock works for tax purposes can best be illustrated by way of an example.

### *Example*

*In November 2017, Grand Slam Limited buys a property in Swansea for £260,000. The company also pays SDLT of £10,800 and legal fees of £1,450. Previously, in October, it had also paid a survey fee of £750.*

*Grand Slam Limited is a property development company and draws up its accounts to 31st December each year.*

*In the company's accounts to 31st December 2017, the Swansea property will be included as trading stock with a value of £273,000, made up as follows:*

|  | £ |
|---|---|
| Property purchase | 260,000 |
| SDLT | 10,800 |
| Legal fees | 1,450 |
| Survey fee | 750 |
|  | ------------ |
|  | 273,000 |
|  | ======= |

### Points to Note

The important point to note here is that, whilst all of Grand Slam Limited's expenditure is regarded as revenue expenditure (because it's a property development company), the company cannot yet claim any deduction for any of it, because it still holds the property.

## Example Continued

Early in 2018, Grand Slam Limited incurs further professional fees of £7,000 obtaining planning permission to divide the property into two separate residences. Permission is granted in July and by the end of the year, Grand Slam Limited has spent a further £40,000 on conversion work.

In the company's accounts to 31st December 2018 the property will still be shown in trading stock, as follows:

|  | £ |
|---|---|
| Costs brought forward | 273,000 |
| Additional professional fees | 7,000 |
| Building work | 40,000 |
|  | ------------ |
|  | 320,000 |
|  | ======= |

Grand Slam Limited still doesn't get any tax relief for any of this expenditure.

By March 2019, Grand Slam Limited has spent another £5,000 on the property and is ready to sell the two new houses. One of them sells quickly for £185,000. Grand Slam Limited incurs a further £3,500 in estate agent and legal fees in the process.

Grand Slam Limited's taxable profit on this sale is thus calculated as follows:

|  | £ | £ |
|---|---|---|
| Sale proceeds |  | 185,000 |
| Less cost: |  |  |
| Total cost brought forward: | 320,000 |  |
| Additional building costs: | 5,000 |  |
|  | ---------- |  |
| Trading stock prior to sale of first property | 325,000 |  |
| Allocated to property sold (50%): | 162,500 |  |
| Add additional costs: | 3,500 |  |
|  | ---------- |  |
|  |  | 166,000 |
|  |  | ----------- |
| Profit on sale |  | 19,000 |
|  |  | ====== |

*This profit will form part of Grand Slam Limited's trading profit for the year ending 31st December 2019.*

## Points to Note

The additional building spend of £5,000 was allocated to trading stock as this still related to the whole property.

The legal and estate agent's fees incurred on the sale, however, were specific to the part that was sold and may thus be deducted in full against those sale proceeds.

In the example, I have split the cost of trading stock equally between the two new houses. If the two new houses are identical then this will be correct. Otherwise, the costs should be split between the two properties on a reasonable basis – e.g. total floor area, or in proportion to the market value of the finished properties.

The latter approach would be the required statutory basis if these were capital disposals. Although it is not mandatory here, it might still be a useful yardstick.

The most important point, however, is that even if Grand Slam Limited fails to sell the second new house before 31st December 2019, its profit on the first new house will still be taxable in full.

There is one exception to this, as we shall now examine.

## Net Realisable Value

Trading stock is generally shown in the accounts at its cumulative cost to date.

On this basis, Grand Slam Limited's second house, if still unsold at 31st December 2019, would have a carrying value of £162,500 in its accounts.

If, however, the market value of the property is less than its cumulative cost then its carrying value in the accounts may be reduced appropriately.

Furthermore, since the act of selling the property will itself give rise to further expenses, these may also be deducted from the property's reduced value in this situation. This gives us a value known in accounting terminology as the property's 'net realisable value'.

## Practical Pointer

Trading stock should always be shown in the accounts at the lower of cost or net realisable value.

To see the effect of this in practice, let's return once more to our example.

### *Example*

*The second new house in Swansea doesn't sell so quickly. Grand Slam Limited therefore decides to take the house off the market and build an extension on the back to make it more attractive to potential buyers.*

*Unfortunately, however, there are some problems with the foundations for the extension and the costs turn out to be more than double what Grand Slam Limited had originally expected.*

*By 31st December 2019, the company has spent £27,500 on the extension work and it still isn't finished. The total costs to date on the second new house are now £190,000. Furthermore, the further expenditure required to complete the extension is estimated at £12,000.*

*The estate agent reckons that the completed property will sell for around £200,000. The agent's own fees will amount to £3,000 and there will also be legal costs of around £750.*

*The net realisable value of the property at 31st December 2019 is thus:*

|  | £ | £ |
|---|---|---|
| Market value of completed property | | 200,000 |
| Less: | | |
| Costs to complete | 12,000 | |
| Professional costs to sell | 3,750 | |
| | ---------- | |
| | | 15,750 |
| | | ------------- |
| Net Realisable Value at 31/12/2019 | | 184,250 |
| | | ======= |

*Since this is less than the company's costs to date on the property, this is the value that should be shown as trading stock in the 2019 accounts.*

The result of this is that Grand Slam Limited will show a loss of £5,750 (£190,000 less £184,250) on the second house in its 2019 accounts. This loss will automatically be set off against the £19,000 profit on the first house.

By June 2020, the second house is ready for sale. Fortunately, there is an upturn in the market and Grand Slam Limited manages to sell the property for £215,000 in October 2020.

The actual additional expenditure on the extension work amounted to £11,800 and the professional fees incurred on the sale were actually £3,900.

Grand Slam Limited's taxable profit on this property in 2020 is thus:

|  | £ | £ |
|---|---|---|
| Sale proceeds |  | 215,000 |
| Less: |  |  |
| Value of trading stock brought |  |  |
| forward, as per accounts: | 184,250 |  |
| Additional building cost | 11,800 |  |
| Professional fees on sale | 3,900 |  |
|  | ---------- |  |
|  |  | 199,950 |
|  |  | ----------- |
| Taxable profit in year to 31/12/2020 |  | 15,050 |
|  |  | ======= |

## Points to Note

When preparing the accounts, we use the most accurate estimates available at that time to calculate net realisable value. In the case of sale price, however, we use the completed property's market value at the accounting date (i.e. 31st December 2019 in this example).

When calculating Grand Slam Limited's profit for 2020, we use actual figures for everything which took place after 31st December 2019, the company's last accounting date (i.e. the sale price, the final part of the building work and the professional fees on the sale). The property's net realisable value in the accounts at 31st December 2019 is, however, substituted for all of the costs incurred up until that date.

In this example, as often happens in practice, the selling price and actual costs incurred after the last accounting date turned out to be different to the estimates previously available. As a result, the apparent loss that the company was able to claim in 2019 effectively reversed and became part of its profits in 2020.

In the end, the net effect is that the true amount of profit that Grand Slam Limited actually made on the development has been taxed. The effect of the net realisable value calculation, however, was to provide some early CT relief for a loss that was reasonably anticipated at that time. For this reason, it will always be worth considering whether properties held as trading stock have a net realisable value less than cost at each accounting date.

## 5.4    WORK-IN-PROGRESS & SALES CONTRACTS

Generally, for speculative property developers, their company's trading stock, as we have seen, is valued at the lower of its cumulative cost to date or its net realisable value.

However, if a contract for the sale of the property exists, the development company has to follow a different set of rules.

This is a complex area of accounting, but, broadly speaking, the company is required to value properties under development, for which a sale contract already exists, at an appropriate percentage of their contractual sale value. This is done by treating the completed proportion of the property as having already been sold.

The same proportion of the expected final costs of the development can be deducted from the sale. Any remaining balance of development costs is included in the accounts as 'Work-in-Progress', which is simply a term for trading stock that is only partly completed.

### Example

*Aayan Limited is building a new house on a plot of land and has already contracted to sell it for £500,000.*

*Aayan Limited draws up accounts to 31st March each year and, at 31st March 2018, the new house is 75% complete. Aayan Limited's total costs to date are £320,000, but further costs of £80,000 are anticipated before the house is completed.*

*Aayan Limited will need to show a sale of £375,000 (75% of £500,000) in its accounts to 31st March 2018.*

*The company will, however, be able to deduct costs of £300,000, which equates to 75% of its anticipated final total costs of £400,000 (£320,000 + £80,000).*

*In other words, Aayan Limited will show a profit of £75,000 in its accounts to 31st March 2018, which is equal to 75% of the expected final profit on the development of £100,000.*

*The remaining £20,000 of Aayan Limited's costs to date will be shown in its accounts at 31st March 2018 as Work-in-Progress.*

*During the following year, Aayan Limited completes the property at an actual cost of £77,000.*

*The company's accounts for the year ending 31st March 2019 will show a sale of £125,000, i.e. the remaining 25% of the total sale proceeds of £500,000.*

*From this, Aayan Limited can deduct total costs of £97,000, which is made up of £20,000 of Work-in-Progress brought forward and actual costs in the year of £77,000.*

*This gives Aayan Limited a development profit of £28,000 for the year ending 31st March 2019.*

As we can see from the example, the effect of this accounting treatment is to accelerate part of the profit on the development.

As there is no specific rule to the contrary, the tax position will also follow the accounting treatment, so that the development company is taxed on part of its property sale in advance.

It follows that the whole profit on a property for which a sales contract exists will need to be included in the company's accounts once the property is fully completed.

Where this accounting treatment applies, the company may nevertheless claim deductions to reflect:

- Any doubt over the purchaser's ability, or willingness, to pay.
- Rectification work that is still to be carried out.
- Administration and other costs relating to completion of the sale.

## 5.5     CAPITAL ALLOWANCES FOR TRADING COMPANIES

As explained in Section 5.2, a property trading company can generally only claim capital allowances on its *own* long-term fixed assets. Any furniture, furnishings or equipment within its trading properties will form part of its trading stock.

In general terms, property development companies are likely to have greater scope for claiming capital allowances than companies with residential property investment businesses but possibly less scope than those with commercial property investments.

Property dealing companies and property management companies, however, are unlikely to be able to claim very many allowances.

The principles outlined below will also apply equally to any assets that a property investment company purchases for use in its own business.

## Plant and Equipment

Subject to the general comments above, plant and equipment purchased for use in the trade will be eligible for the 'plant and machinery' allowances described in Section 4.4.

'Plant and equipment' may include the following items used in the company's trade:

- Building equipment and tools
- Computers
- Office furniture, fixtures and fittings
- Vans

### Example

*During the year ending 31st March 2018, Triple Crown Limited spends £230,000 on plant and equipment for use in its trade. The company is entitled to an annual investment allowance of £200,000 (see Section 4.4) and may claim writing down allowances on the remaining £30,000 of its expenditure.*

*The company's writing down allowances amount to £5,400 (£30,000 x 18%), giving it total capital allowances for the year of £205,400 (£200,000 + £5,400). (For the sake of illustration, I am assuming that the company has no balance brought forward on its main pool.)*

*The remaining £24,600 of expenditure is carried forward to the year ending 31st March 2019, when it is eligible for writing down allowances of 18%, or £4,428. This leaves £20,172 to be carried forward to the year ending 31st March 2020, when it will attract writing down allowances of 18%, or £3,631.*

*Thereafter, the unrelieved balance of expenditure will continue to be carried forward and attract writing down allowances of 18% each year until the remaining unrelieved balance on the company's main pool reduces to £1,000 or less (see Section 4.4).*

It is worth noting that it will take twelve years before Triple Crown Limited has obtained tax relief for 90% of the expenditure in excess of the annual investment allowance. If that expenditure had been incurred in the company's previous, or next, accounting period, 100% tax relief may have been obtained immediately!

**Motor Cars**

The capital allowances regime for cars purchased by companies may be summarised as follows:

- Cars are not eligible for the annual investment allowance

- Cars with $CO_2$ emissions over the 'higher threshold' fall into the special rate pool and attract writing down allowances at just 8%

- Cars with $CO_2$ emissions over the 'lower threshold' but not over the 'higher threshold', fall into the main pool and attract writing down allowances at 18%

- Cars with $CO_2$ emissions of no more than the 'lower threshold' currently attract enhanced capital allowances at 100%

See Section 4.4 for further details on the main and special rate pools.

The 'higher threshold' is currently 130g/km. For cars purchased before 6th April 2013 it was 160g/km; for cars purchased after 31st March 2018 it is to be reduced to 110g/km.

The 'lower threshold' is currently 75g/km. For cars purchased between 1st April 2013 and 31st March 2015 it was 95g/km; for cars purchased before 1st April 2013 it was 110g/km; for cars purchased between 1st April 2018 and 31st March 2021 it is to be reduced to 50g/km. Thereafter, the 100% first year allowance for low emission cars is expected to be abolished.

**Tax Tip**

Companies wishing to maximise their capital allowances claims should consider buying any cars with $CO_2$ emissions over 110g/km but not over 130g/km, or over 50g/km but not over 75g/km, before 1st April 2018.

## Private Use

For cars owned by a company, there is no restriction in the amount of the capital allowances available to reflect any private use of the vehicle.

Instead, however, the person enjoying that private use is subject to Income Tax on a 'Benefit-in-Kind' charge.

Currently, this charge will generally be somewhere between 9% and 37% of the original purchase cost of the car when new.

In addition to the Income Tax charge on the individual, the company itself will have to pay Class 1A NI at 13.8% on the same 'Benefit-in-Kind' charge.

In total, the annual Income Tax and NI costs of running a company car could add up to over 27% of the cost of that car when it was brand new.

Company cars are a complex subject in their own right. Suffice to say, you should carefully review your own situation before deciding to buy a car through your company.


## Capital Allowance Disclaimers

It is worth noting that capital allowances are not mandatory and any proportion of the available allowance may be claimed, from zero to 100%.

Allowances not claimed are generally referred to as 'capital allowance disclaimers'.

Where an allowance is disclaimed in one period, a greater balance of expenditure is carried forward to the next period, thus increasing later capital allowance claims.

Capital allowance disclaimers are generally only worth considering where claiming the allowances would result in losses which are likely to go to waste and the increased allowances available in future periods are likely to be of some benefit.

## 5.6    TRADING LOSSES

Trading losses may be set off against the company's other income *and capital gains* of the same accounting period.

### Loss Carry Back

If the claim for set-off of trading losses within the same accounting period has been made, the company may additionally claim to carry back any surplus loss against its total profits and capital gains in the twelve months preceding the accounting period which gave rise to the loss.

If, however, the loss-making trade was not being carried on by the company throughout the previous twelve months, the relevant period for loss set-off is the period beginning with the commencement of that trade.

An added benefit of setting a trading loss off against other income in the current and previous years is that the resultant tax saving is more or less immediate.

### Loss Carry Forward

Any trading losses which still remain unrelieved after any claim for set-off in the current year or carry back to the previous year, will be carried forward for set-off as follows:

- Losses arising before 1st April 2017 may be set off against future profits from the same trade

- Losses arising after 31st March 2017 may be set off against the company's total income and capital gains, provided that the trade which gave rise to the loss has not ceased or become 'small'. Where the trade has become 'small', the carried forward losses may only be set off against future profits from that trade. Here there is no definition of what 'small' means, although it seems safe to assume it means the trade has become far smaller than it was when it gave rise to the losses.

Companies must now claim these set-offs and are subject to the limits on amounts in excess of £5m discussed in Section 4.8.

Companies which are members of a group of companies may also surrender some or all of their trading losses as group relief.

Loss relief claims must be made within two years of the end of the loss-making accounting period in the case of losses set off against profits and capital gains within the same period or the previous twelve months; or within two years of the end of the period for which relief is claimed in the case of losses carried forward.

Finally, it is worth noting that, whilst companies are subject to the limit on losses in excess of £5m carried forward (discussed in Section 4.8), they are not subject to the rather more restrictive limitations on individuals discussed in Section 13.9.

# Chapter 6

# Corporation Tax on Capital Gains

## 6.1    WHEN DOES A CAPITAL GAIN ARISE?

In Chapter 3, we examined the various different types of property companies and we saw that some property disposals give rise to trading profits.

We also saw, however, that property disposals made by property investment companies (see Section 3.2) give rise to capital gains instead.

Furthermore, other property companies disposing of their long-term fixed assets, such as their own office premises, for example, will also be subject to capital gains treatment.

In each case, the calculation of the amount of capital gain chargeable to CT is as follows:

### Capital Gain Equals Proceeds Less Base Cost

## 6.2    HOW TO CALCULATE THE 'PROCEEDS'

In most cases, the amount of 'Proceeds' to be used in the calculation of a capital gain will be the actual sum received on the disposal of the asset.

However, from this, the company may deduct incidental costs in order to arrive at 'net proceeds', which is the relevant sum for the purposes of calculating the capital gain.

### Example

*Yachvilli Limited sells a house for £375,000. In order to make this sale, the company spends £1,500 advertising the property, pays £3,750 in estate agent's fees and pays £800 in legal fees.*

*Yachvilli Limited's net proceeds are therefore £368,950 (£375,000 less £1,500, £3,750 and £800).*

There are, however, a number of cases where the proceeds we must use in the calculation of a capital gain are not simply the actual cash sum received. Three of the most common such exceptions are set out below.

## Exception 1 – Connected Persons

Where the person disposing of the asset is 'connected' with the person acquiring it, the open market value of the asset at the time of transfer must be used in place of the actual price paid (if any).

A company will be deemed to be 'connected' with any person who controls that company, as well as close relatives of that person and other companies also controlled by that person and/or their relatives.

### Example

*Beckham Limited is a property investment company and is wholly owned by Victoria.*

*Beckham Limited sells a property to Victoria's son, Cruz, for £500,000. The market value of the property at the time of this sale is £800,000. The company pays legal fees of £475 on the sale.*

*Beckham Limited will be deemed to have received net sale proceeds of £800,000 (the market value). The legal fees the company has borne are irrelevant, as this was not an 'arm's-length' transaction.*

The concept of 'connected persons' is important for a number of reasons, as we will see throughout this guide. A list of the persons deemed to be 'connected' with each other is therefore given in Appendix D.

## Exception 2 – Transactions not at 'arm's-length'

Where a transaction takes place between 'connected persons', as above, there is an automatic assumption that the transaction is not at 'arm's-length' and hence market value must always be substituted for the actual proceeds.

There are, however, other instances where the transaction may not be at 'arm's-length', such as:

- A sale of an asset to an employee
- A transaction which is part of a larger transaction
- A transaction which is part of a series of transactions

The effect of these is much the same as before – the asset's market value must be used in place of the actual proceeds, if any.

The key difference from Exception 1 above is that the onus of proof that this is not an 'arm's-length' transaction is on HMRC, rather than there being an automatic assumption that this is the case.

### *Example*

*Brooklyn Limited owns an investment property with a market value of £200,000. If the company sold the property at this price, it would have a capital gain of £80,000.*

*Not wishing to incur a CT liability, Brooklyn Limited decides instead to sell the house to Romeo Limited for £120,000. However, Brooklyn Limited only does this on condition that Romeo Limited gives it an interest-free loan of £80,000 for an indefinite period.*

*The condition imposed by Brooklyn Limited means that this transaction is not at 'arm's-length'. The correct position is therefore that Brooklyn Limited should be deemed to have sold the property for £200,000 and still have a capital gain of £80,000.*

## Exception 3 – Non-cash proceeds

Sometimes all or part of the sale consideration will take a form other than cash. The sale proceeds to be taken into account in these cases will be the market value of the assets or rights received in exchange for the asset sold.

### *Example*

*Little Property Company Limited owns an office block in central London.*

*Big Properties plc (a quoted company) wants to buy the property from Little Property Company Limited but, as it is experiencing some short-term cashflow difficulties, it offers Little Property Company Limited 500,000 shares for the property rather than cash.*

*Little Property Company Limited accepts this offer and takes the shares, which are worth £12.50 per share at the date of sale.*

*Little Property Company Limited's sale proceeds for CT purposes will therefore be £6.25m (500,000 x £12.50).*

**Wealth Warning**

Note that if, as in the above example, you take non-cash consideration for a sale, you will be taxed on the value of that consideration at that date. If the value of the non-cash asset that you receive should subsequently fall, you will still be taxed on the original value! This problem can sometimes possibly be alleviated by disposing of the asset that has fallen in value and thus generating a capital loss, but:

- This is not always desirable, and
- A capital loss cannot be carried back to an earlier accounting period.


## 6.3    HOW TO CALCULATE THE 'BASE COST'

The 'Base Cost' is the amount that may be deducted in the capital gains calculation in respect of an asset's cost. The higher the base cost, the lower the chargeable gain and the less CT payable!

As with proceeds, the basic starting point in most cases will be the actual amount paid to purchase the asset. Added to the actual amount paid are:

i)    Incidental costs of acquisition (e.g. legal fees, SDLT, etc)

ii)   Enhancement expenditure (e.g. the cost of building an extension to a property)

iii)  Expenditure incurred in establishing, preserving or defending title to, or rights over, the asset (e.g. legal fees incurred as a result of a boundary dispute)


**Base Cost – Special Situations**

There are again a number of special situations where base cost is determined by reference to something other than the actual amount paid for the asset.

The major exceptions fall into three main categories:

- The asset was not acquired by way of a 'bargain at arm's length'
- The asset was acquired for non-cash consideration
- The asset was acquired before 1st April 1982

Where one of these exceptions applies, the actual amount paid for the asset is replaced by the amount derived under the rules set out below.

## Assets Not Acquired by Way of a 'Bargain at Arm's Length'

In the case of an acquisition which is not a 'bargain at arm's length', the acquiring company's base cost will generally be the asset's market value at the time of purchase, as this will be the deemed 'proceeds' on which the person selling the asset is taxed.

### *Example*

*Martin owns a property investment company called Johnson Limited. The company buys a warehouse from Martin for £100,000. The warehouse, which Martin held as an investment, has an open market value of £200,000.*

*Johnson Limited will therefore have a base cost for the warehouse of £200,000. (Note that Martin's personal CGT liability will be based on a sale for deemed 'proceeds' of £200,000.)*

### Gifts of Business Assets

In the case of a property that qualifies as a 'business asset' for CGT purposes, the usual rule for a 'bargain not at arm's length' may be over-ridden by a 'hold-over' relief claim (see Section 15.7).

This would alter the position and the acquiring company would then be treated as acquiring the property for the greater of:

i)   The amount actually paid, or
ii)  The property's open market value less the amount of 'held over' gain.

This treatment can generally only apply to furnished holiday letting property or property used as a long-term fixed asset in the transferor's own trading business. We will return to this subject in more detail in Chapter 15.

Where an asset is not acquired by way of a 'bargain at arm's length' (whether 'hold-over' relief is claimed or not), subsequent expenditure incurred by the purchaser under headings (ii) and (iii) above still continues to be added to the base cost in the normal way.

**Assets acquired for non-cash consideration**

Where an asset was acquired for non-cash consideration, its base cost will be determined by reference to the market value of the consideration given.

Expenditure incurred by the purchaser under headings (i) to (iii) above is still added to the base cost in the normal way.

**Assets acquired before 1st April 1982**

Generally speaking, the base cost will usually be the asset's open market value at 31st March 1982.

Expenditure incurred by the purchaser under headings (ii) and (iii) above is added to the base cost: but only when incurred after 31st March 1982. Earlier expenditure is ignored as it has effectively been replaced by the asset's market value at 31st March 1982.

### 6.4    HOW TO CALCULATE THE INDEXATION RELIEF

Indexation relief was introduced in 1982 to eliminate the purely inflationary element of capital gains. Unlike individuals, for whom indexation relief was abolished in 2008, companies continue to be entitled to indexation relief on their capital disposals.

The relief is based on the increase in the retail prices index over the period of the company's ownership of the asset (or from 31st March 1982 until the date of sale, if the asset was acquired before then).

Where the base cost of the asset is made up of original cost and later enhancement expenditure, each element of the base cost will attract indexation relief at its own appropriate rate.

### *Example*

*Wilkinson Limited bought a property for £100,000 in June 1987. In August 1991, the company spent £50,000 building an extension to the property. The property was sold for £600,000 in February 2017.*

*The retail prices index was 101.9 in June 1987, 134.1 in August 1991 and 268.4 in February 2017.*

*The retail prices index increased by 163.4% between June 1987 and February 2017, so the indexation relief due on the company's original purchase cost is £163,400 (£100,000 x 163.4%).*

*The retail prices index increased by 100.1% between August 1991 and February 2017, so the indexation relief due on the company's enhancement expenditure (i.e. the cost of the extension) is £50,050 (£50,000 x 100.1%).*

*Wilkinson Limited's chargeable gain is therefore calculated as follows:*

|  | £ | £ |
|---|---|---|
| *Sale proceeds* | | *600,000* |
| *Less:* | | |
| *Original cost* | *100,000* | |
| *Enhancement expenditure* | *50,000* | |
| | ---------- | |
| | | *150,000* |
| *Indexation relief* | | |
| *On original cost* | *163,400* | |
| *On enhancement expenditure* | *50,050* | |
| | ---------- | |
| *Total:* | | *213,450* |
| | | ---------- |
| *Chargeable gain:* | | *£236,550* |

Indexation relief may not be used to create or increase a capital loss. Hence, in some cases, the amount of relief has to be restricted. Where a capital loss already arises, no relief is given at all. Where there is a capital gain before indexation, the relief cannot exceed the amount of the gain before indexation.

## The Retail Prices Index

A full table of retail prices index factors for use in calculating indexation relief on capital disposals by companies is reproduced in Appendix E.

The rate of indexation relief to be claimed is calculated as follows:

**Indexation Relief Rate = (RD – RA)/RA**

RA is the retail prices index for the month of acquisition, or other allowable expenditure. Where the property's open market value at 31st March 1982 is being used for its base cost (see Section 6.3), use 79.44 for RA.

RD is the retail prices index for the month of disposal.

### Example

*To calculate the indexation relief rate applying to the cost of a property purchased by a company in May 2000 and sold by that company in December 2016, we find from Appendix E that RA is 170.7 and RD is 267.1.*

*The indexation relief rate is therefore (267.1 – 170.7)/170.7 or 96.4/170.7, which equates to 56.5%.*

#### Tax Tip

A close examination of the table in Appendix E reveals that the retail prices index often falls between December and January. From an indexation relief viewpoint, it therefore may be beneficial to try to sell property by the end of December.

The other side of the coin is that it may ultimately prove more beneficial to delay property purchases or enhancement expenditure until January.

Note that the date of sale of a property for capital gains purposes is when an unconditional contract for the sale comes into being.

## 6.5   MAKING THE MOST OF CAPITAL LOSSES

Any capital losses that arise may be set off against capital gains (after indexation relief) arising in the same accounting period.

Surplus capital losses are then carried forward and set off against capital gains arising in later accounting periods.

Capital losses cannot be carried back to earlier accounting periods and nor can they be set against capital gains made by the company owner, even on shares in the company making the capital losses.

**Tax Tip**

It may be worth considering disposing of loss-making properties before the end of an accounting period in which the company has made capital gains.

**Another Tax Tip**

Unless there are strong commercial reasons for doing so, a company which has unused capital losses carried forward should not be wound up as there will always be a possibility of realising tax-free capital gains through it in the future.

# Chapter 7

# Capital Gains Tax on Company Shares

## 7.1    INTRODUCTION

Company owners are not subject to CGT on the capital gains which their company makes on the disposal of properties. As we have seen in previous chapters, the company pays CT on those gains instead. Company owners are, however, subject to CGT on the disposal of shares in their property company. A 'disposal' for this purpose includes:

- A sale of the company,
- A winding up of the company (but see points in Section 7.7), or
- A transfer of shares to another person

In the case of a transfer to a connected person (see Appendix D), or any other transfer which is 'not a bargain at arm's length' (see Section 6.2), the market value of the shares is substituted in place of the actual sale proceeds for CGT purposes.

Holdover relief may sometimes be available in these circumstances (see Section 7.6). Transfers to the owner's spouse are also generally exempt from CGT.

As we saw in Chapter 3, some property company shares will also be eligible for entrepreneurs' relief, which we shall be looking at in detail in Section 7.3.

## 7.2    CAPITAL GAINS TAX RATES

For disposals made by individuals after 5th April 2016, CGT is charged at five rates:

- 10% where entrepreneurs' relief is available (Section 7.3)
- 18% on residential property gains made by basic rate taxpayers
- 28% on residential property gains made by higher rate taxpayers
- 10% on most other gains made by basic rate taxpayers
- 20% on most other gains made by higher rate taxpayers

The 18% and 28% rates continue to apply to:

- Any interest in land or property that has ever included a residential dwelling at any time during the taxpayer's ownership
- Contracts for off-plan purchases of residential property
- A few other, very limited, cases

The lower rates for basic rate taxpayers apply to the extent that the individual has any remaining basic rate tax band available after accounting for their total income for the tax year.

The good news is that, although the rates applying to residential property remain 18% and 28%, the 10% and 20% rates apply to disposals of shares in property investment companies: even if the company is investing in residential property.

Each individual is also entitled to an annual CGT exemption each tax year. The annual exemptions for 2016/17 and 2017/18 are £11,100 and £11,300 respectively.

### Example

*In March 2018, Andy sells some shares in his property investment company and makes a capital gain of £50,000. The shares do not qualify for entrepreneurs' relief.*

*Andy's total taxable income for 2017/18 is £30,000. After deducting his personal allowance of £11,500, his income uses up £18,500 of his basic rate band, leaving £15,000 available for CGT purposes (see Appendix A for details of Income Tax allowances, bands, etc for 2017/18).*

*After deducting his annual exemption of £11,300, Andy is left with a taxable capital gain of £38,700. His CGT bill is therefore as follows:*

| | |
|---|---|
| *£15,000 x 10% =* | *£1,500* |
| *£23,700 x 20% =* | *£4,740* |
| *Total* | *£6,240* |

## 7.3    ENTREPRENEURS' RELIEF

Entrepreneurs' relief operates by substituting a CGT rate of 10% in place of the usual rates.

Each individual may only claim entrepreneurs' relief on a maximum cumulative lifetime total of £10m of qualifying capital gains. Thereafter, the CGT rate on all further capital gains will revert to the normal rates set out in Section 7.2.

Whilst companies themselves do not qualify for entrepreneurs' relief, property company owners may benefit from this relief when they dispose of shares in a qualifying 'personal company'.

The definition of a 'personal company' for the purposes of entrepreneurs' relief is broadly as follows:

    i)    The individual holds at least 5% of the ordinary share capital
    ii)   The holding under (i) provides at least 5% of the voting rights
    iii)  The company is a trading company (see below)
    iv)  The individual is an officer or employee of the company
          (an 'officer' includes a director or company secretary)

Each of these rules must be satisfied for the period of at least one year prior to the disposal in question or, where the company has ceased trading, for at least one year prior to the cessation. In the latter case, the disposal must take place within three years after cessation.

As we saw in Chapter 3, property development companies, property management companies and, in theory, property dealing companies, all qualify as trading companies for the purposes of entrepreneurs' relief.

As discussed in Section 3.2, qualifying furnished holiday lettings are also deemed to be a trade for the purposes of entrepreneurs' relief.

For the availability of entrepreneurs' relief on shares in a company with a 'mixed' property business, see Section 3.6.

To illustrate the impact of entrepreneurs' relief, let's look at an example.

### Example

*Redpath Limited and Delaglio Limited are both property development companies. Both companies were set up for an initial investment of just £1,000 each and started trading immediately afterwards.*

*Both companies also have some rental income, meaning that, in HMRC's view, they have some non-trading activity. Redpath Limited, however, manages to keep the non-trading activity below the level that HMRC regards as 'substantial' (see Section 3.6), meaning that it is accepted as a trading company.*

*The shares in Redpath Limited therefore qualify for entrepreneurs' relief.*

*Brian, who owns all of the shares in Redpath Limited, decides to sell the company in 2017 and receives net proceeds of £5.001m, giving him a capital gain of exactly £5m.*

*Assuming that Brian has already used up his annual exemption on other gains, his CGT liability on the sale of his Redpath Limited shares will be £500,000 (£5m x 10%).*

*Lawrence, the sole shareholder of Delaglio Limited, also sells his company in 2017 and also makes a capital gain of £5m.*

*However, Delaglio Limited's non-trading activities have unfortunately exceeded the level that HMRC regards as 'substantial', meaning that the company is not regarded as a trading company for entrepreneurs' relief purposes.*

*Hence, assuming that Lawrence is a higher rate taxpayer and has used up his annual exemption on other gains, his CGT liability on the sale of his Delaglio Limited shares will be £1m (£5m x 20%).*

*That's £500,000 more than, or **double**, Brian's CGT liability on a sale of very similar shares!*

Note that entrepreneurs' relief is not mandatory and taxpayers may choose whether to claim it.

Where a basic rate taxpayer claims entrepreneurs' relief on a capital gain, this gain uses up their remaining basic rate band in priority to any other gains. In effect, this pushes more (or perhaps all) of those other gains up into the 20% or 28% CGT bracket.

The cumulative lifetime maximum of £10m applies to all entrepreneurs' relief claims on capital gains arising after 5th April 2008.


## 7.4    ENTREPRENEURS' RELIEF FOR PROPERTY INVESTMENT COMPANIES

Subject to the overall limit of £10m, entrepreneurs' relief is available on the whole of a capital gain arising on the disposal of shares in a company which meets the 'personal company' conditions set out in Section 7.3 for the relevant one year period, even if the company did not previously meet those conditions.

Hence, entrepreneurs' relief will be available in full as long as the company qualifies as a 'trading company' for the one year period prior to the disposal of the shares, or the year prior to cessation of its business (provided that the other necessary conditions are met).

### Tax Tip

Entrepreneurs' relief would be available on shares in a former property investment, or other 'non-trading', company which changes its business and becomes a qualifying 'trading company' for the one year period prior to the disposal of the shares or cessation of the company's business.

As usual, qualifying furnished holiday lettings (see Section 4.6) count as 'trading' for this purpose and may therefore provide an easy way for a residential property investment company to undergo the necessary conversion.

## 7.5    ENTREPRENEURS' RELIEF AND COUPLES

It is worth noting that the £10m cumulative lifetime maximum for entrepreneurs' relief applies on a 'per person' basis.

Hence, if both members of a couple own at least 5% of the ordinary shares in a qualifying 'trading company' each, they will potentially be able to claim entrepreneurs' relief on total capital gains of up to £20m. This will provide total CGT savings of up to £2m.

Alternatively, if 5% or more of the ordinary shares in a qualifying 'trading company' are transferred to the owner's spouse at least a year prior to cessation or sale then the spouse may again be entitled to entrepreneurs' relief, once more giving potential relief on total capital gains of up to £20m.

### Wealth Warning

For a disposal of shares to qualify for entrepreneurs' relief, the company must have qualified as the 'personal company' of the individual making the disposal for at least a year prior to cessation or sale.

A pre-sale transfer of shares to a spouse might therefore result in the loss of entrepreneurs' relief if the spouse did not meet all of the necessary qualifying conditions (see Section 7.3) for at least a year prior to cessation or sale.

It is also important to remember that pre-sale transfers to a spouse are only effective if the transferee spouse genuinely obtains beneficial ownership of the transferred shares.

In other words, the transferee must be free to do as they wish with the transferred shares and must be beneficially entitled to their share of the sale proceeds.

## 7.6    HOLDOVER RELIEF

Holdover relief is available on the transfer of shares in an unquoted trading company (except a transfer of shares to or from another company).

Where the transfer is an outright gift, the transferor and transferee may jointly elect to 'hold over' the entire capital gain arising. The effect of this is that no CGT is payable by the transferor and the transferee is treated as having acquired the shares for the same base cost (see Section 6.3) as the transferor.

For sales made for a consideration less than market value, a partial hold over is available. Broadly speaking, the amount of gain held over is equal to the difference between the market value and the sales price. The effect of this is that the transferor pays CGT based on the actual sales price and the transferee's base cost is equal to that price.

The definition of a 'trading company' for holdover relief purposes is the same as for entrepreneurs' relief purposes (see Chapter 3 and Section 7.3 for further details). It follows that most unquoted shares which qualify for entrepreneurs' relief will qualify for holdover relief (but not necessarily vice versa). However, it is important to note that holdover relief will be restricted if the company has not qualified as a 'trading company' throughout the transferor's entire period of ownership.

### Holdover Relief and Entrepreneurs' Relief

A holdover relief claim could be used to make a transfer of shares in a qualifying 'trading company' to another individual other than the owner's spouse free from CGT (e.g. to transfer shares to an unmarried partner or an adult child).

If the transferee then held the transferred shares for at least one year, and met all of the other qualifying conditions set out in Section 7.3, they would then be entitled to entrepreneurs' relief on those shares.


## 7.7   WINDING UP THE COMPANY

When a company is wound up, any remaining assets or funds within the company are distributed to its shareholders. This is known as a 'capital distribution on winding up'. The basic rule is that such distributions are subject to CGT.

Hence, for example, if a property company owner had originally subscribed for their shares in the company for £100 and they receive a distribution of £100,100 when that company is wound up, they will have a capital gain of £100,000. Like any other gain, this will be taxed at the rates set out in Section 7.2. Entrepreneurs' relief may even be available if the criteria discussed in Section 7.3 are met.

From 6th April 2016, however, new 'anti-phoenixing' legislation applies to deem certain distributions on winding up of companies to be income distributions subject to Income Tax, as if they were dividends; instead of capital distributions subject to CGT. (See Section 10.3 for details of the tax rates applying to dividends.)

The provisions apply where:

i)   The recipient held at least 5% of the share capital and voting rights in the company,

ii)  The company was a 'close company' (see Section 16.1) at any time within the two year period prior to the winding up,

iii) The recipient of the distribution participates in a new business operating in a similar trade or business to the company being wound up at any time within the period of two years following the winding up, and

iv)  A tax advantage would otherwise arise as a consequence of the winding up

Given that higher rate taxpayers will always pay a lower rate of tax on a capital distribution (10% or 20%, depending on whether entrepreneurs' relief is available), than on an income distribution (32.5% or more), many commentators fear that HMRC will nearly always regard condition (iv) as having been satisfied.

As we shall see in Section 16.1, most small private companies are close companies, so condition (ii) will usually be satisfied as well.

Hence, if condition (i) applies, it will generally be essential to ensure that you do not fall foul of condition (iii). In other words, if you own at least 5% of the company, it will be important to avoid 'participating' in any similar trade or business for at least two years after the winding up.

Where the company being wound up was a property investment company, this will mean that you are unable to invest in property for the next two years!

For these purposes 'participating' in a trade or business includes:

- Acting as a sole trader/investor
- Investing jointly with one or more other people
- Being a partner in a partnership
- Being a member of an LLP
- Owning at least 5% of the shares in a company

Worst of all, you may also be caught by condition (iii) if a 'connected person' (see Appendix D) participates in a similar trade or business within the critical two year period.

# Chapter 8

# Stamp Duty for Property Companies

## 8.1 INTRODUCTION

Stamp Duty is the oldest tax on the statute books. It was several centuries old already when Pitt the Younger introduced Income Tax in 1799. Even today, we are still governed (to a limited extent) by the Stamp Act 1891.

Since 2003, however, for transfers of real property (i.e. land and buildings or any form of legal interest in them), Stamp Duty has been replaced by SDLT (see Section 8.3).

## 8.2 STAMP DUTY ON SHARES

Despite talk of its abolition a few years ago, this ancient tax continues to apply to transfers of shares. The rate of Stamp Duty on purchases of shares and securities is still unchanged at a single uniform rate of only 0.5%. This has led to many tax-avoidance strategies, designed to avoid the excessive rates applied to property transactions by making use of this more palatable rate. Anti-avoidance legislation has effectively blocked most of the more popular methods, however.

Nevertheless, for those investing in property through a company, there remains the possibility of selling shares in that company at a much lower rate of Duty than would apply to the sale of individual properties within the company.

Sales of private company shares for no more than £1,000 are exempt from Stamp Duty.

## 8.3 STAMP DUTY LAND TAX

SDLT applies to transfers of real property (i.e. land and buildings or any form of legal interest in them). The tax is currently payable on all transfers of real property located in England, Wales or Northern Ireland regardless of where the vendor or purchaser are resident and regardless of where the transfer documentation is drawn up. (See Sections 8.7 and 8.8 regarding property in Scotland and Wales respectively)

The type of property company which you have generally has no impact on the rate of SDLT and the rates applying are mostly the same for companies as they are for individuals except that:

- The higher charges on residential property introduced from 1st April 2016 **always** apply to purchases by companies (subject to the exemptions set out in Section 8.9), and
- A special rate of 15% may apply to certain purchases of residential property for over £500,000 (see Section 8.4)

Subject to the two points above, the rates of SDLT for property purchases by companies are as follows:

### Residential Property

| | |
|---|---|
| Up to £125,000 | 3% |
| £125,000 to £250,000 | 5% |
| £250,000 to £925,000 | 8% |
| £925,000 to £1.5m | 13% |
| Over £1.5m | 15% |

### Non-Residential Property

| | |
|---|---|
| Up to £150,000 | 0% |
| £150,000 to £250,000 | 2% |
| Over £250,000 | 5% |

Both sets of rates are now applied on a 'progressive' basis, as illustrated by this example:

### Example

*The SDLT arising on a residential property purchased by a company for £1.6m for use in its business (see Section 8.4) is:*

| | |
|---|---|
| *First £125,000 @ 3%:* | *£3,750* |
| *Next £125,000 @ 5%:* | *£6,250* |
| *Next £675,000 @ 8%:* | *£54,000* |
| *Next £575,000 @ 13%:* | *£74,750* |
| *Next £100,000 @ 15%:* | *£15,000* |
| *Total:* | *£153,750* |

The rates for residential property purchases set out above include the additional 3% which will always apply where property is purchased by a company. These rates will also generally apply to individual property investors, but for details of the limited circumstances under which the additional 3% charge may be avoided see the Taxcafe.co.uk guide *'How to Save Property Tax'*.

Generally speaking, the SDLT charge is based on the actual consideration paid for the purchase – whether in cash or by any other means.

However, in the case of a transfer of property to a 'connected' company (see Section 6.2), the deemed consideration for SDLT purposes will be the greater of the actual amount of consideration paid and the property's market value. We will explore some of the implications of this in Chapter 15.

Furthermore, it should also be noted that the rate of SDLT to be applied must be determined after taking account of any 'linked transactions'. However, this is not always as disastrous as it once was, following the introduction of 'multiple dwellings relief'. We will examine this issue further in Section 8.6.

## 8.4 RESIDENTIAL PROPERTY PURCHASES BY 'NON-NATURAL' PERSONS

A special SDLT rate of 15% applies to the entire purchase price on purchases of residential properties in excess of £500,000 by companies and other 'non-natural' persons, such as collective investment schemes, unit trusts, and partnerships in which any 'non-natural' person is a partner.

The rate only applies where a single dwelling is purchased for a price in excess of £500,000, or where one or more separate dwellings included in the purchase of a larger portfolio are worth more than £500,000 each.

Properties are exempt from this special rate when acquired for use in a business. This exemption covers both trading businesses and property investment businesses, so property investment companies should not generally have to pay this punitive rate. This issue is examined further in Section 16.7.

Where this special rate applies, neither multiple dwellings relief nor the alternative treatment outlined in Section 8.6 are available.

## 8.5 STAMP DUTY LAND TAX ON LEASES

SDLT is also payable on the granting of a lease. The amount of tax payable is based on the 'net present value' of all the rent payable under the lease over its entire term.

Where the net present value does not exceed £125,000 (for residential property), or £150,000 (for non-residential property), no SDLT will be payable.

For new leases with a net present value exceeding these limits, SDLT is payable at a rate of 1% on the excess. The rate increases to 2% on any amounts in excess of £5m.

VAT is excluded from the rent payable under the lease for the purposes of SDLT calculations <u>unless</u> the landlord has already exercised the option to tax (this applies to commercial property only).

### *Example*

*Woodward Limited is about to take on a ten-year lease over a house in Kent at an annual rent of £18,000.*

*The SDLT legislation provides that the net present value of a sum of money due in twelve months' time is equal to the sum due divided by a 'discount factor'. The applicable discount factor is currently 103.5%.*

*For SDLT purposes, all of the first year's rent is treated as if it were one single lump sum due in twelve months' time. The 'net present value' of the first year's rent is therefore £17,391 (i.e. £18,000 divided by 103.5%).*

*Similarly, the second year's rent, which is due a further twelve months later, must be 'discounted' again by the same amount, i.e. £17,391/103.5% = £16,803.*

*This process is continued for the entire ten-year life of the lease and the net present values of all of the rental payments are then added together to give the total net present value for the whole lease. In this case, this works out at £149,699.*

*The SDLT payable by Woodward Limited is therefore £250 (1% of £149,699 LESS £125,000, rounded up to the nearest £5).*

The current 'discount factor' (103.5%) may be changed in the future, depending on a number of factors, including the prevailing rates of inflation and interest.

### Lease Premiums

Lease **premiums** also attract SDLT, usually at the same rates as for outright purchases.

However, where the lease of a commercial property is also subject to an annual rent of more than £1,000, the 0% rate for the first £150,000 does not apply and SDLT is payable at the rate of 2% on the first £250,000 of any premium.

The restriction of this rule to commercial property only means that it may sometimes be possible to grant a lease over a residential property with a premium of up to £125,000 **and** annual rental with a net present value of up to £125,000 with no SDLT cost whatsoever. (But not where the additional 3% charge discussed in Section 8.3 and in the Taxcafe.co.uk guide *'How to Save Property Tax'* applies to the premium.)

### 8.6    LINKED TRANSACTIONS

The rate of SDLT to be applied is determined after taking account of any 'linked transactions'.

'Linked transactions' can arise in a number of ways, including a simultaneous purchase of several properties from the same vendor.

The effect of the 'linked transactions' depends on whether 'multiple dwellings relief' is claimed. This relief is only available for multiple purchases of residential property.

First, however, let's look at the basic rule applying to linked transactions where multiple dwellings relief is not available.

### Basic Rule without Multiple Dwellings Relief

The basic rule which applies where multiple dwellings relief is not claimed is that the 'linked transactions' are treated as if they were a single purchase for SDLT purposes.

In practice, this will mainly apply to multiple purchases of non-residential property, although it will also apply to any other 'linked transactions' where multiple dwellings relief is not available.

For example, if a property investment company were to buy three commercial properties from the same developer at the same time for £250,000 each, this would be treated for SDLT purposes as if it were one single purchase for £750,000. The SDLT charge would therefore be:

| | |
|---|---|
| £100,000 @ 2%: | £2,000 |
| £500,000 @ 5%: | £25,000 |
| Total: | £27,000 |

## Multiple Dwellings Relief

Multiple dwellings relief is available where multiple **residential** properties are purchased from the same vendor at the same time.

Where multiple dwellings relief is claimed, the rate of SDLT is based on the **average** consideration paid for each 'dwelling'. The relief is not automatic and must be claimed by the purchaser.

For companies, the higher charges detailed in Section 8.3 (including the additional 3%) will always continue to apply to the average price.

### Example 1

*Carter Limited buys five houses from a developer for a total consideration of £1.2m. Without multiple dwellings relief, SDLT would be charged as follows:*

| | |
|---|---|
| *First £125,000 @ 3%:* | *£3,750* |
| *Next £125,000 @ 5%:* | *£6,250* |
| *Next £675,000 @ 8%:* | *£54,000* |
| *Next £275,000 @ 13%:* | *£35,750* |
| *Total:* | *£99,750* |

*However, as the average price for each property is just £240,000, Carter Limited claims multiple dwellings relief. The SDLT calculation is then as follows:*

| | |
|---|---|
| *First £125,000 @ 3%:* | *£3,750* |
| *Next £115,000 @ 5%:* | *£5,750* |
| *Total per property:* | *£9,500* |
| *x 5 =* | *£47,500* |

In a case like this, the charge with multiple dwellings relief is clearly much fairer. The relief goes even further, however, and could actually be used to reduce the SDLT charge on a single large property.

### Example 2

*Lamont Properties Limited is planning to buy a new house in York at a cost of £750,000. The company's SDLT bill will currently amount to:*

| | |
|---|---|
| *First £125,000 @ 3%:* | *£3,750* |
| *Next £125,000 @ 5%:* | *£6,250* |
| *Next £500,000 @ 8%:* | *£40,000* |
| *Total:* | *£50,000* |

*In order to reduce the SDLT cost, however, the company arranges to buy two small flats from the same developer at the same time. The flats cost £60,000 each, bringing the total consideration to £870,000, but the average consideration is now just £290,000. Lamont Properties Limited can therefore claim multiple dwellings relief to give a reduction in the SDLT charge to:*

| | |
|---|---|
| *First £125,000 @ 3%:* | *£3,750* |
| *Next £125,000 @ 5%:* | *£6,250* |
| *Next £40,000 @ 8%:* | *£3,200* |
| *Total per property:* | *£13,200* |
| *x 3 =* | *£39,600* |

*Hence, by buying the flats at the same time as the house, the company has saved £10,400. That's equivalent to getting a discount of almost 9% on the flats!*

### A Major Benefit for Property Investors

Self-contained flats within a single property each constitute a separate 'dwelling' for the purposes of multiple dwellings relief. This provides a major benefit for property investors buying larger properties.

For example, if a property investment company buys a property which has been divided into four flats, this would constitute four dwellings, so that multiple dwellings relief can be claimed and thus significantly reduce the SDLT due.

### Mixed Purchases

Multiple dwellings relief does not apply to non-residential property, even when it forms part of a larger 'mixed' purchase.

### Alternative Treatment

A simultaneous purchase of six or more residential dwellings (from the same vendor) can alternatively be treated as a non-residential property purchase for SDLT purposes. This may sometimes produce a better outcome than claiming multiple dwellings relief. For example, a purchase of six dwellings for a total of £1.8m would attract SDLT of £84,000: even with multiple dwellings relief. The charge at non-residential rates would be £79,500.

## 8.7    PROPERTY IN SCOTLAND

From 1st April 2015, SDLT has been abolished for property located in Scotland and has been replaced by Land and Buildings Transaction Tax ('LBTT'). LBTT operates in a broadly similar way to SDLT, subject to a few variations, as noted below.

Subject to the exemptions set out in Section 8.9, companies purchasing residential property in Scotland will always be subject to the Additional Dwelling Supplement ('ADS') which adds an additional 3% charge in a similar way to the higher rates of SDLT examined in Section 8.3. ADS will generally also apply to purchases of residential property made by individuals for business purposes: for further details see the Taxcafe.co.uk guide *'How to Save Property Tax'*.

### Residential Property
The rates of LBTT on residential property (including ADS) are as follows:

| Purchase Consideration | Rate Applying |
|---|---|
| Up to £145,000 | 3% |
| £145,000 to £250,000 | 5% |
| £250,000 to £325,000 | 8% |
| £325,000 to £750,000 | 13% |
| Over £750,000 | 15% |

### Non-Residential Property
The rates of LBTT on non-residential property are as follows:

| Purchase Consideration | Rate Applying |
|---|---|
| Up to £150,000 | Nil |
| £150,000 to £350,000 | 3% |
| Over £350,000 | 4.5% |

LBTT is applied on a 'progressive' basis for both residential and non-residential property.

### *Example*

*Laidlaw Limited buys a small shop in Aberdeen for £270,000. The company pays LBTT at 3% on £120,000 (£270,000 - £150,000), which amounts to £3,600.*

**Key Differences**

Apart from the rates applying, LBTT operates in broadly the same way as SDLT. Many of the principles examined in Sections 8.3 to 8.6 continue to apply. In particular, the LBTT rates on leases are the same as those for SDLT (see Section 8.5), except that the 2% rate on net present value in excess of £5m does not apply.

Multiple dwellings relief operates differently under LBTT. Instead of taking an average price, the LBTT is calculated separately on each dwelling comprised in the purchase. The total LBTT due cannot be less than 25% of the amount due on the total consideration for the whole transaction.

Purchases of six or more dwellings may again alternatively be taxed at non-residential rates based on the total consideration for the whole transaction.

LBTT applies to 'licences to occupy' in the same way as it applies to leases

The special rate of SDLT examined in Section 8.4 does not apply to LBTT.

This is by no means an exhaustive list of all the differences between LBTT and SDLT, so it remains essential to take legal advice when purchasing property in Scotland (just as it is when purchasing property anywhere else!)

## 8.8    PROPERTY IN WALES

SDLT will cease to apply to property located in Wales from 1st April 2018, when it will be replaced by Land Transaction Tax, the first devolved tax for Wales.

The rates and bands for Land Transaction Tax are to be announced by 1st October 2017.

## 8.9    EXEMPTIONS

The following purchases are exempt from both SDLT and LBTT (including ADS):

- Interests in property worth less than £40,000
- Caravans, mobile homes and houseboats

# Chapter 9

# VAT And Property Companies

## 9.1 VAT ON PROPERTY

VAT, or 'Value Added Tax', to give it its proper name, is the 'new kid on the block' in UK taxation terms, having arrived on our shores from Europe in 1973.

VAT on property is a very complicated area and there are some nasty pitfalls awaiting the unwary property investor at the hands of this indirect form of taxation. Your company's VAT position will depend on its own particular situation and the type (and history) of the properties involved.

VAT is currently charged at three different rates in the UK: a standard rate of 20%, a reduced rate of 5% and a zero rate. All of these rates may be encountered by property companies.

UK VAT generally only applies to properties located in the UK and this is what we will be examining in this chapter. Most other countries in the European Union (see Appendix G) also charge VAT on some or all property transactions taking place there and it is therefore sensible to seek local advice on this issue (and indeed other tax issues) when investing in properties overseas.

## 9.2 RESIDENTIAL PROPERTY LETTING

Generally speaking, a property investment company engaged primarily in residential property letting does not need to register for VAT. (Nor, indeed, very often would it be able to.)

The letting of residential property is an exempt supply for VAT purposes. VAT is therefore not chargeable on rent, although, of course, VAT cannot be recovered on expenses and the company should therefore claim VAT-inclusive costs for CT purposes.

Beware, however, that the provision of ancillary services (e.g. cleaning or gardening) may sometimes be standard-rated, and hence subject to VAT at 20%, if the value of annual supplies of these services exceeds the VAT registration threshold (£85,000 from 1st April 2017).

Some companies making ancillary supplies of this nature prefer to register for VAT, even if they have not reached the registration threshold, as this means they are able to recover some of the VAT on their expenses.

## 9.3    HOLIDAY ACCOMMODATION

The supply of holiday accommodation is standard-rated for VAT purposes. This will certainly apply to any qualifying furnished holiday lets in the UK and may also apply to other holiday lettings.

The landlord will therefore need to register for, and charge, VAT if the total income received from UK holiday accommodation exceeds the VAT registration threshold. For this purpose, 'income' will include both rentals and any charges for ancillary services.

## 9.4    COMMERCIAL PROPERTY LETTING

For commercial property, there is an 'option to tax'. In other words, the landlord company may choose, for each property (on a property-by-property basis), whether or not the rent should be an exempt supply for VAT purposes.

If the 'option to tax' is exercised, the rent on the property becomes standard-rated (at 20%) for VAT purposes.

The landlord company may then recover VAT on all of the expenses relating to that property.

Ancillary services are again likely to be standard-rated regardless of whether the landlord has opted to tax the property and a landlord who has not opted to tax any property will, as usual, need to register and charge VAT on these supplies if they exceed the VAT registration threshold.

Charging VAT on your commercial property rent is usually known as 'exercising the option to tax', although, technically, the proper term, as sometimes used by HMRC, is 'exercising the option to waive exemption from the requirement to charge tax'. Either way, it means the same thing.

**Tax Tip**

If the potential tenants of a commercial property are all, or mostly, likely to be VAT-registered businesses themselves, it will generally make sense to exercise the 'option to tax' on the property in order to recover the VAT on expenses incurred.

If your tenants themselves have a VAT registered and fully taxable business for VAT purposes, then everyone's happy. The problem comes when your tenants cannot recover some or all of the VAT which you are charging them.

And remember that (after a short 'cooling off' period) you cannot change your option on a property for a minimum of 20 years once it has been exercised. Hence, if you opt to charge VAT to a fully taxable tenant, you will probably still need to charge VAT to the next tenant in the same property, even if they cannot recover it.

Sometimes though, with non-taxable (for VAT) tenants, where you have not yet exercised your option to tax, you can refrain from doing so and negotiate a higher rent to compensate you for your loss of VAT recovery on your own costs.

### *Example*

*Benazzi Limited owns an office building and hasn't yet opted to tax the rents. The company incurs monthly costs of £2,000 plus VAT (i.e. £2,400 gross) and expects a monthly rent of £10,000. If Benazzi Limited opts to tax it will recover £400 a month from HMRC and make a monthly profit of £8,000.*

*However, Abdelatif Limited, the prospective tenant, is not registered for VAT. If Benazzi Limited opts to tax the property, Abdelatif Limited's rent will effectively be 20% higher, i.e. £12,000 per month.*

*So, as a better alternative, Benazzi Limited and Abdelatif Limited agree that Benazzi Limited will not opt to tax the building but will, instead, charge Abdelatif Limited rent of £11,000 per month. Now Benazzi Limited is making a monthly profit of £8,600 (£11,000 minus £2,400) and Abdelatif Limited's rent is effectively £1,000 less than it would have been. Benazzi Limited and Abdelatif Limited both win and HMRC loses.*

## 9.5    RESIDENTIAL PROPERTY SALES

Sales of newly constructed residential property are zero-rated for VAT purposes. This means that the developer can recover all of the VAT on their construction costs without having to charge VAT on the sale of the property. (In theory, VAT is charged, but at a rate of zero.)

Furthermore, if your property development company contracts with a builder/contractor for the construction of a residential dwelling house, such services supplied should also be zero-rated, meaning that you will not even need to pay any VAT on these costs in the first place.

Zero-rating is generally also extended to the sale of a property that has just been converted from a non-residential property into a residential property (*e.g. converting a barn into a house*).

Property development companies carrying out construction work under these headings are therefore able to register for VAT and then recover the VAT on the vast majority of their business expenses.

### Other Residential Property Sales

Other sales of residential property are generally an exempt supply meaning, once again, that the company making the sale is unable to recover any of the VAT on its expenses.

This means that VAT cannot be recovered by most residential property investment companies.

Furthermore, property development companies that merely renovate or alter existing residential property prior to onward sale are also generally unable to recover VAT on their costs. Where, however, the work qualifies as a 'conversion', as described in Section 9.8, they may at least be able to reduce the amount of VAT payable.

## 9.6    COMMERCIAL PROPERTY SALES & PURCHASES

Where the 'option to tax' has previously been exercised on a commercial property, the sale of that property will again be standard-rated and this has major implications for such transactions.

Sales of new or uncompleted commercial property are always standard-rated for VAT purposes.

### Wealth Warning

Where VAT must be charged on a commercial property sale, the SDLT arising must be calculated on the basis of the gross, VAT-inclusive price.

For large properties, this could lead to an effective combined VAT and SDLT rate of almost 26%!

This represents a pretty hefty cost if the purchaser is not VAT registered, probably enough to prevent the sale from taking place in some cases.

Imagine a large insurance company buying a new office block in central London – the combined VAT and SDLT cost would be astronomical!

Where a property investment company incurs VAT on the purchase of a commercial property, the only way to recover that VAT will be for the company to exercise the 'option to tax' on the property. In this way, the Government generally forces everyone to maintain the taxable status of the building for VAT purposes.

If a VAT registered property development company incurs VAT on the purchase of a commercial property, it can recover the VAT in the same way as on any other purchase of goods or services for use in the business. This initial recovery is not dependent on exercising the 'option to tax', as the company has a taxable business for VAT purposes, but ...

### Wealth Warning

If VAT has been recovered on the purchase of a commercial property, a sale of that property without first exercising the option to tax would be an exempt supply.

If that property were trading stock, this would result in the loss of all the VAT initially reclaimed on its purchase and on any development, renovation or conversion work carried out on it. Some of the VAT recovered on general overhead costs would probably also become repayable.

Furthermore, when more than £250,000 has been spent on the purchase or improvement of a property for use as the company's own trading premises, a sale of that property within ten years without first exercising the option to tax would also trigger a VAT liability.

## 9.7   VAT ON 'BUILD TO LET'

The 'VAT Refund Scheme' enables a 'DIY Housebuilder' to reclaim any VAT paid on the construction of a new dwelling house. Unfortunately, however, this scheme cannot apply to any person who is constructing the property for business purposes.

We looked at the position for a property development company selling newly constructed residential property in Section 9.5 and, clearly, such companies remain able to recover all of the VAT incurred on construction costs under general principles.

Sadly, however, property investment companies which are building their own properties to hold as long-term investments will not be able to recover any VAT incurred. Nevertheless, if a property investment company contracts with a builder/contractor for the construction of a new residential dwelling house, such services supplied should, again, be zero-rated, thus avoiding the most significant potential VAT cost.

Any work that is closely connected to the construction of a zero-rated building should also be zero-rated. This will include levelling and drainage of land. There must not, however, be any significant time delay between these services being carried out and the physical construction of the building.

Architects, surveyors, consultants and supervisors' fees are normally standard rated at 20%. These fees could be rated differently, however, depending on which type of agreement the company has with the builder/main contractor.

Chapter 3 of VAT Notice 708 gives further information on the usual types of building contracts used.


## 9.8   VAT ON CONVERSIONS

As explained in Section 9.5, the sale of previously non-residential property that has been newly converted for residential use is generally zero-rated. This does, however, depend on the history of the property and, broadly speaking, if it has had *any* residential use in the previous ten years, the sale will, instead, be exempt for VAT purposes.

126

In the case of both 'exempt' sales and conversions carried out by property investment companies planning to hold on to the converted properties for letting purposes, the company will not be able to reclaim any VAT costs incurred.

However, many forms of conversion work are eligible for a reduced VAT rate of 5%, as opposed to the standard rate of 20%.

The reduced VAT rate of 5% is available in respect of any building work carried out on a residential property where the work results in a change to the number of dwellings in the property.

For example, this would apply to the conversion of:

- One house into several flats
- Two or more flats into a single house
- Two semi-detached houses into a single detached house

The reduced rate also applies to work carried out to convert a commercial property into residential use and to renovation work on residential property which had been vacant for two years or more before the work commenced.

Property companies carrying out projects of this nature should ensure that they only pay the appropriate lower VAT rate from the outset, as it is difficult to recover any excess paid in error.


### 9.9    VAT FOR PROPERTY MANAGEMENT COMPANIES

Property management services are standard-rated for VAT and hence a property management company will need to register for VAT if its annual supplies (i.e. fees charged and other sales) exceed the VAT registration threshold. It may still register voluntarily even if the level of its supplies is below the threshold.

Whether the properties under the company's management are residential or commercial makes no difference for this purpose. Naturally, a property management company that is registered for VAT can recover the VAT on most of its business expenses. There are, however, a few exceptions where VAT cannot be recovered (*e.g. on the purchase of motor cars*).

## 9.10   INTERACTION WITH CORPORATION TAX

Any company that is registered for VAT should generally include only the net (i.e. excluding VAT) amounts of income and expenditure in its accounts. Where VAT recovery is barred or restricted (*e.g. on the provision of private fuel for directors or staff*), however, the additional cost arising may generally be claimed as an expense for CT purposes.

A non-registered company should include the VAT in its business expenditure for CT purposes.

# Chapter 10

# Saving Tax When You Extract Profits

### 10.1   PROFIT EXTRACTION PRINCIPLES

As I explained at the beginning of the guide, the need to extract profits from your property company (or, indeed, any company) poses a major drawback. This is why property companies generally work better if the owners do not continually draw out all or most of the profits.

Clearly, if you are able to retain all of the profits within the company, profit extraction is not a problem.

However, sooner or later, almost everyone will want to take something out of the company, or else there wouldn't be much point in having a property business in the first place!

There are two main methods for extracting profits from your own company:

- Paying yourself a salary or a bonus (i.e. employment income), or
- Paying yourself dividends

Where the owner has loaned funds to the company, there is also the option of charging interest on those funds. In many cases, interest charges provide the most tax efficient method for extracting funds from the company where this option is available. We will look at this subject in more detail in Chapter 13.

In most other cases, dividends usually represent the most tax efficient method for extracting funds from your company; although it is often worth paying yourself a small salary equal to the NI primary threshold (see Appendix A) first, depending on what other sources of income you have in the same tax year.

### 10.2   SALARIES, ETC

Employment income is subject to Income Tax and to both employer's and employee's NI.

Payments of wages, salaries or bonuses are deductible against the company's taxable profits for CT purposes, as long as they are incurred for the benefit of the company's business. Some care needs to be taken, therefore, if you do decide to pay yourself, your spouse, your partner or any other members of your family, any wages or salaries, as no deduction will be available if there is no business justification for the payment.

In other words, yes, the recipient does have to actually work in the business!

### Tax Tip

Subject to my comments above, payment of a salary equal to the primary NI threshold (see Appendix A) to yourself, your spouse, your partner or another family member, can be a useful tax-planning measure, where justified.

Generally speaking, it is not tax efficient to make payments in excess of the NI primary threshold as, in most cases, the excess will suffer a total NI cost of 25.8% (12% paid by the employee and 13.8% paid by the employer). This outweighs the CT saving produced by the payment.

There are, however, a few exceptions, where it may be tax efficient to increase the salary payment to a level which fully utilises the recipient's personal allowance. These include cases where:

- The recipient is over state pension age (no employee's NI will be due)
- The recipient is aged under 16 (no NI will be due at all – but see further below)
- The recipient is aged under 21 (no employer's NI will be due on payments up to the higher rate tax threshold)
- The recipient is an apprentice aged under 25 (no employer's NI will be due on payments up to the higher rate tax threshold)
- The £3,000 employment allowance is available (see below)

Any other taxable income received by the recipient needs to be taken into account when determining a salary level which fully utilises their personal allowance. For those over state pension age, this will usually include their state pension.

Children aged 14 or more (sometimes 13 where local by-laws permit) may be employed in your company and salary payments may be made to them.

As always, the amount paid must be justified by the work the recipient does in the business and there are legal restrictions on the type and amount of work which children under 16 may carry out.

Hence, in spite of the NI exemption for payments to children under 16, it will be very rare for a salary in excess of a few thousand pounds to be justified in any case.

For further details on the benefits and restrictions relating to employing children, see the Taxcafe.co.uk guide *'Small Business Tax Saving Tactics'*.

Salary payments to any family member (or indeed yourself) must always be justified by the amount of work they do for the company. Payments in excess of the recipient's personal allowance will seldom be tax efficient but may be necessary where the family member's employment duties are extensive.

Salaries paid to non-directors aged 16 or more must at least equal the national minimum wage; or the living wage in the case of those aged 25 or more.

### The Employment Allowance

Each employer is exempt from a total of up to £3,000 of employer's Class 1 NI in each tax year.

#### Tax Tip

Where the employment allowance has not already been used up on payments to other employees, it will often be worth increasing any salary payments to yourself, your spouse, or other family members, to a level which uses up their Income Tax personal allowance.

Although the recipient will usually suffer employee's NI at 12% on any payment in excess of the primary threshold (see Appendix A), the company will be exempt from employer's NI and will (subject to my comments above) be entitled to CT relief at 19% on the full amount paid: thus providing a net saving of 7% where the employment allowance is available.

**Wealth Warning**

The employment allowance is not available where a single shareholder/director is the company's only employee.

HMRC incorrectly interpret this rule as meaning that at least one other person must be paid in excess of the primary NI threshold whereas, in fact, what the legislation says is that there simply needs to be at least one other employee (on any level of pay).

## 10.3 DIVIDENDS

Subject to the dividend allowance described below, dividends received after 5th April 2016 are subject to Income Tax at the following rates:

| | |
|---|---|
| Basic rate taxpayers: | 7.5% |
| Higher rate taxpayers: | 32.5% |
| Additional rate taxpayers: | 38.1% |

The non-refundable tax credit which attached to dividends paid prior to 6th April 2016 no longer applies: one of the few genuine pieces of simplification that the Government has ever actually achieved! As a consequence, the amount of taxable dividend income is now the same as the dividend actually received and there is no longer any need to 'gross up' dividend income to take account of the tax credit.

**The Dividend Allowance**

Each individual has an annual 'dividend allowance' which reduces the rate of Income Tax on the first part of their dividend income (up to the amount of the allowance) to nil. Dividends falling within the allowance are still included as taxable income for other purposes, however. This means that dividends covered by the dividend allowance will still:

- Use up the basic rate band
- Trigger or increase the High Income Child Benefit Charge where appropriate
- Cause the loss of the individual's personal allowance if they push their total taxable income over (or further over) £100,000
- Count as income for the purposes of the £150,000 additional rate tax threshold
- Count as income for the purposes of restrictions on pension relief for individuals with total deemed income over £150,000

The dividend allowance is £5,000 for 2016/17 and 2017/18, but is being reduced to £2,000 from 2018/19 onwards.

## Example

*In March 2018, Gabby takes dividends of £8,000 out of her property investment company. She has £43,000 of income from other sources for 2017/18.*

*The dividend allowance reduces the rate of Income Tax on the first £5,000 of Gabby's dividends to nil. However, adding her 'tax free' dividends to her other income produces a total of £48,000: which exceeds the higher rate tax threshold for 2017/18.*

*Hence, the remaining £3,000 of Gabby's dividends are subject to higher rate tax at 32.5%.*

An individual's personal allowance is used first before the dividend allowance is considered. Or, put another way, dividends covered by an individual's personal allowance do not use up their dividend allowance.

## Example

*In December 2017, Greg takes a dividend of £10,000 out of his property company. His other income for 2017/18 totals £8,500. The first £3,000 of Greg's dividend is covered by the remaining part of his personal allowance (£11,500 – £8,500); the next £5,000 is covered by his dividend allowance and the last £2,000 is taxed at 7.5%.*

It follows that an individual with no other income could take tax-free dividends of up to £16,500 out of their company during 2017/18. This figure is the total of their personal allowance (£11,500) and their dividend allowance (£5,000). As we shall see in Section 10.4, however, this will seldom be the most optimal approach.

See Appendix A for details of the higher rate tax threshold and personal allowance, as used in the above examples.

## Other Considerations

Dividends represent a distribution of a company's after-tax profits and no deduction is therefore allowed for CT purposes.

No business justification is required for dividends, although company law does require distributable profits to be available.

Hence, having your spouse, partner or another adult family member as a shareholder in your company may be a useful tax-planning measure. (Note that dividends paid to minor children from their parent's own company will be treated as the parent's own income for tax purposes.)

**Jointly Held Shares**

Where shares are held jointly by a married couple, it is no longer possible for the dividend income arising to be automatically split 50/50 for Income Tax purposes. The income must now be split according to the couple's actual beneficial entitlement to it.

### 10.4    OPTIMUM PROFIT EXTRACTION

There are a number of methods for extracting profits from your company but, in most cases, we are usually concerned with either salary or dividends, or a combination of both.

Assuming that these are the only two options available to us, the optimum method for profit extraction is as described below.

**Taxpayers with No Other Income**

- Firstly pay a salary up to the amount of the NI primary threshold
- Pay any further amounts required by way of dividend

**Taxpayers with Other Income Less Than the Personal Allowance**

- Firstly pay a salary equal to the lower of:
    o The NI primary threshold, and
    o The amount required to bring the taxpayer's income up to the level of the personal allowance
- Secondly pay any dividend which is covered by the dividend allowance
- Thirdly pay any further salary required to bring the total salary up to the level of the NI primary threshold
- Pay any further amounts required by way of dividend

**Taxpayers with Other Income Which Is At Least Equal to the Personal Allowance**

- Firstly pay any dividend which is covered by the dividend allowance
- Secondly pay a salary up to the amount of the NI primary threshold
- Pay any further amounts required by way of dividend

This last method covers all higher rate taxpayers, additional rate taxpayers and anyone else whose other income is at least equal to the personal allowance.

Variations to these optimums occur where:
- The employment allowance is available (see Section 10.2)
- The taxpayer is over state pension age (see Section 11.14)

For the relevant amounts of the NI primary threshold, personal allowance, and dividend allowance, see Appendix A for current rates, or Section 11.2 and Appendix B for the amounts used in our forecasts and examples throughout the rest of this guide.

# Chapter 11

# Personal versus Company Ownership

## 11.1 INTRODUCTION

In the previous chapters, we have worked through the principles of how a property company and its owners are taxed.

In the next two chapters, we will be looking in detail at the decision itself: "Should I run my property business through a company?"

Before we do that, however, we are going to take a look in this chapter at the comparative level of tax on a personal property investor or a company investing in property.

There are a great many different criteria which we could choose for our comparison; almost an infinite number, in fact.

However, in order to keep things down to a manageable size, we are just going to look at a few different scenarios that, I believe, should be sufficient to amply demonstrate the principles involved.

In this chapter, we will mostly be looking at income, starting with rental profits and then moving on to income classed as trading profit. Once we get into capital gains, the situation becomes even more complicated and can only really be assessed through the use of detailed examples. This will form a major part of the next chapter.

It is important to remember, as you consider the tables shown in this chapter, that these only represent one-off annual 'snapshots' of the position. Whilst they do provide useful illustrations of the potential tax savings involved, I must urge you to also consider the more detailed and longer-term issues that we will be looking at in the next two chapters.

As explained in Section 2.3, the CT rate is currently 19% and is expected to reduce to 17% from 1st April 2020.

For any investor considering whether to invest in property through a company, it makes sense to consider the long-term position.

136

The long-term position for individual taxpayers is less certain, but we do have some idea of the likely shape of the personal tax regime in the future. We will therefore combine what we do know with what we can reasonably estimate and use this to make a sensible comparison between the tax payable by an individual property investor and the tax payable by an investor using a company.

The forecast future tax rates for individuals which we will be using for our comparison are explained in Section 11.2.

The 17% CT rate currently proposed for accounting periods commencing after 31st March 2020 and the forecast personal tax rates set out in Section 11.2 are therefore the tax rates being used throughout this chapter unless specifically stated to the contrary.

In each of Sections 11.3 to 11.16, I will look at a different scenario and produce a set of conclusions for that scenario. I will then summarise those conclusions in Section 11.17 at the end of the chapter.

Whilst the tax rates being used to reach those conclusions are partly hypothetical, they are based on our latest knowledge of the likely shape of the UK tax system in the near future. Hence, although the figures produced in this chapter may not be precisely accurate, the conclusions which they lead to will remain sound unless there are major changes to the basic structure of the UK tax system.

## 11.2  PERSONAL TAX CHANGES

We have already examined the CT changes that are expected over the next few years in Section 2.5. However, before we can go on to look at our detailed calculations of the comparative forecast levels of tax paid by individuals or property companies, we also need to take a look at how the personal tax regime is expected to develop over the next few years.

As explained in the previous section, when comparing the position of a company investing in property with the position for a personal property investor, it makes sense for us to consider the long-term. For the company's position, this means using the CT rate of 17% currently proposed for accounting periods commencing after 31st March 2020.

To produce an appropriate comparative position for the personal property investor, we also need to produce a set of forecast personal tax rates which will approximate the position which is likely to apply over the next few years.

We know the personal tax rates and allowances for 2017/18, and these are set out in Appendix A, but what about the future?

The main proposals for future years which we know so far are:

- The personal allowance is to be increased to £12,500 by 2020/21
- The higher rate tax threshold is to be increased to £50,000 by 2020/21
- The dividend allowance is to be reduced to £2,000 from 2018/19

Other increases are mostly expected to be based on the consumer prices index, although some items, such as the threshold for withdrawal of personal allowances and the additional rate tax threshold, are not expected to change.

The higher rate tax threshold applying to Scottish taxpayers is now different and we will look at the likely future shape of the Income Tax regime for Scottish taxpayers, and its impact on the conclusions drawn in this guide, in Section 16.9.

Different Income Tax rates may also apply to Welsh taxpayers in the near future. However, since this is unlikely to occur until at least 2020 and we have no information regarding potential future tax rates for Welsh taxpayers, we will assume that 'normal' UK rates will continue to apply to Welsh taxpayers for the foreseeable future.

The increases in the personal allowance and the higher rate tax threshold set out above were part of a Budget 'pledge' made by former Chancellor George Osborne in 2015. Whether this 'pledge' will be honoured remains to be seen but, for the sake of illustration, we will assume that these proposals will indeed come to fruition.

What we can trust, I feel, is the probability that the future reduction in the CT rate will be countered by increases in the Income Tax rates on dividends. As the CT rate will fall by 2% in 2020, I will assume for the sake of illustration that Income Tax rates on dividends will increase by a similar amount from 2020/21 onwards.

Another safe bet is the fact that the rate of Class 4 NI for the self-employed is likely to be increased in the near future. Whilst new Chancellor Philip Hammond's embarrassing U-Turn in March 2017 means that this will probably not happen before the next General Election, I am going to assume for the sake of illustration that the rate will be increased to 11% from 6th April 2020. In reality, this increase is more likely to take place at least a year later, but my objective here is to create a suitable scenario for the long-term forecast tax comparisons set out in the rest of this chapter, so I will include the anticipated Class 4 NI increase in my forecast tax rates set out below.

**2020 Vision**

The best information we have about long-term tax rates is provided by the proposed CT rate applying from 1st April 2020 and the 'pledges' regarding personal tax rates applying by 2020/21.

2020/21 is also the point at which the horrendous restrictions on interest relief for individual landlords will have come fully into force.

The best personal tax rates we can use for our long-term comparisons are therefore the forecast rates for 2020/21 which are set out below.

**Forecast Income Tax Rates (Except on Dividends) 2020/21**

| | |
|---|---|
| Up to £12,500: | 0% |
| £12,500 to £50,000: | 20% |
| £50,000 to £100,000: | 40% |
| £100,000 to £125,000: | 60% |
| £125,000 to £150,000: | 40% |
| Over £150,000: | 45% |

**Forecast Dividend Tax Rates 2020/21**

| | |
|---|---|
| Dividend allowance: | £2,000 |
| Basic rate taxpayers: | 10% |
| Higher rate taxpayers: | 35% |
| Additional rate taxpayers: | 40% |

**Forecast NI Rates for Self-Employed Traders (See Comments Above)**

| | |
|---|---|
| Up to £9,000: | Nil |
| £9,000 to £50,000: | 11% |
| Over £50,000: | 2% |

**Forecast Employee's Primary Class 1 NI 2020/21**

| | |
|---|---|
| Up to £9,000: | Nil |
| £9,000 to £50,000: | 12% |
| Over £50,000: | 2% |

## Forecast Employer's Secondary Class 1 NI 2020/21

Up to £9,000:          Nil
Over £9,000:           13.8%

The forecast tax rates, bands, and allowances on which the above marginal rates are based are set out in Appendix B. I will be referring to them frequently throughout the rest of this guide.


## Keeping it Simple

For the sake of illustration, unless expressly stated to the contrary, some additional complexities in the UK tax system will be ignored for the purpose of all forecasts, examples, etc, throughout the remainder of this guide. These include:

- The High Income Child Benefit Charge (see Section 11.15)
- The £3,000 NI employment allowance (see Section 10.2)
- Different Income Tax rates applying to Scottish taxpayers (but see Section 16.9 for a detailed exploration of their impact on the issues discussed in this guide)
- The marriage allowance (which allows spouses to transfer 10% of their personal allowance  where neither the transferor nor the transferee is a higher rate taxpayer)


## Too Theoretical For You?

For a long-term property investor, comparisons based on long-term forecast tax rates must be the most appropriate measure to use and this is why I have taken this approach in this guide.

For anyone concerned that this is all a bit too theoretical, a comparison of our forecast personal tax rates set out above with the actual rates for 2017/18 in Appendix A will reveal that the differences are generally not too significant.

The most 'radical' assumptions I have made are the increases in the rates of Income Tax on dividends and Class 4 NI on self-employed trading income. I will consider the impact on our forecast results if these increases did **not** occur as we progress, but I feel strongly that including these probable increases provides a more realistic set of forecasts than ignoring them.

Furthermore, as explained in Section 11.1, it is the conclusions summarised in Section 11.17 which matter rather than the detailed figures produced by our calculations – and it would take some pretty fundamental changes to the UK tax system to alter those conclusions!

## 11.3   RENTAL PROFITS KEPT IN THE COMPANY

In this section, we will start out with the simplest situation (albeit a little hypothetical). Here, we look at the tax burden on an individual receiving rental income and compare it with the tax that would have been paid by a company set up to run their property portfolio.

For the time being, in this section, we are also assuming that:

  i)     All profits are retained within the company
  ii)    The individual has no other income
  iii)   No interest or finance costs are incurred

| Annual Rental Profits | Tax Paid Personally | Tax Paid By Company | Tax Saving/(Cost) |
|---|---|---|---|
| £20,000 | £1,500 | £3,400 | (£1,900) |
| £30,000 | £3,500 | £5,100 | (£1,600) |
| £40,000 | £5,500 | £6,800 | (£1,300) |
| £50,000 | £7,500 | £8,500 | (£1,000) |
| £60,000 | £11,500 | £10,200 | £1,300 |
| £75,000 | £17,500 | £12,750 | £4,750 |
| £100,000 | £27,500 | £17,000 | £10,500 |
| £125,000 | £42,500 | £21,250 | £21,250 |
| £150,000 | £52,500 | £25,500 | £27,000 |
| £200,000 | £75,000 | £34,000 | £41,000 |

**Conclusions**

As we can see, using a company is of no benefit to a basic rate taxpayer landlord with no interest or finance costs. A benefit does begin to accrue once the landlord's income exceeds the higher rate tax threshold.

These conclusions are, however, based on the fact that no part of the company's profits are being extracted; neither as salary, dividend, nor by any other means. For a taxpayer with no other income, this is unrealistic but, in the next section, we will consider the position for a taxpayer who already has sufficient other income to make them a higher rate taxpayer.

## 11.4 HIGHER RATE TAXPAYERS WITH RENTAL PROFITS

This time, we will assume that:

i) All profits are retained within the company
ii) The individual has other income totalling £50,000 (our forecast higher rate tax threshold for 2020/21)
iii) No interest or finance costs are incurred

| Annual Rental Profits | Tax Paid Personally | Tax Paid By Company | Tax Saving |
|---|---|---|---|
| £10,000 | £4,000 | £1,700 | £2,300 |
| £20,000 | £8,000 | £3,400 | £4,600 |
| £30,000 | £12,000 | £5,100 | £6,900 |
| £40,000 | £16,000 | £6,800 | £9,200 |
| £50,000 | £20,000 | £8,500 | £11,500 |
| £60,000 | £26,000 | £10,200 | £15,800 |
| £75,000 | £35,000 | £12,750 | £22,250 |
| £100,000 | £45,000 | £17,000 | £28,000 |
| £125,000 | £56,250 | £21,250 | £35,000 |
| £150,000 | £67,500 | £25,500 | £42,000 |
| £200,000 | £90,000 | £34,000 | £56,000 |

'Tax Paid Personally' represents the additional tax arising due to the individual's rental profits. It does not include the tax on their other income.

The above figures are also based on the assumption that the individual's other income does not include dividends, interest or other savings income. Modest amounts of these income sources would only make a slight difference to the forecast savings shown above however.

A dividend which is wholly covered by the dividend allowance (see Section 10.3) could be paid without affecting the savings outlined above.

### Conclusions

A company produces considerable tax savings for a higher rate taxpayer landlord prepared to retain their profits within the company.

For an investor whose existing income is already at least £50,000 (which they could potentially augment with a tax-free dividend of up to £2,000), this is not entirely unreasonable, although the day must surely come when they will wish to extract some profits. This is something that we will be exploring in the next chapter. In the next section, however, we will look at the position for those who cannot wait so long.

## 11.5   RENTAL PROFITS EXTRACTED FROM THE COMPANY

So far, we have looked at the position where rental profits are retained within the company. In this section we will take the opposite approach and assume that the company owner extracts all of the remaining profits after payment of the company's CT liability.

We already know that using a company is of no benefit to a basic rate taxpayer landlord with no interest or finance costs, so we will also assume that the landlord has sufficient other income to make them a higher rate taxpayer.

The table below is therefore based on the following assumptions:

i)    All of the company's after tax profits are paid out to the owner in the optimum manner, as described in Section 10.4

ii)   The individual has other income totalling £50,000 (our forecast higher rate tax threshold for 2020/21)

iii)  That other income does not include any interest or dividends (although, as noted before, modest amounts of these income sources will only make a slight difference to the outcome)

iv)   No interest or finance costs are incurred

| Annual Rental Profits | Tax Paid Personally | Tax Paid Via Company | Tax Saving/(Cost) |
|---|---|---|---|
| £10,000 | £4,000 | £3,446 | £554 |
| £20,000 | £8,000 | £7,966 | £34 |
| £30,000 | £12,000 | £12,571 | (£571) |
| £40,000 | £16,000 | £17,176 | (£1,176) |
| £50,000 | £20,000 | £21,781 | (£1,781) |
| £60,000 | £26,000 | £26,652 | (£652) |
| £75,000 | £35,000 | £36,049 | (£1,049) |
| £100,000 | £45,000 | £49,806 | (£4,806) |
| £125,000 | £56,250 | £61,582 | (£5,332) |
| £150,000 | £67,500 | £74,132 | (£6,632) |
| £200,000 | £90,000 | £99,232 | (£9,232) |

'Tax Paid via Company' summarises the total tax burden using the company route, including both the CT payable by the company and the individual's Income Tax on the salary and dividends received.

The above figures are based on the assumed increases in the dividend tax rates discussed in Section 11.2. Even if dividend tax rates remain at their current level, the position is not much better, as shown below:

| Annual Rental Profits | Tax Paid Personally | Tax Paid Via Company | Tax Saving/(Cost) |
|---|---|---|---|
| £10,000 | £4,000 | £3,446 | £554 |
| £20,000 | £8,000 | £7,787 | £213 |
| £30,000 | £12,000 | £12,185 | (£185) |
| £40,000 | £16,000 | £16,582 | (£582) |
| £50,000 | £20,000 | £20,980 | (£980) |
| £60,000 | £26,000 | £25,643 | £357 |
| £75,000 | £35,000 | £34,730 | £271 |
| £100,000 | £45,000 | £47,967 | (£2,967) |
| £125,000 | £56,250 | £59,257 | (£3,007) |
| £150,000 | £67,500 | £71,412 | (£3,912) |
| £200,000 | £90,000 | £95,724 | (£5,724) |

## Conclusions

As we can see, using a property investment company is of little or no value where the investor extracts all the profits from the company each year and there are no interest or finance costs.

### Wealth Warning

If dividends are paid without there being supporting accounts available to show that the company had sufficient distributable profits (**after tax**) at that time, they are illegal under company law. 'Illegal' dividends may then be treated as salary, resulting in Income Tax and NI at a combined total rate of at least 42% for a higher rate taxpayer, plus a further 13.8% in NI for the company.

In reality, therefore, it is usually best not to extract all of the company's after-tax profits as dividends every year.

It is also important to ensure that the company quite clearly has sufficient distributable profits before any dividend is paid and has the necessary supporting accounts to demonstrate this fact. Supporting accounts would generally consist of either the previous year's statutory accounts or up to date management accounts (e.g. to the end of the previous calendar month).

Documentation minuting the payment of a dividend is also advisable.


## 11.6   HALFWAY HOUSE

In Section 11.4 we saw the potential benefits available to higher rate taxpayers using a property investment company where all the profits are retained within the company. In Section 11.5, however, we saw that there is little or no benefit in using a property investment company if all of the profits are extracted each year.

Between these two extremes, there are many other potential scenarios. The table below illustrates just one of those scenarios: where precisely half of the company's profits after tax are extracted each year. All of the other assumptions remain the same as in Section 11.5 and we assume that profits are extracted in the optimum manner (see Section 10.4).

| Annual Rental Profits | Tax Paid Personally | Tax Paid Via Company | Tax Saving |
|---|---|---|---|
| £10,000 | £4,000 | £2,240 | £1,760 |
| £20,000 | £8,000 | £4,984 | £3,016 |
| £30,000 | £12,000 | £7,945 | £4,055 |
| £40,000 | £16,000 | £11,098 | £4,902 |
| £50,000 | £20,000 | £14,250 | £5,750 |
| £60,000 | £26,000 | £17,403 | £8,597 |
| £75,000 | £35,000 | £22,132 | £12,869 |
| £100,000 | £45,000 | £30,013 | £14,987 |
| £125,000 | £56,250 | £38,422 | £17,828 |
| £150,000 | £67,500 | £48,378 | £19,122 |
| £200,000 | £90,000 | £66,538 | £23,462 |

## Conclusions

As we can see, retaining half of the after tax profits in the company has returned our investor to a position where using the property investment company is highly beneficial once more.

In fact, reasonable levels of savings persist when around two thirds of the after tax profits are extracted from the company (although the savings are quite small where rental profits are less than £20,000).

## 11.7   THE IMPACT OF INTEREST AND FINANCE COSTS

By 2020/21, individual property investors will only get basic rate tax relief for interest and finance costs relating to residential lettings.

These horrendous restrictions are examined in a little more detail in Section 13.10. For a more thorough examination of their impact, see the Taxcafe.co.uk guides *'How to Save Property Tax'* and *'Landlord Interest'*.

The restrictions do not apply to borrowings relating to non-residential property or furnished holiday lettings so the conclusions we have already drawn in Sections 11.3 to 11.6 will remain the same for any investor who is renting out those types of property.

But, for residential lettings, the different treatment of interest and finance costs will make an enormous difference and that is what we will now examine.

To do this, we are going to have to make an assumption about the level of interest being paid by the investor.

We will start with a fairly highly geared investor whose interest costs amount to 75% of their profit before interest. Hence, each £10,000 of rental profit in the tables below is made up as follows:

| | |
|---|---|
| Profit before interest | £40,000 |
| Less: | |
| Interest and finance costs | £30,000 |
| | ---------- |
| Profit after interest | £10,000 |

By 2020/21, the investor will pay tax on their profit before interest of £40,000 and only receive basic rate tax relief on their interest costs of £30,000. For a higher rate taxpayer, this produces an Income Tax liability of £10,000 on a profit of the same amount!

The table below is also based on the following further assumptions:

    i)      All of the company's after tax profits are paid out to the owner in the most tax efficient manner (see Section 10.4)

    ii)     The individual has no other income

146

| Annual Rental Profits | Tax Paid Personally | Tax Paid Via Company | Tax Saving/(Cost) |
|---|---|---|---|
| £10,000 | £0 | £170 | (£170) |
| £20,000 | £7,500 | £2,233 | £5,267 |
| £30,000 | £21,500 | £4,763 | £16,737 |
| £40,000 | £33,000 | £7,293 | £25,707 |
| £50,000 | £45,000 | £9,823 | £35,177 |
| £60,000 | £57,000 | £12,686 | £44,315 |
| £75,000 | £75,000 | £19,593 | £55,407 |
| £100,000 | £105,000 | £31,106 | £73,895 |
| £125,000 | £135,000 | £43,542 | £91,458 |
| £150,000 | £165,000 | £59,406 | £105,595 |
| £200,000 | £225,000 | £83,307 | £141,693 |

It is worth noting that in this scenario, once the individual investor's profits after interest exceed around £75,000, their Income Tax liability is **greater than 100%!**

The savings in the table above are pretty spectacular but we must remember that this is based on a highly geared investor. Keeping all of our other assumptions the same, let's now look at the position where the level of interest is lower.

Firstly, where interest costs amount to 50% of profits before interest:

| Annual Rental Profits | Tax Paid Personally | Tax Paid Via Company | Tax Saving/(Cost) |
|---|---|---|---|
| £10,000 | £0 | £170 | (£170) |
| £20,000 | £1,500 | £2,233 | (£733) |
| £30,000 | £5,500 | £4,763 | £737 |
| £40,000 | £11,500 | £7,293 | £4,207 |
| £50,000 | £17,500 | £9,823 | £7,677 |
| £60,000 | £27,500 | £12,686 | £14,815 |
| £75,000 | £37,500 | £19,593 | £17,907 |
| £100,000 | £55,000 | £31,106 | £23,895 |
| £125,000 | £72,500 | £43,542 | £28,958 |
| £150,000 | £90,000 | £59,406 | £30,595 |
| £200,000 | £125,000 | £83,307 | £41,693 |

Next, where interest costs amount to just 25% of profits before interest:

| Annual Rental Profits | Tax Paid Personally | Tax Paid Via Company | Tax Saving/(Cost) |
|---|---|---|---|
| £10,000 | £0 | £170 | (£170) |
| £20,000 | £1,500 | £2,233 | (£733) |
| £30,000 | £3,500 | £4,763 | (£1,263) |
| £40,000 | £6,167 | £7,293 | (£1,126) |
| £50,000 | £10,833 | £9,823 | £1,010 |
| £60,000 | £15,500 | £12,686 | £2,815 |
| £75,000 | £22,500 | £19,593 | £2,907 |
| £100,000 | £39,167 | £31,106 | £8,061 |
| £125,000 | £51,667 | £43,542 | £8,125 |
| £150,000 | £65,000 | £59,406 | £5,595 |
| £200,000 | £91,667 | £83,307 | £8,360 |

### Conclusions

The tables in this section clearly demonstrate the fact that major savings are available to higher rate taxpayers by using a property investment company to hold residential rental property where there are borrowings against the properties.

Furthermore, as we know from earlier sections, these savings will be greatly enhanced if some or all of the after tax profits are retained within the company.

The tables also show, once again, that a property investment company is of no use to basic rate taxpayers: **BUT** we must remember that anyone with *profits before interest* in excess of the higher rate tax threshold will become a higher rate taxpayer by 2020/21!

For example, in our first table in this section, where interest costs amounted to 75% of profit before interest, even a landlord with just £20,000 of profit after interest achieved major savings by using a company. This is because the restrictions on interest relief for individual landlords will result in them having £80,000 of taxable profit by 2020/21: well in excess of the higher rate tax threshold; and they will only receive basic rate tax relief for their interest.

## 11.8  HIGHER INTEREST RATES IN COMPANIES

The previous section demonstrated the clear advantage of using a property investment company for an investor with residential rental property which has borrowings against it.

Unfortunately, however, the cost of borrowing within a company tends to be higher: with interest rates typically being more than the interest rates available to an individual buy-to-let investor by a factor of somewhere between a quarter and a half.

For the sake of illustration, we will assume that the company's interest and finance costs are greater than the individual's costs by a factor of one quarter.

In the table below, we have also assumed that the individual's interest costs amount to 50% of their profit before interest.

This table has to be presented slightly differently to the tables in previous sections as the company's profit before tax is now different to the individual's. Hence, the best thing to compare is the ultimate net income after both tax and interest.

As before, we will also continue to assume that:

i)      All of the company's after tax profits are paid out to the owner in the most tax efficient manner, as described in Section 10.4

ii)     The individual has no other income

| Annual Rental Profits | Net Income Personally | Net Income Via Company | Tax & Interest Saving/(Cost) |
|---|---|---|---|
| £30,000 | £24,500 | £19,635 | (£4,865) |
| £40,000 | £28,500 | £25,237 | (£3,263) |
| £50,000 | £32,500 | £30,840 | (£1,660) |
| £60,000 | £32,500 | £36,442 | £3,942 |
| £75,000 | £37,500 | £44,846 | £7,346 |
| £100,000 | £45,000 | £55,407 | £10,407 |
| £125,000 | £52,500 | £65,523 | £13,023 |
| £150,000 | £60,000 | £75,638 | £15,638 |
| £200,000 | £75,000 | £90,595 | £15,595 |

**Conclusions**

As we can see, the higher interest cost in the company has significantly reduced the overall savings available.

However, substantial savings are still evident at higher levels of profit.

It must also be remembered that the savings are greatly enhanced when some or all of the profits are retained in the company. The savings will, of course, also be improved if the company's interest and finance costs are not as high as we have predicted here.

## 11.9    THE 'OPTIMUM SCENARIO'

This scenario is what one might call the 'best of both worlds', where we use the lessons from the previous sections in this chapter to produce an optimum position. That optimum position is basically as follows:

Firstly, the taxpayer builds a 'private' portfolio held in their own name as an individual which is large enough to use up their basic rate band. By the year 2020/21, we anticipate this meaning that the following amounts will total £50,000:

a)    Profits from residential lettings **before** interest

b)    Profits from non-residential and furnished holiday lettings **after** interest

c)    Income from other sources

If (c) alone exceeds £50,000 then the individual is already a higher rate taxpayer and we will assume that there is no 'private' portfolio.

The benefit of any residential lettings within the 'private' portfolio will, of course, be maximised if these properties are debt free and this is an ideal position for the investor to aim for.

The tables below compare the position arising on any further property investments beyond the 'private' portfolio included under (a) and (b) above. For ease of reference, we will refer to these further investments as the 'second portfolio'. The tables are based on the following assumptions:

| | | |
|---|---|---|
| i) | The investor has £50,000 of taxable income from other sources (including income from their 'private' portfolio, as described under (a) and (b) above) | |
| ii) | That other income does not include any interest or dividends (although, as noted before, modest amounts of these income sources will only make a slight difference to the outcome) | |
| iii) | The properties in the 'second portfolio' are all residential lettings | |
| iv) | The rental profits arising on the 'second portfolio' when held as an individual are shown after interest costs equal to 50% of the profits before interest | |
| v) | The interest costs incurred by the company are greater than those incurred by an individual by a factor of one quarter | |
| vi) | When profits are extracted from the company, this is done in the optimum manner, as described in Section 10.4 | |

The first table shows the position where all after tax profits are extracted from the company:

| Annual Rental Profits | Net Income Personally | Net Income Via Company | Tax & Interest Saving |
|---|---|---|---|
| £10,000 | £4,000 | £5,054 | £1,054 |
| £20,000 | £8,000 | £9,337 | £1,337 |
| £30,000 | £10,000 | £13,383 | £3,383 |
| £40,000 | £11,000 | £17,430 | £6,430 |
| £50,000 | £15,000 | £21,476 | £6,476 |
| £60,000 | £18,000 | £25,522 | £7,522 |
| £75,000 | £22,500 | £31,591 | £9,091 |
| £100,000 | £30,000 | £38,951 | £8,951 |
| £125,000 | £37,500 | £46,823 | £9,323 |
| £150,000 | £45,000 | £56,938 | £11,938 |
| £200,000 | £60,000 | £75,868 | £15,868 |

Next, we look at the position where half of the after tax profit is extracted from the company:

| Annual Rental Profits | Net Income Personally | Net Income Via Company | Tax & Interest Saving |
|---|---|---|---|
| £10,000 | £4,000 | £5,945 | £1,945 |
| £20,000 | £8,000 | £11,388 | £3,388 |
| £30,000 | £10,000 | £16,831 | £6,831 |
| £40,000 | £11,000 | £22,055 | £11,055 |
| £50,000 | £15,000 | £27,190 | £12,190 |
| £60,000 | £18,000 | £32,326 | £14,326 |
| £75,000 | £22,500 | £40,029 | £17,529 |
| £100,000 | £30,000 | £52,869 | £22,869 |
| £125,000 | £37,500 | £65,708 | £28,208 |
| £150,000 | £45,000 | £78,547 | £33,547 |
| £200,000 | £60,000 | £101,622 | £41,622 |

'Net Income Via Company' now includes after tax profits retained within the company.

Finally, let's look at the position where all of the after tax profits are retained within the company:

| Annual Rental Profits | Net Income Personally | Net Income Via Company | Tax & Interest Saving |
|---|---|---|---|
| £10,000 | £4,000 | £6,225 | £2,225 |
| £20,000 | £8,000 | £12,450 | £4,450 |
| £30,000 | £10,000 | £18,675 | £8,675 |
| £40,000 | £11,000 | £24,900 | £13,900 |
| £50,000 | £15,000 | £31,125 | £16,125 |
| £60,000 | £18,000 | £37,350 | £19,350 |
| £75,000 | £22,500 | £46,688 | £24,188 |
| £100,000 | £30,000 | £62,250 | £32,250 |
| £125,000 | £37,500 | £77,813 | £40,313 |
| £150,000 | £45,000 | £93,375 | £48,375 |
| £200,000 | £60,000 | £124,500 | £64,500 |

If the individual's other income is made up of rental income or pensions and they have no interest or finance costs on any residential lettings within their 'private' portfolio, they will have net income after tax of £42,500, so the idea of leaving all of the profits in the company is not unreasonable.

Small dividends covered by the dividend allowance will make no difference to the outcome in the last table though, so there is the opportunity to bring net income up to £44,500 and still retain these savings.

## Conclusions

Even after factoring in the probability that higher interest rates will apply to any borrowings within a company, we see that a property investment company can provide major savings for a higher rate taxpayer.

Remember that, when we refer to higher rate taxpayers, by 2020/21 this will include any residential landlords whose profit *before interest* pushes them over the higher rate tax threshold.

The tables also demonstrate the fact that the available savings are greatly enhanced when some or all of the after tax profits are retained within the company.

## 11.10   TRADING PROFITS

Having covered rental profits, we will now look at the same comparison where the income from the property business is treated as trading income.

This makes no difference to the rates of CT applying. The individual's tax position is significantly altered, however, due to the fact that Class 4 NI is payable where this income is received personally (unless the individual is over state pension age – see Section 11.14).

For our first trading scenario, we will consider the position where the individual has no other income and all of the company's after tax profits are paid out in the most tax efficient manner, as described in Section 10.4 (but see the 'Wealth Warning' in Section 11.5 which applies equally here).

Remember, we are also using the forecast Class 4 NI rate of 11% discussed in Section 11.2.

| Annual Trading Profits | Tax Paid Personally | Tax Paid Via Company | Tax Saving/(Cost) |
|---|---|---|---|
| £10,000 | £110 | £170 | (£60) |
| £20,000 | £2,710 | £2,233 | £477 |
| £30,000 | £5,810 | £4,763 | £1,047 |
| £40,000 | £8,910 | £7,293 | £1,617 |
| £50,000 | £12,010 | £9,823 | £2,187 |
| £60,000 | £16,210 | £12,686 | £3,525 |
| £75,000 | £22,510 | £19,593 | £2,917 |
| £100,000 | £33,010 | £31,106 | £1,905 |
| £125,000 | £48,510 | £43,542 | £4,968 |
| £150,000 | £59,010 | £59,406 | (£396) |
| £200,000 | £82,510 | £83,307 | (£797) |

As before, the table above is based on the forecast dividend tax increases discussed in Section 11.2, so it is probably also worth looking at the situation if dividend tax rates are *not* increased. This is covered by the table below.

| Annual Trading Profits | Tax Paid Personally | Tax Paid Via Company | Tax Saving/(Cost) |
|---|---|---|---|
| £10,000 | £110 | £170 | (£60) |
| £20,000 | £2,710 | £2,142 | £568 |
| £30,000 | £5,810 | £4,465 | £1,345 |
| £40,000 | £8,910 | £6,787 | £2,123 |
| £50,000 | £12,010 | £9,110 | £2,900 |
| £60,000 | £16,210 | £11,765 | £4,445 |
| £75,000 | £22,510 | £18,361 | £4,149 |
| £100,000 | £33,010 | £29,355 | £3,655 |
| £125,000 | £48,510 | £41,207 | £7,304 |
| £150,000 | £59,010 | £56,530 | £2,480 |
| £200,000 | £82,510 | £79,499 | £3,011 |

Lastly, it is probably also worth looking at the position where neither dividend tax rates nor Class 4 NI rates are increased, as shown below:

| Annual Trading Profits | Tax Paid Personally | Tax Paid Via Company | Tax Saving/(Cost) |
|---|---|---|---|
| £10,000 | £90 | £170 | (£80) |
| £20,000 | £2,490 | £2,142 | £348 |
| £30,000 | £5,390 | £4,465 | £925 |
| £40,000 | £8,290 | £6,787 | £1,503 |
| £50,000 | £11,190 | £9,110 | £2,080 |
| £60,000 | £15,390 | £11,765 | £3,625 |
| £75,000 | £21,690 | £18,361 | £3,329 |
| £100,000 | £32,190 | £29,355 | £2,835 |
| £125,000 | £47,690 | £41,207 | £6,484 |
| £150,000 | £58,190 | £56,530 | £1,660 |
| £200,000 | £81,690 | £79,499 | £2,191 |

Personally though, for the reasons described in Section 11.2, I feel that the first table represents the most likely outcome.

## Conclusions

Many people will be surprised by the results shown in the above tables, but it is clear that, with a few exceptions, there is generally little or no tax benefit in putting a trading business into a company if all of the profits are to be extracted each year (bearing in mind that there are extra costs involved in running a company which have not been factored into the above figures).

This is mostly due to the overall marginal rate of tax applying to profits which are first taxed in the company and then taxed again when paid out to a higher rate taxpayer shareholder as dividends.

Even if dividend tax rates are **not** increased from current levels, that marginal rate will be 44% after 1st April 2020, as shown below:

| | |
|---|---|
| Corporation Tax | 17.0% |
| Income Tax on after tax profit paid as dividend (83% x 32.5%) | 27.0% |
| | -------- |
| Overall marginal rate | 44.0% |

This compares with the overall marginal tax rate (Income Tax and NI) of 42% applying to a self-employed higher rate taxpayer. In other words, the company is *costing extra tax!*

Plus, if dividend tax rates increase as predicted in Section 11.2, this overall marginal tax rate will rise to 46.1%. At present, with the current CT rate of 19%, this overall marginal rate is currently 45.3%.

As we can see from the above tables, there are some quirks in the tax system which mean reasonable savings can arise at certain profit levels but, generally speaking, the overall picture suggests that it is not worth using a company for a property trade where all of the profits are being extracted.

## 11.11  RETAINING TRADING PROFITS IN THE COMPANY

In the previous section, we saw that a property trading company was of little or no benefit where all of the profits were being extracted each year.

A taxpayer with no other income will almost certainly need to extract some profits but, in this section, we will look at the position where the amount extracted is limited so that the company owner does not become a higher rate taxpayer.

The table below is therefore based on the following assumptions:

i)      The taxpayer has no other income

ii)      Company profits are extracted by first taking a salary of £9,000, then taking any remaining profits as a dividend up to a maximum of £41,000 (thus bringing the taxpayer's income up to the forecast higher rate tax threshold for 2020/21 of £50,000)

(We will also return to our forecast tax rates as set out in Section 11.2, including the forecast increases to dividend tax and Class 4 NI.)

| Annual Trading Profits | Tax Paid Personally | Tax Paid Via Company | Tax Saving |
|---|---|---|---|
| £50,000 | £12,010 | £9,823 | £2,187 |
| £60,000 | £16,210 | £12,220 | £3,990 |
| £75,000 | £22,510 | £14,770 | £7,740 |
| £100,000 | £33,010 | £19,020 | £13,990 |
| £125,000 | £48,510 | £23,270 | £25,240 |
| £150,000 | £59,010 | £27,520 | £31,490 |
| £200,000 | £82,510 | £36,020 | £46,490 |

## Conclusions

A property trading company can produce considerable tax savings where the profits extracted are limited to an amount which prevents the company owner's income from exceeding the higher rate tax threshold.

This still leaves the owner with net income after tax of £46,450 (once the company's trading profits exceed around £58,400).

## 11.12  HIGHER RATE TRADERS

Where a property investor already has sufficient income from other sources to make them a higher rate taxpayer, they could make considerable savings by using a property trading company: provided that they do not extract all of the profits each year.

Some savings are possible where only part of the profits are extracted each year, but the best savings arise where all of the after tax profits are retained in the company: which is what we will look at in this section. Hence, the tables below are based on the following assumptions:

  i)     The trader has £50,000 of taxable income from other sources (as detailed further for each table below)
  ii)    All of the company's after tax profits are retained

The nature of the trader's other income will influence the outcome considerably due to the different ways in which this other income is treated for NI purposes. As usual, we will assume that the other income does not included interest or dividends, although modest amounts of these types of income will only make a slight difference to the results shown below.

The first table deals with the situation where the trader's other income is made up of rental profits or pensions. (Remember that for residential lettings, by 2020/21, it will be the rental profit *before interest* which will form the individual's taxable income.)

| Annual Trading Profits | Tax Paid Personally | Tax Paid Via Company | Tax Saving |
|---|---|---|---|
| £10,000 | £4,110 | £1,700 | £2,410 |
| £20,000 | £9,210 | £3,400 | £5,810 |
| £30,000 | £14,310 | £5,100 | £9,210 |
| £40,000 | £19,410 | £6,800 | £12,610 |
| £50,000 | £24,510 | £8,500 | £16,010 |
| £60,000 | £30,710 | £10,200 | £20,510 |
| £75,000 | £40,010 | £12,750 | £27,260 |
| £100,000 | £50,510 | £17,000 | £33,510 |
| £125,000 | £62,260 | £21,250 | £41,010 |
| £150,000 | £74,010 | £25,500 | £48,510 |
| £200,000 | £97,510 | £34,000 | £63,510 |

For the next table, we will assume that the trader's other income is employment income:

| Annual Trading Profits | Tax Paid Personally | Tax Paid Via Company | Tax Saving |
|---|---|---|---|
| £10,000 | £4,110 | £1,700 | £2,410 |
| £20,000 | £8,400 | £3,400 | £5,000 |
| £30,000 | £12,600 | £5,100 | £7,500 |
| £40,000 | £16,800 | £6,800 | £10,000 |
| £50,000 | £21,000 | £8,500 | £12,500 |
| £60,000 | £27,200 | £10,200 | £17,000 |
| £75,000 | £36,500 | £12,750 | £23,750 |
| £100,000 | £47,000 | £17,000 | £30,000 |
| £125,000 | £58,750 | £21,250 | £37,500 |
| £150,000 | £70,500 | £25,500 | £45,000 |
| £200,000 | £94,000 | £34,000 | £60,000 |

Note that the savings are slightly reduced here because the self-employed trader would be able to claim a partial repayment of their Class 4 NI. This repayment must be claimed: it is not automatic.

If the trader's other income is other self-employed trading income, the results would be exactly the same as in the table above except that:

i) 'Tax Paid Personally' and the saving arising by using a company would both be £90 more where the trading profit is £10,000, and

ii) The reduction in Class 4 NI on the additional trading income would be automatic and there would be no need to claim a repayment

**Conclusions**

A property trading company can produce considerable tax savings for a higher rate taxpayer prepared to retain all of the after tax profits in the company. (The same level of savings will be maintained where small dividends covered by the dividend allowance are paid.)

## 11.13  PARTIAL EXTRACTION FOR HIGHER RATE TRADERS

The previous section demonstrated the benefits of a property company for higher rate taxpayers with a property trade who were prepared to retain their after tax profits in the company.

Now let's look at the position where the company owner extracts half of the company's after tax profits. As before, we will assume that this is done in the most tax efficient manner, as described in Section 10.4. Other assumptions remain the same as in the previous section.

Firstly, here is the position where the trader's other taxable income consists of £50,000 of rental profits or pensions (see previous comments regarding taxable income from residential lettings):

| Annual Trading Profits | Tax Paid Personally | Tax Paid Via Company | Tax Saving |
|---|---|---|---|
| £10,000 | £4,110 | £2,240 | £1,870 |
| £20,000 | £9,210 | £4,984 | £4,226 |
| £30,000 | £14,310 | £7,945 | £6,365 |
| £40,000 | £19,410 | £11,098 | £8,312 |
| £50,000 | £24,510 | £14,250 | £10,260 |
| £60,000 | £30,710 | £17,403 | £13,307 |
| £75,000 | £40,010 | £22,132 | £17,878 |
| £100,000 | £50,510 | £30,013 | £20,497 |
| £125,000 | £62,260 | £38,422 | £23,838 |
| £150,000 | £74,010 | £48,378 | £25,632 |
| £200,000 | £97,510 | £66,538 | £30,972 |

And here is the position where the other income consists of £50,000 of employment income:

| Annual Trading Profits | Tax Paid Personally | Tax Paid Via Company | Tax Saving/(Cost) |
|---|---|---|---|
| £10,000 | £4,110 | £2,240 | £1,870 |
| £20,000 | £8,400 | £4,984 | £3,416 |
| £30,000 | £12,600 | £7,945 | £4,655 |
| £40,000 | £16,800 | £11,098 | £5,702 |
| £50,000 | £21,000 | £14,250 | £6,750 |
| £60,000 | £27,200 | £17,403 | £9,797 |
| £75,000 | £36,500 | £22,132 | £14,369 |
| £100,000 | £47,000 | £30,013 | £16,987 |
| £125,000 | £58,750 | £38,422 | £20,328 |
| £150,000 | £70,500 | £48,378 | £22,122 |
| £200,000 | £94,000 | £66,538 | £27,462 |

As in the previous section, this is subject to the comments regarding the need to claim a repayment of some of the Class 4 NI suffered as a self-employed individual.

This table can again be applied equally where the other income is self-employed trading income, subject to the same small difference of £90 discussed in the previous section.

**Conclusions**

A property trading company still produces considerable tax savings for a higher rate taxpayer prepared to retain half of the after tax profits in the company.

**11.14  OLDER PROPERTY INVESTORS**

Investors over state pension age are exempt from all classes of NI.

As a result, anyone over state pension age will suffer the same effective tax rates on trading income as they do on rental income. For these investors, a property trading company will produce more or less the same results as a property investment company where there are no interest or finance costs on residential rental property. Hence, see Sections 11.3 to 11.6 for the appropriate savings available to property investors over state pension age running a property business classed as a trade for tax purposes (subject to the further points discussed below).

There is a slight additional advantage to taxpayers over state pension age using any type of property company. Payment of a salary in excess of the NI threshold will not attract primary Class 1 employee's NI; although it will still be subject to employer's NI unless the employment allowance is available (see Section 10.2).

Paying additional salary to a taxpayer over state pension age (i.e. beyond the amount of the NI threshold) is, however, only worthwhile in the following situations:

i) Where they have no other income (a salary up to the amount of the personal allowance is beneficial)

ii) Where they are a higher rate taxpayer and they do not use the CT saving arising by paying a larger salary to pay out additional dividends (unless those dividends are covered by the dividend allowance)

iii) In any case where the employment allowance is available

Point (ii) is valid at the current rate of CT (19%) but will only remain valid after the CT rate is reduced to 17% if the rates of tax on dividend income are increased as forecast in Section 11.2.

The employment allowance may cover salaries up to £21,739 in excess of the NI threshold (i.e. up to £30,739 for the purposes of our forecasts in this chapter). See Section 10.2 for more details regarding the availability of the employment allowance. Note also that higher salaries will only generate additional savings where those salaries can be claimed as an expense for CT purposes: this issue is also examined in Section 10.2.

## 11.15  INVESTORS WITH CHILDREN

Investors with young children may be able to realise additional benefits by investing in property via a company. By keeping profits in the company and thus ensuring that their personal income is kept at a lower level, they may be able to avoid some or all of:

• The withdrawal of their Tax Credit entitlement, where applicable
• The High Income Child Benefit Charge

Avoiding the High Income Child Benefit Charge will be a major benefit for many investors where the highest earner in the household faces additional tax charges on personal taxable income between £50,000 and £60,000.

As each investor's position is different, it is not possible to take these extra savings into account in all of the calculations in the rest of this guide, but the additional savings available in 2017/18 alone could be as much as those shown in the table below.

| No. of Qualifying Children | Additional Saving |
|---|---|
| 1 | £1,076 |
| 2 | £1,789 |
| 3 | £2,501 |
| 4 | £3,214 |
| 5 | £3,926 |
| Each Extra | £712 |

'No. of Qualifying Children' represents the number of children living in the investor's household for whom Child Benefit is being claimed.

The 'Maximum Additional Saving' is the amount of additional tax saved (on top of any savings calculated elsewhere in this guide) where:

i) Using a property company enables the personal taxable income of the highest earner in the household for the year to be kept to £50,000 or less, and

ii) Without the company, the highest earner in the household for the year would have had taxable income of £60,000 or more.

Smaller savings also remain available in other cases where using the company enables the personal taxable income of the highest earner in the household for the year to be reduced within or below the £50,000 to £60,000 bracket.

In considering these potential savings, it should be borne in mind that the High Income Child Benefit Charge is always based on the income of the highest earner in the household. Reducing one person's income may result in the other adult in the household becoming the highest earner instead and this would limit the savings available: unless their income can also be reduced.

Please note that the potential additional savings available by avoiding the High Income Child Benefit Charge or by avoiding the withdrawal of

Child Tax Credits, where applicable, are not taken into account throughout the rest of this guide.


## 11.16   CAPITAL GAINS

For our final scenario in this chapter, we will take a quick look at the difference in the tax on a typical capital gain on a property held by an individual investor or by a property investment company. In this scenario, we will assume the following:

i)   The property is sold producing a total gain before exemptions and reliefs equal to the amount shown in the first column below

ii)   The gain arising is equal to 50% of the property's purchase price

iii)   The individual investor is a higher rate taxpayer

iv)   The gain does not qualify for entrepreneurs' relief

v)   The indexation relief rate over the relevant period is 25%

vi)   The individual has not made any other capital gains during the same tax year

vii)   The annual CGT exemption for the relevant tax year is £12,500

viii)   No other reliefs or exemptions are available to either the individual or the company

ix)   CT is payable at 17% (see Section 2.3)

x)   Company profits are retained

First, we will look at the position for a residential property:

| Capital Gain Before Reliefs | Tax Paid Personally | Tax Paid By Company | Tax Saving/(Cost) |
|---|---|---|---|
| £10,000 | £0 | £850 | (£850) |
| £25,000 | £3,500 | £2,125 | £1,375 |
| £50,000 | £10,500 | £4,250 | £6,250 |
| £100,000 | £24,500 | £8,500 | £16,000 |
| £200,000 | £52,500 | £17,000 | £35,500 |

And next, for a non-residential property:

| Capital Gain Before Reliefs | Tax Paid Personally | Tax Paid By Company | Tax Saving/(Cost) |
|---|---|---|---|
| £10,000 | £0 | £850 | (£850) |
| £25,000 | £2,500 | £2,125 | £375 |
| £50,000 | £7,500 | £4,250 | £3,250 |
| £100,000 | £17,500 | £8,500 | £9,000 |
| £200,000 | £37,500 | £17,000 | £20,500 |

Naturally, all of this is rather contrived, but it is perhaps the best that we can come up with by way of a simple illustration of the impact of the different tax regimes.

The company benefits in two ways:

i)      It pays CT on capital gains at just 17% (for accounting periods beginning after 31st March 2020)

ii)     It is eligible for indexation relief

By contrast, the individual's only advantage is that they have an annual CGT exemption. As a result, whilst the individual is better off with a small capital gain, the company is more advantageous for larger capital gains. In this scenario, based on the assumptions set out above, the company produces savings whenever the gain exceeds £17,950 for a residential property or £21,740 for a non-residential property.

Basic rate taxpayer individuals pay CGT at lower rates (see Section 7.2). Individual investors can also save CGT through joint ownership (so that two annual CGT exemptions are available).

These factors can mean that it takes a greater capital gain before the company is beneficial. Keeping all the other assumptions set out above the same, the amount of capital gain required before the company becomes beneficial is as follows:

- Individual owner with income not exceeding the personal allowance: residential property £23,690; non-residential property £54,350
- Joint owners, both higher rate taxpayers: residential property £35,900; non-residential property £43,480
- Joint owners, both with income not exceeding the personal allowance: residential property £47,370; non-residential property £108,700

As we can see, the impact of indexation relief means that, for large enough capital gains, the company will probably eventually prove beneficial in all cases.

It is important to remember, however, that no account has been taken here of the additional tax costs involved in extracting the sale proceeds from the company.

We will look at this factor in the next chapter, which includes a far more detailed analysis of the impact of the difference between the company and personal tax regimes for capital gains.


## 11.17  SUMMARY

I will attempt here to briefly summarise our findings in this chapter. Before I do so, however, I would like to make a few key points:

i)      As explained in Section 11.1, these findings are based on our current best estimate of the long-term tax regime for both companies and individuals in the UK. To do this, we have used an estimated forecast of the tax rates applying over the next few years

ii)     These findings are based on tax considerations only and are thus subject to the important non-tax considerations examined in Chapter 1

iii)    These findings are also based simply on a 'snapshot' of the position for a single year. In the next chapter we will look at the more detailed factors that should be considered in the long term

iv)     These findings do not take account of a property investment company's ability to set interest and finance costs off against other types of income or capital gains. We will look at the importance of interest relief in more detail in Chapter 13

v)      These findings are subject to any special circumstances that may apply

### Rental Income

Property investment companies are of little or no benefit to basic rate taxpayers. (It must be borne in mind, however, that, by 2020/21, it is the rental profit **_before interest_** from residential property that will be counted as an individual landlord's taxable income and this will mean that many landlords who are currently basic rate taxpayers will become higher rate taxpayers by that time.)

Major savings are available to higher rate taxpayers who are prepared to retain a significant proportion of their company's rental profits within the company. The more profit that is retained, the greater the savings.

The savings are always reduced where profits are extracted and, indeed, in any case where there are no interest costs relating to residential lettings, a property investment company will be of no benefit where all profits are being extracted.

Where there are interest costs relating to residential lettings, higher rate taxpayers will enjoy an even greater benefit by using a company. Some benefit is likely to remain even if all profits are extracted. The benefit is so great that it may even compensate for higher interest costs suffered in the company.


## Property Trades

A property trading company is generally of little or no benefit where all of the company's profits are being extracted each year. There are a few exceptions to this at certain profit levels due to some particular quirks in the UK tax system.

Even when profits are retained, the benefit to basic rate taxpayers remains questionable as the amount of savings involved may not be significant enough to compensate for the higher costs of running a company.

However, major benefits remain for higher rate taxpayers prepared to retain a significant proportion of profits within the company.


## Capital Gains

Generally speaking, capital gains arising within a company enjoy a better overall effective tax rate once the investor's annual exemption has been exhausted.

This, however, is before considering the additional costs of extracting sale proceeds from the company.

# Chapter 12

# Making the Big Decision

## 12.1 THE 'BIG PICTURE'

Before you can decide whether a company is for you or not, you will need to look at what I call the 'Big Picture'.

Many investors concentrate almost exclusively on the taxation treatment of their income. Others are mainly concerned with capital gains.

Neither approach is correct. The only way to carry out effective tax planning is to take every applicable tax into account. In the case of property companies, we are not concerned only with income, nor solely with capital gains, but with both. On top of that, we must also consider the costs of extracting profits and sale proceeds from the company.

VAT, Stamp Duty, SDLT and any other tax costs should also be considered and, if one is taking the really long view, it makes sense to give some thought to IHT as well.

Fully effective tax planning is only possible once all potential tax costs have been taken into account, however and whenever they are likely to arise. But, even this is still not truly the 'Big Picture'.

### *Bayley's Law*

'The truly wise investor does not seek merely to minimise the amount of tax paid, but rather to maximise the **wealth** remaining once all taxes have been taken into account.'

### Taking the Long Term View

The more favourable regime for obtaining tax relief for interest and finance costs may sometimes provide the greatest benefit when using a property company. Undoubtedly, this is an important factor and we will therefore be looking at this issue in detail in Chapter 13.

The most effective tax planning, however, is always based on a long-term view. This is seldom more true than it is when looking at the issue of whether or not to use a property company. My aim in this chapter is therefore to show you the likely outcome provided by using a property company in the long-term.

In the long-term, history shows that UK property tends to grow in value at an average annual rate of around 7.5%. Due to the compound effect of this growth, this roughly equates to properties doubling in value every ten years.

In order to take a long-term view, therefore, we will use this growth rate for the models which we will explore in this chapter.

Readers will, of course, be acutely aware that actual growth rates fluctuate significantly and we do not always see these sort of growth rates in the short term.

Nevertheless, our purpose in this chapter is to look at the 'Big Picture' and to plan for the long-term. This necessitates taking a hypothetical approach based on long-term trends. I make no apologies for this, because this is the right approach when considering effective long-term planning.

In reality, however, the short-term position will, of course, often be very different and it is imperative that readers form their own opinion on current and likely future market conditions. The models used in this chapter are entirely hypothetical and are in no way intended to be a true indication of the likely performance of the property market over the next few years.

## 12.2   TYPES OF PROPERTY BUSINESS REVISITED

Following on from our conclusions in Section 11.17, it is already reasonable to surmise that the current tax regime produces the potential to make significant tax savings by operating most property development, property trading or property management businesses through a company where:

- The company owner is a higher rate taxpayer (or would be if they had not used a company), and
- A significant proportion of after tax profits are retained in the company

This arises mainly because of the preferential CT rate when compared with the combined Income Tax and NI cost of trading on a personal basis.

Add to this the fact that a trading company's shares will usually qualify for entrepreneurs' relief (see Section 7.3) and the position appears fairly clear-cut in the case of any property trade producing a substantial level of annual profits. The only dangers lie in potential future changes to the tax regime or, perhaps, with the investor's inability to comply with the more stringent administrative necessities involved in operating a company.

We will return to take a more detailed look at the advantages of property trading companies in Section 12.15.

As far as property investment companies are concerned, our findings in Chapter 11 tell us that these are not generally beneficial for basic rate taxpayers. (But readers should bear in mind that many more residential landlords will become higher rate taxpayers in the near future due to the restrictions in interest relief which we will be looking at in Section 13.10.)

Property investment companies do appear to be beneficial for higher rate taxpayers under certain circumstances: namely when a significant proportion of profits are retained in the company, or when there are interest costs relating to residential lettings.

But, in most cases, we also need to factor in the costs involved in extracting both rental profits and property sale proceeds. Even if the company owner does not extract all their profits and gains every year, they are usually going to want to extract them eventually!

This is therefore where we are going to concentrate for most of the remainder of this chapter.


## 12.3    THE RENTAL INCOME POSITION

In the preceding chapters, we have looked at the mechanics of how UK resident companies are taxed. We will now begin to look at how this all affects property investment businesses and whether a company therefore becomes beneficial or not.

The best way to illustrate this is by way of an example. We will start with a simple scenario which does not involve any interest or finance costs. Taking the long-term view, we will assume that the CT rate is now 17% and the other tax changes set out in Section 11.2 have also taken place.

## Example 'A', Part 1

Humphrey has decided to begin investing in property with the intention of building up a property portfolio over the next few years. He is already a higher rate taxpayer, even before taking any rental income into consideration.

Although his friend Charlie said "you'd be daft not to use a company, old boy", Humphrey goes ahead and buys three flats in his own name for £130,000 each and begins to rent them out.

During the following year, Humphrey receives rental income of £10,000 from each flat, but has deductible expenditure totalling £6,000, leaving him with a profit of £24,000. Humphrey's accountant, Edmund, therefore advises him that he has an Income Tax liability of £9,600 (£24,000 at 40%), leaving him with net income of £14,400.

Feeling somewhat frustrated by his inability to persuade Humphrey to invest through a limited company, Charlie decides to try it out for himself. He sets up a company, Murrayfield Limited, and, through this, he too buys three flats for £130,000 each. He incurs the same level of expenses as Humphrey and Murrayfield Limited therefore also has a profit of £24,000.

Murrayfield Limited's profits are taxed at 17%, meaning that the CT payable by the company would be £4,080.

At first glance, therefore, Charlie appears to be some £5,520 better off than Humphrey, indicating that a company seems to be highly beneficial.

Now feeling rather pleased with himself, Charlie shows what he has done to Edmund (who happens to be his accountant too). Unfortunately for Charlie, Edmund has two pieces of bad news for him.

Firstly, as using a company has a few extra complications, Edmund's fees to Charlie will be rather more than he charged Humphrey. However, the difference is not a huge sum compared with the tax he has saved, and is a tax-deductible expense in itself, so Charlie is not too concerned by this. (We will also ignore Edmund's additional fees for the sake of illustration.)

Secondly though, Edmund points out that if Charlie wants any of the money that Murrayfield Limited has made, he will have to pay himself a salary or a dividend. Edmund advises that the best course of action in this case is to first take a salary of £9,000, since this will attract CT relief; then to pay out the remaining after tax profits to himself as a dividend.

*The salary reduces the taxable profit to £15,000, meaning that the company's CT bill will now be £2,550. That leaves a profit after tax of £12,450 which can be paid out as a dividend.*

*Charlie suffers Income Tax of £3,600 on his salary (at 40%) and £3,658 on his dividend (at 35%, except for the first £2,000 which is covered by the dividend allowance).*

*This leaves Charlie with total net income of £14,192 (£9,000 – £3,600 + £12,450 – £3,658), or **£208 less** than Humphrey!*

For the sake of illustration, I have treated Charlie's salary and dividends as arising in the same year as his company's rental profits. In practice this may not always be the case: especially in view of the 'Wealth Warning' in Section 11.5.

**Analysis of Example 'A' so Far**

In tax terms alone, Charlie is worse off than Humphrey. Furthermore, after taking account of Edmund's higher fees and other costs associated with running a company, Charlie will be even worse off. This is mainly because Charlie has withdrawn all of his rental profits from the company.

In this example, we have examined the position of two higher rate taxpayers with no interest or finance costs who both want to spend all of the profits from their property business. The example confirms our findings in Chapter 11 that a company is of no benefit in this situation.

Humphrey and Charlie are typical of the type of property investor who already has a good level of income from other sources and wishes to supplement it through property investment.

**Conclusion**

**Using a property investment company is of no benefit when there are no borrowings relating to residential lettings and all of the profits are needed to fund the investor's current lifestyle**

## 12.4 REINVESTING RENTAL PROFITS

In the previous section, we saw that a property investment company was of no benefit when all of its profits were being withdrawn by the proprietor and there were no borrowings relating to residential lettings.

However, where a property investment company can really produce significant financial benefits is when the property investor does not need their rental income immediately and reinvests their profits in order to build up a substantial investment portfolio over a number of years.

To see how a company may benefit these investors, let's return to our friends Humphrey and Charlie.

### Example 'A', Part 2

*Humphrey and Charlie both continue to accumulate a property portfolio. After a few years, each of them has ten properties, which have cost a total of £1.5m. Each of them now has total annual rental income of £125,000 and annual expenditure of £15,000, leaving rental profits of £110,000.*

*Let us also assume that Humphrey and Charlie each have existing annual income from other sources of £60,000 and that our forecast tax rates (see Appendix B) still prevail at this time.*

*Humphrey will therefore face Income Tax on his rental income as follows:*

| | |
|---|---|
| *£90,000 (£150,000 - £60,000) x 40% =* | *£36,000* |
| *£20,000 (£110,000 - £90,000) x 45% =* | *£9,000* |
| *£12,500 (lost personal allowance) x 40% =* | *£5,000* |
| *Total* | *£50,000* |

*This will leave him with net income of £60,000 (£110,000 – £50,000).*

*If Charlie continues to pay himself a salary of £9,000, this will reduce Murrayfield Limited's taxable profit to £101,000, giving the company a CT bill (at 17%) of £17,170. This would leave a profit after tax of £83,830 and, if this were paid out to Charlie as a dividend, he would suffer Income Tax as follows:*

| | |
|---|---|
| *Salary - £9,000 x 40% =* | *£3,600* |
| *Dividend - £2,000 x 0% =* | *£0* |
| *£79,000 x 35% =* | *£27,650* |
| *£2,830 x 40% =* | *£1,132* |
| *£12,500 (lost personal allowance) x 40% =* | *£5,000* |
| *Total* | *£37,382* |

*This would leave Charlie with net income of £55,448 (£9,000 + £83,830 – £37,382), or **£4,552 less** than Humphrey!*

*Let us suppose instead, however, that Humphrey and Charlie each wish to reinvest £60,000 of their rental profits in a new property.*

*In Humphrey's case, this makes absolutely no difference to his Income Tax bill, which remains £50,000. Similarly, this reinvestment makes no difference to Murrayfield Limited's CT bill of £17,170. What the reinvestment **does** mean, however, is that, since Murrayfield Limited is reinvesting £60,000 of its rental profits in a new property, Charlie will only be taking out a dividend of £23,830, thus reducing his Income Tax bill as follows:*

| | |
|---|---|
| *Salary - £9,000 x 40% =* | *£3,600* |
| *Dividend - £2,000 x 0% =* | *£0* |
| *£21,830 x 35% =* | *£7,640* |
| *Total* | *£11,240* |

*Between Charlie and his company, the total tax burden for the year will be reduced to only £28,410, which is £21,590 less than Humphrey's Income Tax bill!*

### Analysis of Example 'A', Part 2

To begin with, the example reinforces the fact that there is no benefit in using a company, even at higher levels of profit, if there are no interest costs relating to residential lettings and all of the income continues to be withdrawn.

However, it can also be seen that using a company can save a considerable amount of tax on the investor's rental profits where these are **not** all withdrawn.

**Hence, a property investment company can prove highly beneficial for income purposes when a substantial proportion of the profits are being reinvested**

### 12.5 CAPITAL GAINS

In Chapter 6, we looked at the basic mechanics of how a company is taxed on its capital gains.

Now, in order to illustrate the impact of the differences between how capital gains are taxed in a company and how individuals are taxed on capital gains, let's turn to another example.

## Example 'B', Part 1

*Michelle and Yvonne share a lottery win and each decide to invest £250,000 of their proceeds in residential property.*

*Yvonne buys her property personally; Michelle forms a company, Dawson Limited, to buy her property. Both properties are rented out to provide income. Ten years later, Michelle and Yvonne both sell their properties for £500,000. They are both higher rate taxpayers at this time.*

*Over this ten-year period inflation has totalled 40% and the CGT annual exemption has increased to £15,000.*

*Yvonne has made a capital gain of £250,000. After deducting her annual exemption, her taxable gain therefore amounts to £235,000, giving her a CGT liability of £65,800 (£235,000 x 28%).*

*Dawson Limited also has a gain of £250,000, but may deduct indexation relief at 40% on cost (£250,000), i.e. £100,000. This leaves Dawson Limited with a chargeable gain of £150,000 and a CT bill, at 17%, of just £25,500.*

*Again, at first glance, we see that the corporate investor appears to be better off. However, once again, we must also consider how to extract the after-tax proceeds from the company.*

*If Michelle removes the net proceeds of £474,500 from Dawson Limited as a dividend, as a higher rate taxpayer she would have to pay Income Tax of at least £187,850 (using our forecast rates set out in Appendix B, as usual).*

### Analysis of Example 'B', Part 1

Clearly, Michelle now appears to be much worse off than Yvonne, but could she have done something better than simply paying herself this enormous dividend?

The answer is yes, but we will need to look at what happens to a property company which is no longer required (Section 12.6) before we can see how it works. The position also depends on how the company was financed in the first place (we will cover that topic in detail in Chapter 13).

Another alternative for Michelle might be to leave the proceeds in the company for reinvestment in new property (or some other form of investment). Again, we can see from this example that a property company works best in a reinvestment environment.

In practice, it is highly unlikely that a property investor like Michelle would have simply taken a dividend of this magnitude out of the company.

Firstly, Michelle's case is unusual as she did not have any borrowings, thus meaning that the proceeds which she wished to remove from the company were somewhat inflated.

Secondly, company law would prevent her from taking a dividend out of Dawson Limited in excess of its distributable profits. (We will cover the extraction of the original capital invested in the company in Section 12.6.) For the sake of illustration, therefore, let's consider Michelle's tax position if she only withdraws her after-tax profit on the property from Dawson Limited, rather than her entire proceeds.

### Example 'B', Part 2

*Michelle takes a dividend of £224,500 out of Dawson Limited, representing her after-tax profit on the sale of the property. As a higher rate taxpayer, her Income Tax liability on this dividend will be at least £87,850 (using our forecast rates set out in Appendix B).*

*Combining this with the CT already suffered in Dawson Limited (£25,500) gives a total tax cost on the property disposal of at least £113,350.*

### Analysis of Example 'B', Part 2

Now that we have altered the situation so that we are only looking at the profit element of the proceeds, we can clearly see that Michelle, the corporate investor, is still considerably worse off than Yvonne, the private investor. As a higher rate taxpayer, Michelle would, in fact, be at least £47,550 worse off (£113,350 - £65,800).

Michelle could possibly improve the situation by taking her dividends over a few years, so that she kept her taxable income under £100,000 in each year, retained her personal allowance and avoided any additional rate tax. Nonetheless, as a higher rate taxpayer, spreading the dividends over, say, five years, she would still suffer a total of £75,075 in Income Tax; leaving her £34,775 worse off than Yvonne (£75,075 + £25,500 = £100,575 - £65,800 = £34,775).

And, in case you think this problem only arises because I am forecasting increases in the dividend tax rates applying in the future, Michelle's total Income Tax cost in the last scenario, based on **current** dividend tax rates would still be £69,713, so she would still be £29,413 worse off than Yvonne (£69,713 + £25,500 = £95,213 - £65,800 = £29,413).

This clearly demonstrates that a company is not a good investment vehicle if the investor wishes to realise capital gains and extract them from the company for private use, rather than reinvest them within it.

## 12.6   WINDING UP THE COMPANY TO REDUCE TAX

In Section 12.5 we encountered a situation where an investor was left with funds in a company that had perhaps outlived its usefulness. In such a case, the most tax-efficient procedure may be to wind the company up. Unfortunately, this can be a very expensive process if the company still has assets and liabilities or has recently been in active business.

For the sake of illustration, however, let us return to Example 'B' and ignore the impact of these costs.

### Example 'B', Part 3

*Rather than pay herself a huge dividend, Michelle decides instead to wind Dawson Limited up.*

*First, however, she pays herself her small tax-free dividend of £2,000, which is covered by the dividend allowance (see Section 10.3). The remaining net proceeds left in Dawson Limited now amount to £472,500 (£474,500 - £2,000).*

*Ignoring costs, this sum can now be distributed to Michelle on the winding up and will therefore be treated in her hands as a capital disposal subject to CGT and not Income Tax (but see the 'Wealth Warning' below).*

*Michelle originally invested £250,000 in Dawson Limited in order to enable it to purchase the property. Hence, her capital gain on her shares in Dawson Limited is £222,500. After deducting her annual exemption of £15,000, this leaves a taxable gain of £207,500.*

*Michelle's CGT liability at 20% (not 28% - see below) will therefore be £41,500. Combining this with the CT paid by Dawson Limited (£25,500) gives Michelle a total tax cost on this disposal of £67,000.*

## Analysis of Example 'B', Part 3

Firstly, it is worth noting that entrepreneurs' relief is not available on the disposal of Michelle's property company shares. As explained in Section 3.2, this will generally be the case for property investment companies (but see Section 7.4 for a possible way to obtain this relief). The shares do, however, benefit from the lower, 'non-residential', rate of CGT (see Section 7.2) because the shares themselves are not residential property (even though Dawson Ltd had invested in residential property).

By winding up the company rather than merely paying herself a single huge dividend, Michelle has dramatically improved her position from Part 2 (Section 12.5). In effect, changing the way that most of her sale proceeds are treated to a capital gain instead of a dividend has reduced the tax rate on a large part of her profits from 40% to 20%.

It's a big improvement, but still not enough to match the private investor's position. In fact, Michelle would still remain £1,200 worse off than Yvonne (£67,000 - £65,800). Hence, it appears quite conclusive that a company is not beneficial when we are looking at fairly static levels of capital growth, without any serious reinvestment activity, which are ultimately being returned into the hands of the individual investor.

### Wealth Warning (A *Major* Wealth Warning in Fact!)

As discussed in Section 7.7, there is a risk that sums distributed on a winding up of the company could be treated as dividends if the company owner, or a connected person (see Appendix D), continues to invest in a similar property business in any way within the next two years after the winding up. This would return an investor like Michelle back to the position shown in Part 2 (Section 12.5), leaving her at least £47,550 worse off than the private investor.

### 12.7 WHAT IF THE COMPANY STILL HOLDS PROPERTY WHEN WOUND UP?

Generally, this would not be a good idea:

- Firstly, the costs of the winding up would be considerably greater
- Secondly, the company would be treated as having made a disposal of the property at its market value and taxed accordingly
- Thirdly, the shareholder would be taxed on the 'disposal' of the company shares, again based on the market value of the property!

In Michelle's case, for example, tax liabilities of at least £67,400 would be incurred without there being any actual sale proceeds from which to fund them. This demonstrates the fact that, once you have your investments in a company, it can be very difficult (or expensive) to get them out if you should want to!

## 12.8  NON-RESIDENTIAL PROPERTY

So far, we have looked at the position on residential property investments. How would things differ if we were investing in non-residential property?

Firstly, any interest and finance costs incurred by the individual investor would be fully relieved, meaning that the position described in Example 'A' (Sections 12.3 and 12.4) would remain the same even if there were borrowings against the properties.

Secondly, the individual investor would suffer CGT on a property disposal at the lower, non-residential, rates of 10% for basic rate taxpayers and 20% for higher rate taxpayers. Hence, for example, Yvonne's CGT liability in Example 'B' (Sections 12.5 and 12.6) would be reduced to just £47,000 (£235,000 x 20%), whereas the tax incurred by both Michelle and Dawson Limited would remain unaltered.

Overall, therefore, the conclusions which we have drawn so far would simply be further reinforced if the investor is looking to invest in non-residential property.

## 12.9  FURNISHED HOLIDAY LETTINGS

The position also differs significantly where the investor is looking to invest in furnished holiday lettings.

Once again, any interest and finance costs incurred by the individual investor would be fully relieved, meaning that the position described in Example 'A' (Sections 12.3 and 12.4) would remain unaltered where there were borrowings against the properties.

The private investor might be eligible for entrepreneurs' relief on a disposal of their property: providing that they were disposing of an entire furnished holiday letting business (see the Taxcafe.co.uk guide 'How to Save Property Tax' for a detailed examination of the considerations involved).

The corporate investor should definitely be eligible for entrepreneurs' relief on a disposal of their shares (provided all the conditions described in Section 7.3) are met.

Assuming both investors are eligible for entrepreneurs' relief, the results in Example 'B' would differ as follows:

Yvonne's CGT liability (see Section 12.5) would be reduced to £23,500 (£235,000 x 10%).

Michelle's final CGT liability in Part 3 (Section 12.6) would be reduced to £20,750 (£207,500 x 10%). However, the total tax incurred by both Michelle and Dawson Limited would be £46,250 (£25,500 + £20,750), leaving her £22,750 worse off than Yvonne. (The 'Wealth Warning' in Section 12.6 would also still be highly relevant!)

Once again, therefore, the conclusions which we have drawn so far would simply be further reinforced if the investor is looking to invest in furnished holiday lettings.


## 12.10  INTEREST RELIEF

What we have not factored in so far in this chapter is the impact of the dreadful interest relief restrictions applying to individual landlords investing in residential property.

In Example 'C' below, we are now going to include this additional consideration. We will assume that the forecast tax rates set out in Appendix B apply and that the interest relief restrictions are fully in force (i.e. we are looking at a period falling after 5th April 2020).

### Example 'C'

*James and Robert both have similar residential property portfolios yielding profits before interest of £100,000. They both have £50,000 in other income.*

*James holds his properties personally and has annual interest and finance costs of £40,000.*

*Robert holds his properties through Tipp Holdings Limited which has annual interest and finance costs of £50,000 (a quarter more than James).*

*James suffers Income Tax on his property profits as follows:*

| | |
|---|---|
| £100,000 x 40% = | £40,000 |
| £12,500 (lost personal allowance) x 40% = | £5,000 |
| Less interest relief | |
| £40,000 x 20% | (£8,000) |
| Tax liability | £37,000 |

This leaves James with net income of £23,000 (£100,000 - £40,000 - £37,000).

Robert takes a salary of £9,000 out of Tipp Holdings Limited, leaving the company with a taxable profit of £41,000 (£100,000 - £50,000 - £9,000). The company therefore pays CT of £6,970 (£41,000 x 17%) leaving it with profits after tax of £34,030, which it pays out to Robert as a dividend.

Robert then has an Income Tax liability made up as follows:

| | |
|---|---|
| Salary - £9,000 x 40% = | £3,600 |
| Dividend - £2,000 x 0% = | £0 |
| £32,030 x 35% = | £11,210 |
| Total | £14,810 |

This gives Robert net income of £28,220 (£9,000 + £34,030 - £14,810), leaving him £5,220 better off than James.

**Analysis of Example 'C'**

As we can see, using a property investment company can yield savings for a residential property investor even when the company's interest costs are higher than they would have suffered as an individual *and* they are extracting all of their company's after tax profits.

**12.11 LONG-TERM REINVESTMENT**

What we have not yet considered is how the incorporated property business's long-term capital growth might benefit from its ability to reinvest a greater share of its profits owing to the fact that its tax bill is much reduced under the CT regime.

## Reinvesting Profits Over a Number of Years

We now know that a property company can produce a significantly better outcome in the short term, year on year, when either:

    a) Its profits are being reinvested, or
    b) There are borrowings on residential rental property

In Example 'A', we assumed that the investors had built up identical portfolios over a period of time. However, in practice, it is likely that if both investors reinvest all or most of their profits, the company investor will eventually build up a larger portfolio of properties. This is because the lower CT rates will leave the company investor with extra resources to invest in new properties.

The long-term effect of reinvestment through a property company is best illustrated by way of the example that follows (Example 'D'). In this example, we will have to make many assumptions, including rates of return, interest rates and the rate of growth of property values. Here again we will follow the hypothetical long-term trend for the reasons discussed in Section 12.1.

Whilst the real outcome over the coming years will almost certainly be different to that which is predicted here, the example will still serve as a valid illustration because we will apply all of our assumptions equally to the company investor and the personal investor, except for:

- Their different tax environments, and
- An assumed higher interest rate for the company investor

The numbers will get quite messy in this example but please bear with me, as it is worth persevering to see the ultimate result.

### Example 'D', Part 1

*Lenny and Dawn are both higher rate taxpayers and they each own residential rental properties worth £320,000. They each earn annual rents of £24,000 and, after deducting costs of £4,000, are left with annual profits of £20,000. At present, neither of them is paying any interest.*

*Lenny's property is owned personally and, because he is a higher rate taxpayer, he is left with after-tax profits of £12,000.*

*Dawn uses a company, Saunders Limited, to invest. Saunders Limited's rental profits will be subject to CT at 17%. On a profit of £20,000 this will give rise to a CT bill of £3,400, leaving the company with £16,600.*

*Each investor is using their property business to save for retirement, so all after-tax profits are saved and reinvested.*

*After three years, Lenny will have £36,000 available for reinvestment. With a 70% Buy-to-Let mortgage, this will enable him to buy a new property at a cost of £120,000. This brings in rental income of £9,000, less interest of £3,360 and other costs of £1,100, leaving him with an annual rental profit of £4,540.*

*Lenny's total annual rental profit for both properties is now £24,540 (£20,000 + £4,540) but he is subject to Income Tax at 40% on his profit before interest of £27,900 and only gets basic rate tax relief at 20% on his interest cost. This gives him an Income Tax liability of £10,488, leaving him with after-tax profits of £14,052.*

*Dawn, the company investor, also buys a new property after three years, but she has £49,800 available (3 x £16,600). This enables her to buy a property for £166,000, which produces rental income of £12,450. After interest of £5,810 and other costs of £1,330, Dawn's company receives an additional annual rental profit of £5,310 from this property.*

*Saunders Limited's annual profits are now £25,310, giving rise to CT, at 17%, of £4,303, leaving profits after tax of £21,007.*

## Analysis of Example 'D', Part 1

Already, we can see that Dawn is moving ahead of Lenny. Her company's second property purchase is worth £46,000 more and her annual after-tax profits are now almost £7,000 greater (assuming she continues to keep them within the company).

For the sake of illustration, I have had to make a number of assumptions here, which are worth explaining:

- Rental income, or yield, is assumed to be 7.5% of the property's value
- Mortgage interest is at 4% for individuals and 5% for a company
- Other annual costs amount to a fixed element of £500 per property, plus a variable element equal to 0.5% of the property's value

182

We are now going to move forward many more years, assuming that Lenny and Dawn continue to reinvest all of their available after-tax profits in new property every three years using 70% Buy-to-Let mortgages.

The result in Part 2 will be based on all of the same assumptions as in Part 1 above, assuming, in turn, that these all remain valid throughout that period.

Additionally, and purely for the sake of simplicity, we will also assume that:

- The rentals are never increased on any of the properties
- There is no capital repayment of any of the mortgages (i.e. we assume they are all interest-only mortgages)
- Lenny and Dawn's other taxable income amounts to £50,000 each
- Our forecast tax rates (see Appendix B) apply throughout the relevant period

### Example 'D', Part 2

*After continuing in the same way for 15 years, Lenny and Dawn will each have a portfolio of six properties.*

*Lenny's properties now produce total annual rental profits of £52,222 but he is taxed on his profit before interest of £75,370 and only gets basic rate tax relief on his interest costs of £23,148. This gives rise to a net Income Tax bill of:*

| | |
|---|---|
| *£75,370 x 40% =* | *£30,148* |
| *£12,500 (lost personal allowance) x 40% =* | *£5,000* |
| *Less interest relief* | |
| *£23,148 x 20%* | *(£4,630)* |
| *Tax liability* | *£30,518* |

*This leaves him with just £21,704 of annual after-tax income.*

*Dawn's property company is now receiving annual rental profits of £67,145, leaving a sum of £55,731 after CT.*

*Let us suppose that, at this point, both Lenny and Dawn wish to stop reinvesting, retire and start spending their rental profits privately. We already know how much net income Lenny will receive.*

*For Dawn, we now need to take account of the Income Tax that she will suffer when she withdraws her after tax profits from the company. First, she takes a salary of £9,000. This reduces the company's taxable profit to £58,145, leaving £48,260 after CT, which is available for her to take as a dividend. Her Income Tax liability will be as follows:*

| | |
|---|---|
| *Salary - £9,000 x 40% =* | *£3,600* |
| *Dividend - £2,000 x 0% =* | *£0* |
| *£46,260 x 35% =* | *£16,191* |
| *Partial loss of personal allowance –* | |
| *£3,630 x 40% =* | *£1,452* |
| *Total* | *£21,243* |

*Dawn will therefore be left with net annual income from her property business of £36,017 (£9,000 + £48,260 - £21,243), or £14,313 more than Lenny.*

### Analysis of Example 'D', Part 2

What this example shows is that the ability to reinvest a greater share of the annual rental profits over a number of years has ultimately provided Dawn, the corporate investor, with a greatly increased income.

In fact, in this example, **the company investor has an after-tax income almost 66% greater than that enjoyed by the personal investor!**

**This example has shown that, in a long-term reinvestment scenario, a property investment company really can provide enormous tax benefits to those who build up a portfolio of properties and ultimately use it to generate income.**

### 12.12 RETAINING THE WEALTH

So far, so good, but we still haven't tackled the issue of capital gains. Although Lenny and Dawn have now stopped reinvesting, they do still have the pressure of a property-letting business to worry about. To genuinely retire, they may, in fact, wish to now sell all of their properties.

To look at the final outcome on the ultimate sale of the property portfolios, let's move on one final three-year period and assume that Lenny and Dawn each then sell all of their properties.

We also need to make three other major assumptions for this purpose:

i)  Property values have increased at an average compound rate of 7.5% per annum (see Section 12.1)
ii) Inflation has averaged 2.5% per annum
iii) There have been no changes to the tax system beyond our forecasts in Appendix B, other than an increase in the annual CGT exemption to £20,000

### Example 'D', Part 3

*Eighteen years after we started, Lenny's property portfolio is worth a total of £2,739,320. The total cost of this portfolio was £1,146,716, thus giving him total capital gains of £1,592,604.*

*Let's assume that Lenny's disposals are spread over two tax years, with annual exemptions of £20,000 in each year.*

*Deducting these two annual exemptions leaves Lenny with total taxable gains of £1,552,604, thus giving rise to total CGT liabilities (at 28%) of £434,729.*

*After paying his CGT and also repaying all of his mortgages, Lenny will be left with net proceeds of £1,725,890.*

*Now let's look at Dawn.*

*The property portfolio in Dawn's company will now be worth a total of £3,745,328. The cost of the portfolio was £1,738,439, producing total capital gains of £2,006,889. Indexation relief will amount to a total of £480,198, leaving taxable indexed gains of £1,526,691.*

*The CT on the company's capital gains therefore amounts to a total of £259,537 (at 17%).*

*After paying this CT and repaying all of the mortgages that the company took out, the remaining funds in the company will be £2,492,883.*

*Dawn now winds up Saunders Limited in order to get these proceeds into her own hands.*

*Here, we will assume that Dawn originally invested £320,000 in the company (the value of her first property), meaning that she will have a capital gain of £2,172,883. (We are again ignoring the costs of the winding up as we did in Section 12.6.)*

*Dawn is entitled to an annual exemption of £20,000, leaving her with a taxable gain of £2,152,883. Her CGT liability at 20% on the winding up of her property investment company will therefore amount to £430,577, leaving her with net proceeds of £2,062,306 (£2,492,883 - £430,577).*

### Analysis of Example 'D', Part 3

So how much better off is the company investor compared with the private investor?

**Ultimately, our corporate investor, Dawn, has emerged £336,416, or almost 20%, better off than Lenny, our personal investor.**

This represents **over 105% of the original amount invested by each investor!**

In short, what this means is that, over a reasonable period of time, the reinvestment of the additional net income receivable through the use of a company should eventually produce a sufficiently improved position to more than compensate for the disadvantages of realising capital gains in a company and suffering a second layer of tax when extracting the net sale proceeds.

Readers should, however, bear in mind the 'Wealth Warning' in Section 12.6 and the 'anti-phoenixing' rules described in Section 7.7 which could mean that the eventual proceeds received on the winding up of the company could be treated as dividends.

In Dawn's case, this would have led to an Income Tax liability of £867,653, reducing her net proceeds to £1,625,230 and leaving her **just over £100,000 worse off** than Lenny.

Readers in this sort of position should seek professional advice regarding the potential application of the rules in Section 7.7.


### 12.13  AN ALTERNATIVE FUTURE

In Section 12.12 we saw that a long term investor could end up almost 20% better off by using a property investment company. However, we also considered the risk that the anti-phoenixing' rules described in Section 7.7 might result in a less beneficial outcome.

Alternatively, another option might simply be to reinvest the proceeds of the company's property disposals within the company and thus avoid the risk of the 'anti-phoenixing' rules applying.

This could have huge benefits, and we will illustrate these by returning to Example 'D'.

### Example 'D', Part 4

*Lenny takes his net proceeds of £1,725,890 and invests them in a share portfolio. Let's say this yields an annual return of 5%, or £86,295. Let's also say that this is all in the form of dividends.*

*Lenny will suffer tax on this income as follows:*

*£84,295 (£86,295 - £2,000) x 35% =     £29,503*
*£12,500 (lost personal allowance) x 40% =  £5,000*
*Total                                      £34,503*

*This leaves him with £51,792 of annual after-tax income (£86,295 - £34,503).*

*Dawn takes the net proceeds of £2,492,833 held by Saunders Limited and invests these in a share portfolio held by the company. This yields an annual return at 5% of £124,642. The company is exempt from CT on dividend income so it is able to redistribute all the dividends it receives to Dawn, again in the form of dividends. Her Income Tax liability on this income will be as follows:*

*£2,000 x 0% =                                £0*
*£98,000 x 35% =                         £34,300*
*£24,642 x 40% =                          £9,857*
*£12,500 (lost personal allowance) x 40% =  £5,000*
*Total                                   £49,157*

*This leaves her with £75,485 of annual after-tax income (£124,642 - £49,157) or £23,693 more than Lenny.*

### Analysis of Example 'D', Part 4

**Reinvesting her ultimate sale proceeds within her company has left our corporate investor, Dawn, with almost 46% more after tax income than Lenny, our personal investor.**

## 12.14  LONG-TERM REINVESTMENT CONCLUSIONS

After taking a long and detailed look at the possible outcomes for two investors (one corporate and one personal) over many years, we can now see that using a property investment company can be hugely beneficial when building a portfolio over a long period of time.

The benefits come in three possible forms:

- By building the portfolio for an extended period and then beginning to extract income: we saw an increase of almost 66% in after-tax income for the corporate investor (Example 'D', Part 2, Section 12.11)
- By eventually selling off the portfolio after an extended period of growth: we saw an increase of almost 20% in the total net proceeds for the corporate investor (Example 'D', Part 3, Section 12.12)
- By selling the portfolio after an extended period of growth and then reinvesting the funds in other, more 'passive' forms of investments within the company: we saw an increase of almost 46% in after-tax income for the corporate investor (Example 'D', Part 2, Section 12.11)

## 12.15  THE BENEFITS OF REINVESTMENT FOR A TRADING COMPANY

The one thing that we have not yet covered is the situation where the profits from a property **trade** are being reinvested over a long period.

I did suggest in Section 12.2 that this was almost a 'no-brainer', with a property company being the obvious winner in most cases. However, I feel that this stance does warrant an illustrative example to back up my assertions!

As usual, for the sake of illustration, we will use the forecast future tax rates set out in Appendix B as a good approximation of the actual position over the next few years.

### Example 'E' Part 1

*Andrew and Lianne are both property developers. Each of them acquires a derelict property in Southampton at a cost of £180,000, which they plan to renovate and convert into flats which they will then sell. Andrew is going to carry on his business as a sole trader. Lianne, on the other hand, forms a property development company, Rainbow Developments Limited.*

*Neither Lianne nor Andrew has any other income, so each will need £20,000 out of their net profits to cover modest living expenses.*

*In their first year of trading, each of them manages to develop their property and sell all of the flats. After building costs, interest costs and other trading expenditure, each makes a total profit of £100,000 which they plan to reinvest in their business, together with their original capital of £180,000.*

*At our forecast tax rates (Appendix B), Andrew will have a total Income Tax and NI liability of £33,010, leaving him only £66,990 of net, after-tax profit. £20,000 of this goes on living expenses, leaving £46,990 available to reinvest, plus his original capital of £180,000, making a total of £226,990.*

*Lianne, on the other hand, pays herself a salary of £9,000 (the NI primary threshold). This leaves a taxable profit in the company of £91,000. After CT of £15,470 (at 17%), the company is left with a net profit of £75,530. From this, Lianne pays herself a dividend of £11,611: of which £3,500 is covered by the remainder of her personal allowance (£12,500 - £9,000), £2,000 by her dividend allowance, and the final £6,111 is taxed at 10%. After paying tax of £611, she is left with a final sum of £20,000 to cover living expenses as required (£9,000 + £11,611 - £611 = £20,000).*

*The company is therefore left with £63,919 (£75,530 - £11,611) to reinvest plus Lianne's original capital of £180,000, making a total of £243,919.*

## Analysis of Example 'E' Part 1

Already we can see that Rainbow Developments Limited, the property development company, has an extra £16,929 available for reinvestment. This is because the company has been able to retain over 36% more of its profits than Andrew was able to keep himself.

## *Example 'E' Part 2*

*The following year, Andrew and Lianne both reinvest their available profits and capital in a new development. In each case, they double the amount available by borrowing the same sum as they are investing themselves.*

*After all relevant expenditure, each development yields a profit of 25% before interest costs at 7.5%.*

*Throughout the rest of this example, I'm also going to assume that Lianne and Andrew's requirements for living expenses will each increase by £2,000 per annum and the forecast future tax rates set out in Appendix B will continue to apply.*

*On the basis of the above assumptions, Andrew will make a profit of £96,471 and will have total Income Tax and NI costs of £31,528. After living expenses of £22,000, he will have total profits and capital left for reinvestment the next year of £269,933.*

*In the same year, Rainbow Developments Limited will make a net profit before tax of £103,666, which is £7,195 more than Andrew, owing to the greater amount of profit available for reinvestment from the previous year.*

*Rainbow Developments Limited will then pay Lianne a salary of £9,000 and the CT at 17% on the remaining £94,666 profit will be £16,093. Lianne will take out a dividend of £13,833 to top up her total income after tax to the level required to cover her living expenses for the year.*

*This will leave the company with net retained profits of £64,739 which, this time, is £21,796 more than Andrew had left for reinvestment. Rainbow Developments Limited's total funds available for reinvestment at this point are £308,658. This is £38,725, or over 14%, more than Andrew is able to invest.*

*In fact, by using a company, Lianne has experienced 43% more growth than Andrew when compared to the £180,000 of capital which they each invested originally.*

**Analysis of Example 'E' Part 2**

After only two years of trading, the property development company is producing almost 7.5% higher profits before tax and has accumulated 43% more after-tax profit for reinvestment. Through her company, Lianne is already seeing the twin benefits of:

- Having greater funds available for reinvestment, whilst
- Being able to do so within a lower tax environment

**Example 'E' Part 3**

*Lianne and Andrew both continue trading for several years in exactly the same vein.*

*After five years, Andrew will be making profits after tax of £95,964 and will have accumulated funds available of £442,985.*

190

*By the same point in time, Rainbow Developments Limited will be making profits after tax of £171,463, even after paying Lianne a salary of £9,000. The total funds being generated will therefore be £180,463, which is over **88% more** than Andrew's business.*

*By this time, Rainbow Developments Limited will have total accumulated funds available of £658,214, over £215,000, or 49%, more than Andrew!*

## Analysis of Example 'E' Part 3

After five years of trading, the property development company is clearly substantially more successful than the sole trader property developer. All of this simply because of the ability to reinvest a greater proportion of each year's profits.

As with property investment companies, however, we must also now consider the position on a final dissolution of each business.

## *Example 'E' Part 4*

*Lianne and Andrew each reinvest their available funds in one last new development.*

*By the time he has completed and sold his last development, Andrew will be left with a sum of £524,258 after tax and his usual living expenses.*

*What about Rainbow Developments Limited and Lianne, though?*

*Rainbow Developments Limited **started** its last development with funds available for investment of £658,214, already over £215,000 ahead of Andrew.*

*Let us suppose that the company then invests in a new development in the usual way. On completion, the new development will be worth £1,645,535.*

*After accounting for borrowings, including accumulated interest, the CT on its final development, and Lianne's usual salary of £9,000, the net worth of the company will be £882,929. Even if Lianne takes out her maximum tax free dividend of £5,500, it will still be worth £877,429.*

*By this point, a business like Rainbow Developments Limited's property development trade could have some substantial goodwill value, although we are going to ignore that here for the sake of illustration.*

*Nevertheless, by selling the company, rather than the property development within the company, Lianne may effectively be able to avoid the costs of winding it up.*

*At this stage, therefore, Lianne might potentially be able to sell the company for the net value of its assets: £877,429.*

*After deducting her original investment of £180,000, Lianne would therefore have a capital gain of £697,429. Deducting her annual CGT exemption of, say, £15,000 would then leave a taxable gain of £682,429.*

*Lianne's shares in the company will qualify for entrepreneurs' relief, so her gain will be subject to CGT at just 10%, giving her a tax bill of a mere £68,243.*

*This would leave Lianne with net proceeds from her company sale of £809,186 (£877,429 - £68,243). Adding her salary of £9,000 and dividends of £5,500, and then deducting £30,000 to cover her usual living expenses, would leave her with a final sum of £793,686.*

### Analysis of Example 'E' Part 4

After one last development, Lianne has been able to sell her company and retain almost £270,000, or over 51%, more than Andrew, her sole trader rival.

In the final period, she was able to add the benefit of a CGT rate of just 10% (see Section 7.3) to the advantages that she had already accumulated over the preceding years.

### And The Purchaser Can Save Money Too!

If Rainbow Developments Limited's final development was a commercial property, then a purchaser who bought the property directly would suffer SDLT of £88,232 (£1,645,535 + VAT at 20% = £1,974,642 taxed at the rates set out in Section 8.3).

If it were one or more residential properties, the SDLT is likely to be between £49,366 and £160,580, depending on the exact circumstances.

By purchasing the company for £877,429 instead, the Stamp Duty charge will be just £4,387 (0.5%), giving the purchaser a saving of somewhere between £44,979 and £156,193.

## Wealth Warnings

The VAT position on the final development held by Rainbow Developments Limited would need to be considered, as there is some risk of a 'claw back' of any VAT claimed by the company on this last project, depending on the purchaser's future intentions for the company.

There is also a risk of SDLT anti-avoidance legislation applying under some circumstances.

Hence, if you are buying a property development company of this nature, take professional advice!

# Chapter 13

# The Importance of Interest Relief

## 13.1  INTRODUCTION

A property company which borrows to finance property purchases or other aspects of its property business obtains CT relief for interest and finance costs.

Relief may follow either the special rules explained in Section 4.7, or the general principles for any trading deduction explained in Chapter 5, depending on the type of property business which the company has. Either way, as long as the interest or finance costs are incurred for business purposes, the company does get full, unrestricted CT relief on annual costs up to £2m (see Section 4.7).

Investors themselves may obtain Income Tax relief for interest on borrowings invested in the property company, provided that it is a 'Close Company', but not classed as a 'Close Investment Holding Company'. Both of these terms are explained in Section 16.1. This relief is subject to some limitations, however, which we will look at in Section 13.9.

To obtain relief, the investor must also either have a 'material interest' in the company, or must hold <u>some</u> ordinary shares in the company <u>and</u> work for the greater part of their time in the actual conduct or management of the company's business.

A 'material interest' is broadly defined as more than 5% of the company's share capital and shares held by 'connected' persons (see Appendix D) may usually be counted for this purpose, as long as the individual concerned does hold some of the shares personally.

In the case of most private property companies, the investor will qualify as having a 'material interest', although, for a large property company, it may be that some new investors come on board who qualify for relief through the second criterion instead.

Where the investor qualifies for relief, they are equally eligible for interest relief on funds borrowed to purchase shares in the company or funds borrowed to lend to the company.

**Top Tax Tip**

The important point to note, therefore, is that, in most cases, an investor who borrows funds to invest in their own property company can claim tax relief for their interest against their other income.

For this purpose it does not matter what form the investor's other income takes and it does not have to be in any way related to the property business.

We will look at an illustration of the potential benefits of interest relief claimed directly by the investor personally later in this chapter.

This form of interest relief is not subject to the dreadful new restrictions now applying to residential landlords: **even when the property company itself is investing in residential property!**

**Wealth Warning**

Whilst the above 'Tax Tip' is true in most cases, investors may not always be able to obtain full relief for interest on funds borrowed to invest in their property company, especially (but not exclusively) where annual interest costs exceed £50,000. See Section 13.9 for details.

Nonetheless, despite the 'Wealth Warning' above, combining the potential for personal interest relief for the investor with the beneficial regime enjoyed by the company itself (see Section 4.7) will often make a property investment company very attractive.


## 13.2   WHO SHOULD BORROW THE FUNDS?

When investing in property through a company, there are three possible approaches to the financing structure:

i)   Borrow the funds personally and then invest them in shares in the company
ii)  Borrow the funds personally and then lend them to the company
iii) Borrow the funds within the company

These three different structures make several important differences to the overall tax situation:

- Tax relief on the interest paid
- Additional tax arising due to the need to extract funds to service personal debt held outside the company
- The CGT position on an ultimate winding up or sale of the company
- Stamp Duty on a sale of the company's shares

They do not, however, make any difference to the capital gains position on property disposals made by the company itself.

An additional non-tax issue is the impact on the investor's ability to withdraw the sums invested back out of the company.

Over the next few sections, we will take a look at the implications of each structure in turn. In each case, we will assume that the company is a Close Company, but not a Close Investment Holding Company.

We will also assume that the rate of interest charged will be unaffected by the funding method used. In practice, this may not be the case and investors will therefore also need to weigh up the impact of any differences in interest rates.

Throughout Sections 13.3 to 13.8, we will assume that the investor is able to obtain full Income Tax relief for interest paid on sums borrowed to invest in the company and is not affected by the limitations discussed in Section 13.9.

Where those limitations do apply, however, it will generally make sense for funds to be borrowed within the company whenever possible and not by the investor personally: or at least for the investor's personal borrowings to be limited to a suitable level so that the restrictions in Section 13.9 do not affect them.

Finally, we will assume throughout this chapter that the company's total annual interest cost is less than £2m, so there is no risk of the restrictions discussed in Section 4.7 applying.

## 13.3 BORROWING TO INVEST IN SHARES

The individual will obtain interest relief on the borrowings. This can be highly advantageous, as relief is being given at a higher rate than the CT paid by the company on its profits.

If the individual is able to service the debt from other resources then this is all well and good and in Section 13.8 we will take a look at the significant benefits which this can produce.

In many cases, however, it will be necessary to extract funds from the company in order to service the debt.

### Example

*Gill, a higher rate taxpayer, borrowed £100,000 to invest in her own property company. She pays annual interest totalling £7,000, thus providing her with effective relief of £2,800 (at 40%).*

*However, in order to pay this interest, Gill takes a dividend of £7,000 out of her company. This costs her an additional £2,275 (32.5%) in Income Tax, meaning that her effective relief for the interest is only £525 (7.5%).*

Clearly, if personal debt needs to be serviced through the withdrawal of funds from the company, this will generally eliminate any apparent advantage of obtaining interest relief personally: Gill's effective rate of relief is only 7.5%; the company would obtain CT relief at 17% if it were paying the interest.

Alternatively, Gill might take a salary of £7,000 to fund her interest. This would attract Income Tax at 40% leaving Gill with no effective relief at all. However, the company would obtain CT relief at 17% for the salary (subject to the points in Section 10.2). In effect, this transfers the relief for the interest from Gill to the company, although it is generally only worth pursuing this option if the total salary required does not exceed the NI primary threshold.

Note that we have only considered the payment of interest here and have ignored capital repayments. These would, of course, only serve to further increase the Income Tax cost on the withdrawal of the necessary funds from the company.

Hence, corporate borrowings will generally provide better tax relief than individual borrowings invested in property company shares in most circumstances.

On a winding up where borrowings have been invested in company shares, the individual will have a high base cost in the shares, thus reducing the potential CGT impact (as was the case for Michelle in Example 'B', Part 3 in Section 12.6).

A sale of the company's shares could give rise to a fairly substantial Stamp Duty bill for the purchaser, as much of its value will be held as non-distributable share capital.

Another big drawback to this structure is the difficulty in withdrawing the funds invested. This requires a winding up, corporate restructuring or company purchase of own shares. We have covered winding up in Section 12.6. While in some cases they can prove worthwhile, the other possible methods are likely to prove costly in terms of both the tax charges arising and the professional fees which will inevitably be incurred.


## 13.4   BORROWING TO LEND TO THE COMPANY

Lending funds to the company will produce the same interest relief as in Section 13.3 above, as long as the loan is structured properly.

All of the same issues regarding withdrawal of the necessary funds to service the debt, etc, apply here in equal measure except that the investor can, if desired, also charge the company interest on the outstanding loan from them to the company.

Provided that the interest charged does not exceed a normal commercial rate, the company will obtain CT relief on interest paid to the investor, although the investor will, of course, be taxed on this income. This is a useful third alternative for 'profit extraction' (see Chapter 10), as CT relief is obtained without any NI costs arising.

A slight cashflow disadvantage does arise due to the fact that the company must deduct 20% Income Tax at source from payments of interest to the individual investor and account for this to HMRC on a quarterly basis. The tax deducted can later be set off against the individual's Income Tax liability under Self-Assessment, but this can leave investors 'out of pocket' when they have to service personal borrowings whilst only receiving 80% of the interest due from the company.

The major advantage of this structure (over Section 13.3) is that the funds invested can be withdrawn from the company at any time (with no tax liability), if the cash is available.

On a winding up, the amounts due to the investor can be repaid without any tax implications. This would leave the same level of CGT as in Section 13.3 above.

On a sale of the company, the funds due to the investor would effectively be deducted from the value of the company's shares, thus reducing the amount of Stamp Duty payable by the purchaser.

All in all, lending funds to the company is generally to be preferred to borrowing to invest in shares and still has the potential to produce the significant benefits which we will explore in Section 13.8 near the end of this chapter. The company will, of course, need some share capital but this can be kept at a minimal level in most private companies (e.g. £100).

### 13.5    CORPORATE BORROWINGS

Where the company obtains funds through its own direct borrowings, this will, of course, mean that it is the company which claims relief for the interest costs. However, it also means that there will be no need to extract funds from the company in order to service the debt.

Whether this is better than the position which results through personal borrowings invested into the company will depend on whether the investor would have had to withdraw funds from the company to service any private debt.

Borrowings in the company will generally produce a better overall effective result for interest relief where it would otherwise be necessary to pay out dividends in order to service personal debt.

Where, however, a taxpayer is able to service the debt from other resources, a better rate of tax relief is usually obtained by borrowing funds personally for investment into the company.

Where the company pays interest to any investor to enable them to service personal debt, the position regarding interest relief is effectively the same as for corporate borrowings, except for the slight cashflow disadvantage discussed in Section 13.4.

The position on a winding up where corporate borrowings have been used will depend on whether the borrowings are still in place at that time. If, at that time, there are still loans to be repaid out of property disposals, then the total sums to be distributed on the winding up will be reduced.

Hence, if all of the borrowings were still in place, the position would again be much the same as in Example 'B', Part 3 in Section 12.6. However, if the borrowings have been repaid, this means that the sum distributed on the winding up is increased.

### Example 'B', Part 4

*Returning to our earlier example in Sections 12.5 and 12.6, let us now suppose that Michelle set Dawson Limited up with only a small nominal sum in share capital (so small, in fact, that we will ignore it for the sake of illustration). Dawson Limited borrowed £250,000 to finance the property purchase and these borrowings have now been completely repaid out of rent received by the company.*

*As before (see Section 12.6), we will assume that Michelle first takes a small dividend of £2,000 which is covered by her dividend allowance, leaving net proceeds of £472,500 in Dawson Limited.*

*This sum is then distributed to Michelle on the winding up (once more ignoring professional fees, etc). Again, this represents a capital disposal by Michelle but, this time, she has no (or very little) base cost to set off. She will therefore have a capital gain of £472,500. Even after deducting her future estimated annual exemption of £15,000, her taxable gain will be £457,500.*

*Michelle's CGT bill on this gain, at 20%, will therefore be £91,500, meaning that the total tax burden on this property disposal would be £117,000! (Including the CT paid by Dawson Limited on the property sale, £25,500.)*

### Analysis of Example 'B', Part 4

Clearly, this is a very poor result for Michelle.

However, we must bear in mind that the company has repaid its borrowings from rental profits. To repay £250,000 out of after tax profits will have required pre-tax profits of at least £301,205 (based on CT at 17%).

If Michelle had received rental profits of £301,205 personally, she would have suffered at least £120,482 in additional Income Tax (at 40%). Hence, by using a company, Michelle has achieved a cumulative tax saving on her rental income of at least £69,277 (£120,482 - £51,205).

If we factor in this cumulative tax saving, the actual overall net cost of the property disposal becomes £47,723 (£117,000 - £69,277): which is almost £20,000 less than the overall cost achieved in Part 3 of this example (see Section 12.6), indicating that using corporate borrowings which are then repaid out of rental profits can produce further long-term financial benefits.

As usual, it is for individual investors to weigh up the conflicting factors in order to decide which approach is best for them.

Of course, in practice, the investor does not always have the luxury of being able to choose which financing structure is wanted, as banks will sometimes only be prepared to lend to the individual.

### Loss-Making Companies

Our analysis so far has all been based on the assumption that the company will obtain CT relief for any interest costs it incurs.

If the company is loss-making, or would make a loss if it incurred the interest costs, then it may be more beneficial for the investor to borrow personally. This, in turn, however, is based on the assumption that the investor would obtain Income Tax relief on the interest and would be able to service the debt from other resources without the need to extract funds from the company.

It should also be borne in mind that a property investment company can effectively 'roll up' its interest costs for set off against future capital gains. We will look at the benefits of this in Section 13.7.

On the other hand, where property trading companies or companies engaged in furnished holiday lettings are making losses, it may be difficult for them to obtain relief for their interest costs. Personal borrowings by the investor may then be preferable – *if* Income Tax relief is available!

### 13.6   DEEDS OF TRUST

As explained in Section 1.2, it is sometimes difficult for a company to be able to borrow funds for the purchase of investment property at the same level as the personal investor.

Whereas a loan to value ('LTV') of 85% may sometimes be possible for an individual investor, the maximum borrowing afforded to corporate investors is often just 70%. This, in effect, means having to raise twice as much deposit money if investing via a company.

One way to resolve this dilemma is for the individual investor to take legal title to the property in their own name, thus enabling borrowings to be made at the desired level.

The investor then enters into a 'Deed of Trust' with the company. This is effectively a legal agreement under which the investor agrees that the beneficial ownership of the property actually lies with the company and the company agrees to recompense the investor for any costs incurred in relation to the property.

The effect of the Deed of Trust is therefore to put both the company and the individual investor into the same position as they would have been if the company had purchased the property, whilst allowing a more favourable level of borrowings to be obtained.

As long as the Deed of Trust is prepared and executed correctly and its terms actually adhered to in practice, the position for most tax purposes will be just as if the company had legal title to the property. One exception to this, however, is that a SDLT or LBTT charge could arise on a later transfer of the legal title in the property to the company due to the market value rule explained in Section 15.2.

Deed of Trust arrangements have some important legal implications, so professional advice is essential. In particular, it is important to ensure that the arrangement does not invalidate any mortgage agreements relating to the properties involved.


### 13.7    ROLLING UP INTEREST IN A COMPANY

As explained in Section 4.7, a property investment company can effectively 'roll up' its accumulated interest costs and set them off against the capital gains arising on the sale of its investment properties.

This is clearly much better than the position for individual investors, for whom any surplus interest costs can generally only be relieved against future rental profits: and only at basic rate!

To see what an enormous advantage this provides in practice, let's look at an example.

### Example

*Brian and Jason both buy a portfolio of residential investment properties for £1m each. They each borrow £750,000 to fund their purchases, on which the interest charge, at 6%, is £45,000 per annum.*

Each investor has other allowable costs relating to his portfolio of £40,000 per annum and each portfolio yields annual rental income of £70,000. Each portfolio is therefore making an overall profit of £30,000 per annum before interest costs.

Brian makes his investments through his company, Habana Properties Limited. The company sets £30,000 of its annual interest cost against its rental profits each year and carries the excess (£15,000) forward. (If the company had other sources of income it could set this excess cost against them.)

Jason makes his investments personally and therefore has unrelieved surplus interest costs of £15,000 each year which he can only carry forward for basic rate tax relief against future rental profits from UK property (assuming his current portfolio is made up of UK property).

After ten years, Habana Properties Limited has unrelieved interest costs carried forward of £150,000 and Jason has rental losses of £150,000.

We will assume here that both Habana Properties Limited and Jason have had to borrow a further £150,000 to fund the deficit in their rental income over this ten year period, bringing their total borrowings to £900,000 each. (We will, however, ignore the additional interest costs arising for the sake of simplicity.)

At this point, both investors decide to sell off their portfolio. They each sell their properties for a total sum of £1.6m making total capital gains of £600,000 before any reliefs.

Jason deducts his annual exemption of, say, £15,000 and is left with taxable gains of £585,000. He is a higher rate taxpayer, so his CGT liability at 28% amounts to £163,800 leaving him with net proceeds of £536,200 after repaying his borrowings (£1.6m - £900,000 - £163,800).

Habana Properties Limited claims indexation relief at, say, 40%, leaving a taxable gain of £200,000 (£600,000 - £1m x 40%). The company is then able to set its unrelieved 'rolled up' interest costs of £150,000 against this gain leaving just £50,000 chargeable to CT. The company's CT bill, at 17%, therefore amounts to just £8,500.

### At this stage, we see that the company has saved over £155,000 compared with the individual investor!

But what if the investor now wishes to wind the company up so that he can obtain his net sale proceeds?

Taking account of its borrowings, the company's remaining net funds amount to £691,500 (£1.6m - £900,000 - £8,500). Of this, £250,000 represents the original equity invested by Brian ten years previously and can therefore be returned to him tax free. Hence, if Brian winds up Habana Properties Limited at this point, he will have a capital gain of £441,500 (£691,500 - £250,000).

*After deducting his estimated future annual exemption of £15,000, Brian is left with a taxable gain of £426,500 which, as a higher rate taxpayer, gives him a CGT liability, at 20%, of £85,300.*

*Hence, deducting his CGT bill from his net proceeds of £691,500 (ignoring the costs of the winding up as usual) we see that Brian eventually keeps a net sum of £606,200, or £70,000 more than Jason.*

*(Brian may have been able to reduce his tax bill slightly by paying himself a small dividend covered by the dividend allowance prior to the winding up.)*

As we can see from this example, the ability to 'roll up' interest in the company provides the opportunity to make enormous CT savings. In this case, the CT bill on a gain of £600,000 was slashed to just over 1.4%!

Where sale proceeds are being retained in the company for reinvestment, this will therefore provide a massive advantage over individual investors.

Admittedly, as we can see from the last part of the example, a large part of the initial CT savings may effectively be lost if the proceeds are returned to the individual investor but, even then, a fairly significant saving may still arise.

Note that, in the above example, Jason's accumulated unrelieved interest of £150,000 simply goes to waste. In practice, an investor such as Jason would be well advised to keep at least part of their portfolio in order to be able to utilise these costs. More advice on getting value out of unrelieved interest is contained in the Taxcafe.co.uk guide *'How to Save Property Tax'*.

Finally, it is also important to remember the 'Wealth Warning' in Section 12.6 which might potentially apply to Brian in this situation.


### 13.8 PERSONAL INTEREST RELIEF

Finally, to (almost) finish off this chapter, it is worth taking a look at the benefits of personal Income Tax relief for interest on funds invested in a property company.

Before we do that, however, I must reiterate that all of the points made in this section are based on the assumption that the investor will obtain full Income Tax relief for their interest costs. Everything in this section is therefore subject to the limitations on Income Tax relief for interest costs which we will examine in Section 13.9.

As we saw in Section 13.4, it will generally be sensible to lend borrowed funds to the company rather than use them to purchase company shares.

In Section 13.3, we saw that borrowing to invest in a property company is not beneficial where the debt has to be serviced by paying dividends to the investor.

Where the personal debt can be serviced by paying interest to the investor, the position is effectively neutral, since the taxable income matches the personal interest relief obtained (subject to the cashflow issue discussed in Section 13.4).

What we have not yet looked at, however, is the position where interest relief is being obtained personally without the need to extract funds from the company to service the debt.

Here again, the use of a property investment company will provide enormous advantages over the personal investor due to the more beneficial interest relief situation.

### *Example*

*Patrick and Francois both have large salaries of £100,000. Each of them borrows £1m to invest in property and incurs annual interest charges, at 5%, of £50,000.*

*Patrick invests his borrowed funds directly into his own personal property portfolio. Patrick's properties yield a rental profit of £40,000 before interest. This gives rise to an Income Tax charge of £21,000 (including an additional £5,000 due to the loss of his personal allowance). He can then claim basic rate tax relief for £40,000 of his interest costs, reducing his tax bill to £13,000.*

*The remaining £10,000 of Patrick's interest costs can only be carried forward for basic rate tax relief against future rental profits.*

*Francois lends his borrowed funds to his company, Wadyamin Fudpoiznin Limited, and the company invests the funds in a property portfolio. The company's properties also yield a rental profit of £40,000 before interest.*

*Wadyamin Fudpoiznin Limited therefore pays CT at 17% on its rental profits, i.e. £6,800.*

*Meanwhile, Francois claims interest relief for £50,000. As he is a higher rate taxpayer, this will provide him with a tax repayment of £20,000 (£50,000 x 40%).*

*In net terms therefore, Francois and his company receive an overall tax **refund** of £13,200 (£20,000 - £6,800).*

*Remarkably, this net refund actually exceeds the overall deficit of £10,000 on Wadyamin Fudpoiznin Limited's property portfolio (i.e. the deficit which arises after taking Francois' interest costs into account: £50,000 - £40,000).*

*In other words, Francois' interest relief has turned an effective **loss** before tax of £10,000 into an effective **profit** after tax of £3,200 (£13,200 - £10,000).*

*The Government is therefore effectively funding Francois' property portfolio and adding a little extra too!*

*Meanwhile, poor Patrick, who is also making an effective loss before tax of £10,000, has an Income Tax bill of £13,000, giving him a loss after tax of £23,000!*

As we can see from this example, where a taxpayer borrows to lend funds to their property company, the tax relief on the interest arising is highly beneficial.

The example also demonstrates that, where rental income is insufficient to cover interest costs, using a company can actually enable the investor to recover their deficit from the Government!

Even when rental profits are being made, the fact that tax relief can be obtained at 40% or even 45% on interest when company profits are being taxed at only 17% will continue to provide a significant benefit.

## 13.9 LIMITATIONS ON INCOME TAX RELIEF

There is an annual limit on the total combined amount of Income Tax relief available under a number of reliefs.

The total amount of relief which any individual may claim under all of these reliefs taken together is limited to the greater of:

- £50,000, or
- 25% of their 'adjusted total income' (see below)

Hence, for anyone with total income of no more £200,000, the limit is £50,000.

The limit applies to individuals only, so it will not directly affect companies; but it will affect investors using a company.

**The Affected Reliefs**

Eleven different reliefs are affected. The most important ones to be aware of include:

- Qualifying loan interest
- Relief for trading losses against other income
- Property loss relief
- Share loss relief

'Qualifying loan interest' is precisely the relief which we have been talking about throughout this chapter: relief for interest on personal borrowings used to invest funds in a qualifying company (or partnership – although the relief is now denied where the partnership invests in residential rental property).

Individuals with trading losses can set them off against their other income in the same tax year or the previous one. Additional relief applies in the early years of a trade. (See the taxcafe.co.uk guide *'How to Save Property Tax'* for further details.)

'Property loss relief' refers to an individual's ability to set capital allowances within rental losses against their other income for the same tax year. (Again, see *'How to Save Property Tax'* for further details.)

'Share loss relief' applies in certain limited circumstances and allows owners of some private companies to claim Income Tax relief for losses on their shares. Sadly, it is not usually available to property company owners.


**Adjusted Total Income**

Broadly speaking, 'adjusted total income' means an individual's total taxable income for the year after deducting gross pension contributions (i.e. including tax relief given at source) but before deducting any other reliefs.


**Summary for Property Company Investors**

In effect, in most cases, individuals with total taxable income of no more than £200,000 now have an annual limit of £50,000 on the amount of Income Tax relief they may claim for interest on funds borrowed to invest in property companies (i.e. a maximum deduction from taxable income of £50,000).

Those with total income over £200,000 are subject to a limit equal to the greater of £50,000, or 25% of their income after deducting gross pension contributions.

Further restrictions will apply in all cases where the individual is also claiming relief for trading losses, capital allowances within rental losses, or losses on shares in a different (non-property) company.

## 13.10 INTEREST RELIEF FOR INDIVIDUAL LANDLORDS

To assist in understanding just how beneficial the regime for interest relief in companies is, it is worth briefly examining the horrendous new restrictions applying to individual landlords.

Before we look at these dreadful restrictions in detail, it is worth pointing out that they do **not** affect furnished holiday letting businesses or landlords renting out non-residential property.

Most importantly, of course, they do **not** apply to companies. Furthermore, they also do **not** apply to individuals claiming relief for interest on funds invested in their own property company (although they do apply to funds invested in a partnership which holds residential rental property).

### The Restrictions in Detail

Income Tax relief for interest and finance costs relating to residential property lettings is being restricted to basic rate only. This is being done by phasing out higher rate tax relief for interest and finance costs over a four year period, commencing in 2017/18. This will work as follows:

- 2017/18: 75% deducted as normal, 25% relieved at basic rate
- 2018/19: 50% deducted as normal, 50% relieved at basic rate
- 2019/20: 25% deducted as normal, 75% relieved at basic rate
- 2020/21 onwards: all relieved at basic rate

Any unrelieved excess interest and finance costs which are eligible for relief at basic rate may be carried forward for relief in future years.

For further details see the Taxcafe.co.uk guides *'How to Save Property Tax'* and *'Landlord Interest'*.

# Chapter 14

# How to Set Up Your Own Property Company

## 14.1 WHO CAN HELP AND HOW MUCH DOES IT COST?

If you decide to go ahead and form a property company, it is pretty easy to do. There are a number of websites available which enable you to complete the task online at minimal cost.

If you feel you need further assistance, most lawyers can form a company for you, as well as many accountants. Some have so-called 'off-the-shelf' companies available for use at a moment's notice.

If you use a lawyer or accountant to assist with the task, or need to set up a specialised share structure, the costs may well be significantly more, perhaps as much as £500 to £1,500 in some cases.

Whoever you use to form your company, you will find that they ask a great many questions about the prospective officers of the company for the sake of 'security'. This is all in the name of the 'anti-money laundering' regulations. Details requested have been known to include eye colour, mother's maiden name and certain digits from NI numbers.

## 14.2 THE COMPANY'S CONSTITUTION

The company's constitution is embodied in two documents:

- The company's Memorandum of Association, and
- The company's Articles of Association

The Memorandum covers what the company is empowered to do and sets out the framework for its share structure. Most modern Memorandums of Association empower the company to do pretty much anything. For a property company, it is important to ensure that the company has the power to:

- Borrow money,
- Buy or sell land and property, and
- Rent out, or grant leases over, property

As well as anything else that you are expecting to need the company to do.

The Articles of Association govern the rights of the holders of each class of shares (there only needs to be one class, but there can be more), as well as the power to appoint or remove directors or auditors (where necessary) and the conduct of general meetings of the company's members.

The company will need a registered office address, which must be occupied and cannot be a mere P.O. box. The company's name should be displayed prominently at the registered address and its statutory books and records should usually be kept there.

A UK company can be registered in Scotland, in Northern Ireland or in England and Wales, depending on where its registered office is located.

You will need to appoint at least one person to serve as a director. You may also need to appoint a company secretary if required by your company's Articles of Association. (A company secretary is no longer a mandatory requirement but many company's constitutions will still require one.)

Directors and company secretaries are referred to as the company's 'officers'. You will need to provide Companies House with a home address for each officer. You can also provide a 'service address' for each officer. The service address will appear on the public record and can therefore be used to keep the officers' home addresses private. If you do not provide a service address, the officer's home address will be made public!

The company's registered office address can be used as the service address for one or more of the company's officers, if desired. A service address must again be occupied and not a mere P.O. box.

The owners of shares in the company are referred to as 'members'. A company must have at least one member. Until a few years ago, companies had to have at least two members.

A UK company may either be a private company or a public limited company (PLC). Most companies are private companies and there is little point in being a PLC unless you are seeking a stock-market quotation.

It is also possible to form a 'Societas Europaea' (or 'SE' for short), a special form of European company available throughout the European Union. The tax treatment of an SE will depend entirely on where it is resident

210

and hence, if you form one of these companies, and base it in the UK, it will be subject to CT in exactly the same way as any other UK company.

The act of forming a company is often referred to as 'incorporation' and the day on which the company is formed is known as its date of incorporation.

Once you have formed your company, it can go ahead and borrow money or purchase new properties. Provided, of course, that the lenders are willing to co-operate!


## 14.3    OTHER COMPANY FORMATION FORMALITIES

Shortly after you register your company with Companies House, you will receive a letter from them congratulating you on your new company and advising you of some of your responsibilities as a company director.

You will also receive a form CT41G from HMRC. You should complete and return this form in order to get the company into the CT system. It is important to do this within three months of when the company commences any business activities, as penalties will be imposed if you do not return the completed form within this timescale.

You will usually need to register the company as an employer for PAYE purposes. Remember that paying yourself, or your spouse or partner, a small salary will be enough to mean that the company must register as an employer. You may also need to register the company for VAT, if applicable (see Chapter 9).

In some cases, you will also need to submit a 'Form 42' to HMRC by 6th July following the end of the tax year in which the company's shares are issued. This form provides details of shares issued to a company's employees, including directors, and may also need to be submitted again following any further subsequent issues of shares by the company.

Form 42 is not generally required in the simple case of a new company incorporation where the new company issues a single class of ordinary shares to one or more shareholder/directors who have no previous employment relationship with the business being run by the company.

## 14.4 CHANGING YOUR COMPANY'S ACCOUNTING DATE

Initially, the company's accounting date will automatically be set as the date falling twelve months after the end of the month in which the company was incorporated.

However, a company's accounting year-end date does not need to permanently remain as the same calendar date and can generally be changed.

Generally speaking, in order to change the company's accounting date, you will simply need to submit a form AA01 to Companies House any time before the earlier of the filing deadline for the accounts based on its original accounting date and the filing deadline based on the revised accounting date which you are now requesting.

See Section 14.6 for details of Companies House accounts filing deadlines. Take note of the additional requirement in respect of the company's first accounting period, which is particularly relevant here.

Subject to a few restrictions, a company may change its accounting date at any time. However, this generally happens most often at the beginning of a company's life due to the application of the initial rule explained above.

Naturally, where a change is made to the accounting date, for whatever reason, the company will have a short or long accounting period (i.e. a period other than a year). This has some important consequences for the company's CT position and we will look at these in Section 16.5.

## 14.5 DEALING WITH COMPANIES HOUSE

Once your company is set up, you will need to advise Companies House of any changes in the company's:

- Directors (or their particulars – i.e. their name, home address or service address)
- Company Secretary (or their particulars)
- Registered Office
- Accounting Date (as explained in Section 14.4)
- Issued share capital
- Charges (i.e. mortgages and other secured loans)

The last point is particularly significant for property companies and it is important to ensure that any charges over the company's property are registered with Companies House and these details are kept up to date.

There are also two things that Companies House will require from you on an annual basis:

- Statutory Accounts (see Section 14.6) and
- An Annual Return

The annual return provides details of the company's share capital and shareholders. A notice to complete the annual return will be sent to the company's registered office address a few weeks in advance of the filing deadline.

The filing deadline for the return will usually be 28 days after each anniversary of the company's date of incorporation.

### Wealth Warning

Do not confuse the Companies House requirements with HMRC's requirements.

Both institutions require a set of accounts and a return from you each year, with different deadlines. Complying with one institution's requirements will not satisfy the other institution and you will suffer penalties if you make the mistake of thinking that it does.

### 14.6    STATUTORY ACCOUNTS

Every company must prepare a set of statutory accounts for each of its accounting periods. These accounts must adhere to a standard format specified by Company Law and either UK generally accepted accounting practice (sometimes referred to as 'GAAP') or International Financial Reporting Standards ('IFRS').

The full set of statutory accounts must always be submitted to HMRC together with the company's Corporation Tax Return, as explained in Section 2.8.

Small and medium-sized companies (see below) may, however, file a set of abbreviated statutory accounts with Companies House.

These abbreviated accounts must be prepared on the same basis as the full statutory accounts but provide less detail on the company's activities. This is to ensure that smaller companies do not need to make too many of their business dealings public.

Remember that accounts held at Companies House are part of the public record and can be seen by anyone, so I would generally recommend that abbreviated accounts are filed whenever possible.

Broadly speaking, a company is 'Small' for these purposes if it meets at least two of the following three tests:

i)   Turnover (i.e. gross income) does not exceed £6.5m per annum
ii)  Total asset value does not exceed £3.26m
iii) It has no more than 50 employees

Most property companies will tend to qualify as 'Small' on the basis that they meet tests (i) and (iii).

It is important to note that test (ii) is based on **gross** asset values (i.e. the total value of all the company's properties and other assets, with no deduction in respect of borrowings and other liabilities).

A 'Medium-Sized' company is one which fails to meet the 'Small' company test but which does meet at least two out of the following three tests:

i)   Turnover (i.e. gross income) does not exceed £25.9m per annum
ii)  Total asset value does not exceed £12.9m
iii) It has no more than 250 employees

Statutory accounts are usually prepared on an annual basis, although other accounting periods, up to a maximum length of 18 months, may sometimes be used. We will return to the CT consequences of this in Section 16.5.

Where it has been necessary to prepare additional, more detailed, accounts for CT purposes, these do not need to be filed with Companies House.

Whether abbreviated accounts are used or not, private companies must generally file the appropriate statutory accounts at Companies House within nine months of their accounting date. The company's **first** set of accounts must, however, be filed by the **earlier** of nine months from the accounting date or 21 months from the date of incorporation.

As with taxation, there are harsh penalties for late filing of the accounts. Extensions to the filing deadline are, however, sometimes granted. You must apply to Companies House directly (preferably in advance), for these.


**New Financial Reporting Standards**

A new set of financial reporting standards ('FRSs') have recently been introduced to update UK GAAP and bring it more into line with IFRS. For small companies, the new standards are mandatory for accounting periods commencing after 31st December 2015.

In most cases (assuming a twelve month accounting period) the new standards will therefore be mandatory for accounting periods ending on or after 31st December 2016.

Subject to the points considered below, the new standards will not generally make much of a difference for most small property companies.

'Micro-entities' can prepare 'abridged' accounts rather than the usual full statutory accounts and abbreviated accounts discussed above. At present, there are some concerns regarding how HMRC will react to 'abridged' accounts however, so it may be more sensible to stick with the full and abbreviated accounts – for the time being at least.


**Investment Property Revaluations**

Investment properties (including most rental properties) must be shown in statutory accounts at their current market value.

This creates the need to carry out regular valuations on investment properties: an additional administrative burden resulting from the use of a property company.

In practice, most companies only carry out formal valuations of their investment properties every few years. This is considered acceptable provided that the previous valuation still provides a reasonable reflection of the properties' value during the intervening years.

Where investment properties are still held by the company at its accounting date, any increase in their values over and above their original cost is not included in the company's taxable profits and is not considered to be part of the company's distributable profits for the purpose of paying dividends.

It is only when an investment property is sold that the resultant profit is taxed (as a capital gain) and is available for distribution as a dividend (after accounting for the resultant tax liability).

Under the old UK GAAP, the increase in value in investment properties still held at the accounting date was included in a 'revaluation reserve' and not in the company's profit and loss account.

Under the new accounting standards, these increases in value must be included in the company's profit and loss account. This, however, is only a change in presentation and will not alter the position described above regarding the taxation of these profits and the payment of dividends.

## 14.7  CHOOSING AN ACCOUNTANT OR AUDITOR

Not every company requires an audit. Generally speaking, companies which qualify as 'Small' (as defined in Section 14.6) do not usually need to be audited.

Failing to qualify as a 'Small' company makes an audit mandatory, but there is nothing to stop you having your company audited in other cases. You might wish to do this, for example, if you have left the running of your company in the hands of managers and would like some independent verification of the company's financial results.

An audit of the company's accounts *must* be carried out by a firm of qualified accountants registered to carry out audit work.

Most other people operating a business through a company will usually also find that they need the services of an accountant, even if they don't need an audit.

In this case, there are no legal requirements regarding the type of accountant you must use. Nevertheless, whilst there are some very good unqualified accountants, I would generally recommend that you use a qualified firm of accountants who are members of one of the major recognised accountancy bodies, such as the Institute of Chartered Accountants in England and Wales ('ICAEW') or the Institute of Chartered Accountants of Scotland ('ICAS').

Furthermore, as property is a specialised area, you should try to find a firm with experience in the property sector.

You might also like to ask your prospective accountant where your accounts will actually be prepared. Some accountancy firms are now adopting the rather reprehensible habit of sending client files half way around the world for processing, without even telling the client what they are doing!

# Chapter 15

# How to Put Existing Property into a Company

## 15.1 INTRODUCTION

The basic problem with transferring anything into your company is the fact that you and the company are 'connected'. As explained in Section 6.2, this means that, in principle, any transfers of assets between you and the company will be deemed to take place at market value for CGT purposes. Furthermore, as explained in Chapter 8, any transfer of property to a connected company will also be deemed to take place at market value for SDLT or LBTT purposes.

Potentially, therefore, you could face a huge tax bill if you try to transfer existing properties into a company.

Most people tend to worry more about the potential CGT on the transfer and we will return to this issue later in this chapter. Since the introduction of the higher SDLT charges on residential investment property on 1st April 2016 (and the ADS on similar property in Scotland), however, this has been a far more important issue, so we will examine this problem first!

## 15.2 STAMP DUTY LAND TAX ON TRANSFERS

Transfers of UK property to your company will generally give rise to SDLT or LBTT liabilities based on the greater of the amount of consideration actually paid by the company for the transfer, or the market value of the properties transferred. The higher SDLT charges for investment property (or the ADS on property in Scotland) will apply in the case of residential property (see Sections 8.3 and 8.7 for details of the rates applying).

'Consideration' for this purpose will include not only any amount actually paid, or payable, by the company, but will also include the amount of any mortgages or other loans over the properties which the company takes over. 'Consideration' also includes the value of any shares issued in exchange for the properties transferred.

## 15.3    MULTIPLE TRANSFERS

Where a whole business is transferred (e.g. to obtain incorporation relief or entrepreneurs' relief – see Sections 15.8 and 7.3 respectively), all of the property transfers will amount to 'linked transactions' (see Section 8.6). Any other simultaneous transfers of more than one property will also be 'linked transactions', as will all of the transfers in any pre-arranged series of transfers.

### Residential Property

Even taking multiple dwellings relief (see Section 8.6) into account, the SDLT (or LBTT) applying to multiple transfers of residential property into a company is likely to be at least 3% of the total value of the properties transferred: more in some cases.

### *Example*

*Finn has a residential property portfolio made up of 20 properties with a total value of £3m. He transfers the properties to his company, Russell Rentals Ltd, and claims multiple dwellings relief. The average value of each property is £150,000, so the SDLT charge is as follows:*

| | |
|---|---|
| *First £125,000 @ 3%:* | *£3,750* |
| *Next £25,000 @ 5%:* | *£1,250* |
| *Total per property:* | *£5,000* |
| *x 20 =* | *£100,000* |

*The overall effective rate of SDLT on the transfer is thus 3.33%.*

Transfers of six or more residential dwellings may be treated as non-residential property instead for the purposes of SDLT or LBTT charges. Whether this is helpful or not depends on the exact circumstances of the case. In Finn's case, for example, this would increase the SDLT charge to £139,500, so it would not be beneficial (but see Section 8.6 for an example of a case where a saving does arise).

Where any residential dwelling within the transfer has a value in excess of £500,000 and is not being used for business purposes, the rate of SDLT applying to that property will be 15%. (See Sections 8.4 and 16.7 for further details.)

## Non-Residential Property

The rates applying to non-residential property will again be based on the total value of the properties transferred and could therefore be almost 5% in some cases, or almost 4.5% for property in Scotland (see Sections 8.3 and 8.7).

### Example

*Sonia owns a portfolio of commercial property (shops and offices) with a total value of £1.5m. She transfers the portfolio to her company, Pitchside Properties Ltd. The SDLT arising is as follows:*

| | |
|---|---|
| *First £150,000 @ 0%:* | *£0* |
| *Next £100,000 @ 2%:* | *£2,000* |
| *Next £1.25m @ 5%:* | *£62,500* |
| *Total:* | *£64,500* |

*The overall effective rate of SDLT on the transfer is thus 4.3%.*

### Summary

Transfers of property into a company are likely to lead to SDLT or LBTT charges at effective overall rates of at least 3% for residential property and up to 5% for non-residential property. In many cases, these charges are quite prohibitive and can even make it impractical for the property owner to make the transfer.

There is one major exception to these rules: which we will examine in Section 15.5.

### 15.4   TRANSFERRING OTHER ASSETS

SDLT (or LBTT) only applies to the transfer of land and property, so the value of other assets can be disregarded for these purposes. Hence, when transferring a whole business it will be necessary to make an apportionment.

## Example

*Chris transfers his property development business, worth £1m, to Paterson Developments Limited in exchange for shares. The business value is made up as follows:*

|  | £ |
|---|---|
| *Office premises* | *100,000* |
| *Work-in-progress & land bank* | *300,000* |
| *Building materials in stock* | *50,000* |
| *Plant and machinery* | *100,000* |
| *Motor vehicles* | *50,000* |
| *Debtors* | *550,000* |
| *Goodwill* | *100,000* |
|  | *1,250,000* |
| *Less Creditors* | *-250,000* |
|  | *1,000,000* |

*Of these, only the office premises and work-in-progress would be subject to SDLT. This gives a total value of £400,000 subject to Duty. The exact amount of SDLT payable would depend on the nature of the properties within work-in-progress, but it would be at least £9,500.*

### Tax Tip

When transferring a property development business to a company, it is worth trying to time the transfer at a point when the business has as little work-in-progress on hand as possible, including its land bank. This will help to reduce the amount of SDLT or LBTT arising on the transfer.

Alternatively, by using the 'gifts of business assets' route (see Section 15.7), the transferor could refrain from transferring any work-in-progress, thus reducing their exposure to SDLT or LBTT.

## 15.5 PARTNERSHIP TRANSFERS

It may be possible to transfer properties which are part of a property business run by a partnership into a company and enjoy substantial or complete exemption from either SDLT or LBTT (as appropriate).

To obtain the exemption, the company needs to be 'connected' with one or more of the partners. If it is 'connected' with all/both of the partners, complete exemption is possible.

The good news is that a company will generally be 'connected' with all/both of the partners if all/both of those partners are:

- Spouses or civil partners,
- Siblings, or
- Parents and their adult children

And these individuals also own the company.

Hence, the most obvious example is where a married couple, or a family, have been running a property business as a partnership and they transfer the business to their own company.

In many such cases, complete exemption from SDLT or LBTT will be possible.

The exemption applies equally to LLPs (although these are not usually a good medium through which to invest in property due to some even more restrictive rules on interest relief and loss relief).

Some people have been taking the view that a property portfolio which is jointly owned by a married couple, or by any two individuals, is effectively a partnership even if it has not been formally constituted as one. I am afraid that I disagree and would regard a formally constituted partnership as being necessary for the exemption to apply. It will also be essential that Partnership Tax Returns have been submitted by the partnership (see the Taxcafe.co.uk guide 'How to Save Property Tax' for further details).

Others are suggesting that it is only necessary to form a partnership for a brief period before transferring property into a company in order to obtain the exemption. Again, I am not comfortable with this idea as there is anti-avoidance legislation which could be used to overturn the exemption in such a case.

One thing which is clear, however, is that a transfer of property from a long-term, well established, property partnership run by a married couple, or other qualifying relatives, to a company owned by the same individuals is completely exempt from both SDLT and LBTT.

Nonetheless, the rules governing this exemption are highly complex, so professional advice is essential.

## 15.6 CAPITAL GAINS TAX ON TRANSFERS

As far as CGT is concerned, there are two important reliefs available which may potentially resolve the problem discussed in Section 15.1 in some cases. Careful use of these reliefs may even create additional tax advantages for those with the 'right kind' of property business.

These important CGT reliefs are:

- Relief for 'Gifts Of Business Assets', and
- 'Incorporation Relief'

Whether either or both of these reliefs are available, and the extent to which they may be used to defer, or even reduce, your potential CGT liabilities, will depend on the exact nature of your property business in the past, the present and the future.

### Tax Tip

Both of these CGT reliefs are available when the business qualifies for them at the time of the transfer of the assets. The business does not need to continue to qualify for any particular period after the transfer.

This creates some significant tax-planning opportunities, which we will explore later in this chapter.

I would, however, suggest that the business needs to continue for some period after the transfer, or else the qualifying activity would probably be regarded as no more than an artificial sham.

Where the business qualifies for one of the above CGT reliefs, the relief is equally available to transferor individuals, partnerships or trusts. However, for the rest of this chapter, I will refer just to individual transferors for the sake of simplicity.

## 15.7 GIFTS OF 'BUSINESS ASSETS'

The first of the two potential CGT reliefs available is something of a misnomer since, in fact, the relief will generally only apply to trading assets, rather than what the average person would regard as a business asset. Within tax legislation, 'business' is a much wider term than 'trade' and, as we have discussed already, property investment or property letting is not usually considered to be a 'trade' for tax purposes.

Hence, this relief is unlikely to be available to a property investment or property letting business, although we will return to this subject in Section 15.13.

The relief for 'gifts of business assets' will, however, be available to a property development business or a qualifying furnished holiday letting business. It should, in fact, be available to any business classed as a 'trade' (see Chapter 3), although we will return to this point in Section 15.11.

The relief for 'gifts of business assets' works where you transfer qualifying 'trading' properties to your company for no consideration, or for a consideration less than market value. For this relief, it is not necessary to actually transfer the whole business, as the relief can be claimed in respect of any asset used in a qualifying trade.

Hence, for example, an individual who used both an office and a warehouse in their property development business could claim relief on a 'gift' of the warehouse to a company while still retaining personal ownership of the office.

The relief works by allowing the capital gain that arises on the transfer under the normal rules to be 'held over'. This means that the individual making the transfer has no CGT liability, but it also means that the assets transferred to the company have a lower base cost (see Section 6.3). The assets' base cost is reduced by the amount of gain 'held over'.

Where the asset is only partly used in the qualifying trade, or has been used in the qualifying trade for only part of the transferor's period of ownership, the amount of gain that may be 'held over' is proportionately reduced. This will usually mean that some CGT liability will still arise on the transfer.

Note that this relief is not automatic and a claim must be made jointly by the transferring taxpayer and the recipient company using a prescribed form.

The relief cannot be used to transfer shares in one company from an individual's ownership into the ownership of another company.

### Example

*Tom runs a property development business from his office in Glasgow. He decides that he would like to transfer the whole business, including his office, into a new company, Smith Developments Limited. Tom bought his office for £100,000 in March 2000 and has used it as his trading premises ever since.*

*Its current market value is £250,000, but Tom 'gifts' the property (i.e. transfers it for no consideration) to Smith Developments Limited in March 2018.*

*Under the normal rules, Tom would have had a capital gain of £150,000. However, if Tom and his company jointly elect to 'hold over' the gain, Tom will have no chargeable capital gain. Smith Developments Limited's base cost in the office property will be its market value, £250,000, less the 'held over' gain of £150,000, i.e. £100,000.*

As we can see, the company ends up with the same base cost for the office property as the individual owner had. (Plus the additional SDLT cost, which I have ignored here for the sake of illustration.)

Note that Tom's actual capital gain (had he not elected to 'hold over') would have qualified for entrepreneurs' relief and therefore would probably have been subject to CGT at just 10% (see Section 7.3). Hence, assuming that his annual exemption of £11,300 (for 2017/18) was available, his actual potential CGT bill may have been as low as £13,870.

Against this, we must weigh the fact that a sale of the property by the company after the transfer would give rise to a CT bill of at least £25,500 (once again ignoring the SDLT cost for the sake of illustration, and assuming the long-term 17% rate of CT applies).

It's a case of a small amount of tax now versus a much greater amount of potential tax in the future. This presents us with a bit of a dilemma and we will return to this point in Section 15.10.

### Tax Tip

Rather than 'gifting' assets to the company for no consideration, it is often worth selling them for a small sum in order to utilise the transferor individual's available reliefs.

The 'gifts of business assets' relief can still be used to 'hold over' the element of the gain that arises only due to the 'deemed' sale proceeds at market value rule, with the individual's CGT calculation then proceeding on the basis of the actual consideration.

With many new companies, this is often done by agreeing a sale price for the asset and allowing that sum to be left outstanding as a loan from the transferor to the company.

The loan may be paid back to the transferor as the company's funds permit, giving the transferor what is, to all practical intents and purposes, a tax-free income from the company until the loan is paid off.

*Example Revisited*

*In the above example, Tom could have transferred the office property to Smith Developments Limited for £111,300. After electing to 'hold over' the amount representing the difference between market value and actual consideration (£138,700), this would leave him with a capital gain of £11,300.*

*This gain would then be covered by his annual CGT exemption, leaving him with no tax to pay and a 'tax-free' sum of £111,300, which he can draw upon as funds permit.*

*Meanwhile, Smith Developments Limited's base cost is £11,300 more than it would have been and this will save at least £1,921 in CT on a sale of the property (at the future CT rate of 17%).*

## 15.8 INCORPORATION RELIEF

Technically, this relief should be available whenever any 'business' is transferred to a company wholly or partly in exchange for shares.

A huge area of difficulty arises, however, in determining exactly what constitutes a 'business' for this purpose. Certainly, anything that may be deemed to be a 'trade' (see Chapter 3) must also qualify as a 'business', as will any qualifying furnished holiday letting businesses.

Beyond this, however, matters become unclear. There is no statutory definition of what constitutes a business for the purposes of incorporation relief.

For a long time, there was no relevant case law to fall back on either but the case of 'Elisabeth Moyne Ramsay v Revenue and Customs Commissioners' (the 'Ramsay case') finally shed some light on this issue a few years ago and we will therefore return to the tricky question of what constitutes a qualifying business for the purposes of incorporation relief in Section 15.14.

In the meantime, however, let's just concentrate on how the relief works. Incorporation relief works along similar principles to the relief for 'gifts of business assets', except that:

- The transferor must transfer the whole of their business as a 'going concern'
- The assets transferred only need to be in use in the business at the point of transfer. Unlike the relief for 'gifts of business assets', there is no restriction to the relief if the assets have not been in business use throughout the transferor's ownership (but see the 'Tax Tip' in Section 15.11)

- The transfer must be made wholly or partly in exchange for shares in the transferee company (the relief will only apply to the part of the sale consideration which is satisfied in shares)
- The gain 'held over' is deducted from the transferor individual's base cost in the shares and not from the value of the underlying assets transferred. In effect (where the transfer is made wholly in exchange for shares), this means that the transferor's CGT base cost for those shares becomes the same as the base cost which they previously had for the underlying assets.
- It also follows that the new base costs which the company has in the business assets transferred to it are those assets' market values at the date of transfer. This provides a unique opportunity to 'step up' the base cost of those assets and thus save a fortune on their ultimate sale. We will look at this further in Section 15.14.
- Where the necessary conditions apply, the relief is given automatically. The transferor may, however, elect to disapply the relief. (Why would they want to disapply it? – see the warning below.)

**Wealth Warning**

Incorporation relief will eliminate, or at least reduce, the CGT arising on the transfer of an individual's qualifying business to a company.

However, it is essential to remember that this will mean any available entrepreneurs' relief is not claimed.

Usually, of course, where entrepreneurs' relief was available on the business, then it will also be available on the company shares and it is only necessary to hold the shares for one year for this purpose.

In some cases, however, there may be a risk that the company will not qualify as the transferor's 'personal company' for entrepreneurs' relief purposes (see Section 7.3) and the chance to claim entrepreneurs' relief will effectively have been lost. In these cases, it may therefore sometimes be better to disapply this relief.

There is, of course, also the possibility that the transferor ends up selling their shares within less than a year after the transfer. Again, in such cases, an election to disapply incorporation relief will often be beneficial.

An election to disapply incorporation relief must normally be made by the second anniversary of the 31st January after the tax year in which the transfer took place. For example, for a transfer made during 2017/18, the normal deadline to elect to disapply is 31st January 2021.

However, if the transferor has disposed of all of the shares received as consideration for the transfer by the end of the next tax year after the transfer, the deadline is accelerated by a year.

## 15.9 WHICH RELIEF IS BEST?

In some cases, the relief for 'gifts of business assets' and incorporation relief may both potentially be available to prevent any CGT liability from arising on the transfer of a property business into a company. In such cases, it is generally possible to choose which one of the two reliefs you wish to use.

Actually, when I say it is possible to 'choose' which relief is used, this choice is generally made by the way in which you structure the transaction used to transfer your business.

In essence, by making the transfer of your whole business wholly or partly in exchange for shares, you will effectively be 'choosing' incorporation relief (as it is then automatic). Alternatively, by transferring qualifying trading properties into a company for no consideration, or a consideration that is less than market value (and, if you are transferring your whole business, does not consist wholly or partly of shares), you will be able to claim relief for 'gifts of business assets'.

All of this assuming that you do have a business which qualifies for the reliefs of course!

The best choice will depend on your future plans and expectations for the properties and business being transferred.

In general, however, the relief for 'gifts of business assets' offers far greater flexibility, both in terms of the assets that are to be transferred and in the choice of the level of CGT to be paid.

Furthermore, the ability to use the relief for 'gifts of business assets' to create what is effectively a source of tax-free income, as we saw in Section 15.7, means that this is often the preferred route.

In the second part of the example in Section 15.7, we looked at a situation where the consideration was fixed at the maximum level that still left the transferor with no CGT to pay.

228

In practice, however, where entrepreneurs' relief is available, many transferors will choose to pay some CGT at just 10%, in order to increase the level of the loan account, which they can later draw upon tax free.

This is because, for higher rate taxpayers, the 10% CGT bill is far less than the tax arising on withdrawals made by way of salary or dividend (see Chapter 10).

Hence, in effect, by using the relief for 'gifts of business assets' (where available) you can actually choose how much CGT you want to pay on the transfer and you can effectively 'bank' the sum which has been taxed and withdraw it later with no further tax to pay.

Admittedly, similar results can be achieved with incorporation relief, by using a mixture of shares and cash as consideration for the transfer of the business, but it is much more difficult to judge this correctly in order to achieve the optimum, or desired, result.

The relief for 'gifts of business assets' also enables you to keep the share capital in your company at a low level, thus enabling you to withdraw your investment far more easily. By contrast, to use incorporation relief, you will generally need to issue large amounts of share capital, making it difficult for you to withdraw your investment from the company.

Incorporation relief also requires you to transfer your whole business. This could mean having to transfer properties and other assets that you did not wish to transfer and it also maximises your SDLT or LBTT exposure (see Section 15.2).

By using the relief for 'gifts of business assets' you can effectively 'cherry pick' the properties and other assets that you wish to transfer. Note, however, that entrepreneurs' relief is only available where the assets transferred constitute a distinct part of the business which is capable of being operated as a going concern in its own right.

Incorporation relief does, however, have two major advantages over relief for 'gifts of business assets'.

Firstly, as explained in Section 15.8, with incorporation relief there is no reduction in the amount of gain that may be 'held over' if the assets have not been used in the business throughout the transferor's ownership. In some cases, this may enable the owner of business property to obtain relief for their whole capital gain, rather than just part of it.

Secondly, of course, there is the ability for the company to get a 'step up' in the base cost of the assets transferred to their current market values.

In some cases, however, the 'step up' in base cost will be of limited value when the business is eligible for entrepreneurs' relief and the maximum CGT exposure for the transferor is thus only 10%.

Add to this the fact that most property business transfers will attract SDLT or LBTT (see Section 15.2) and we can see that the benefit of the 'step up' may sometimes be quite doubtful when entrepreneurs' relief is also available.

Nevertheless, there are occasions when the 'step up' in base cost offered by incorporation relief will be valuable, especially when the use of the properties being transferred is expected to change.

We will explore some opportunities for tax planning with incorporation relief in Section 15.14.

In general, however, it is fair to say that where both reliefs are available, most people will benefit more from the relief for 'gifts of business assets'.

## 15.10  PAY NOW, SAVE LATER

As we have already discussed, where a property business, or a part of a property business capable of operating as a going concern in its own right, is eligible for entrepreneurs' relief, the CGT rate which the owner will suffer on a transfer into a company is just 10% (on the first £10m of capital gains per person).

There is therefore a strong argument for saying that, in these circumstances, it is better not to claim either of the two major hold over reliefs discussed in the previous section since, by paying tax at 10% now, the transferor may achieve far greater tax savings in the future.

Furthermore, as we discussed in the previous section, this will allow the transferor to withdraw substantial sums from the company tax free.

### *Example*

*Leigh is a higher rate taxpayer with a qualifying furnished holiday letting business in Devon. In May 2018, Leigh transfers all of his furnished holiday letting properties into Halfpenny Lettings Limited, a new property investment company which he has just set up.*

*Leigh bought the properties many years ago for a total of £200,000 and, at the time of the transfer, they are worth a total of £1.2m.*

*If Leigh does not claim to hold over his gain arising on the transfer of the properties, his CGT liability will be as follows:*

|  | £ |
|---|---|
| *Deemed sale proceeds* | *1,200,000* |
| *(market value on transfer)* | |
| *Less:* | |
| *Original cost* | *200,000* |
|  | *1,000,000* |
| *Less:* | |
| *Annual exemption for 2018/19 (say)* | *11,600* |
| *Taxable gain* | *988,400* |

*CGT payable at 10%:               £98,840*

*Whilst Leigh is not exactly happy to pay this tax, he nevertheless appreciates that, at less than 10%, it does represent a very good rate of tax. He therefore decides to transfer his properties for a sum of £1.2m, which he can leave outstanding on loan account, rather than attempt to hold over the gain arising.*

*Over the next few years, Leigh is able to take £1.2m out of the company tax free (although he has to use the first £98,840 to pay his CGT bill).*

*If he took this sum out of the company by way of dividends at, say, £50,000 per year, he would have to pay a total of at least £400,800 in Income Tax (based on current rates for the first two years and forecast rates as per Appendix B for the rest).*

*By paying £98,840 in CGT up front, Leigh is therefore likely to save more than £300,000 in the long run.*

*Furthermore, the company will also have a base cost of £1.2m for the properties rather than the £200,000 that it would have had if Leigh had 'held over' his capital gains. On a sale of the properties, this higher base cost will save the company at least £170,000 (at 17%).*

*Hence, the £98,840 'up front' payment of CGT could eventually save Leigh and the company together a total of over £470,000!*

Note that, in this example, Halfpenny Lettings Limited would also have a SDLT bill of at least £36,000 on the transfer of Leigh's properties. This would actually increase the company's base cost in the properties although, once again, I have ignored this in the example for the sake of illustration.

The important point to note is that it makes no difference to the SDLT liability whether or not Leigh holds over the capital gain arising on the transfer of his properties.

The 'pay now save later' strategy will be even more beneficial when the availability of entrepreneurs' relief is about to be lost. So beneficial sometimes, in fact, that it can make the transfer of property into a company a tax saving strategy in itself.

### *Example*

*Frank is a higher rate taxpayer and has a small villa which he purchased many years ago for £50,000, but which is currently worth £250,000. He used the property as qualifying furnished holiday accommodation until 5th April 2015 and then changed over to long-term residential lettings. This means that the property will cease to qualify for entrepreneurs' relief after 5th April 2018.*

*In March 2018, however, Frank transfers his property to a new company, Hadden Lettings Limited.*

*Frank has a capital gain of £200,000. He deducts his 2017/18 annual exemption of £11,300, leaving £188,700 which is subject to CGT at just 10%, i.e. £18,870.*

*The company also has a SDLT liability of £10,000 on the property, bringing its total base cost up to £260,000.*

*Five years later, in March 2023, Hadden Lettings Limited sells the property for £350,000, thus producing a capital gain of £90,000. After indexation relief of £34,166 (based on the company's base cost for the property of £260,000 and assuming inflation at 2.5% per annum), Hadden Lettings Limited has a chargeable gain of just £55,834, which is then subject to CT at 17%, i.e. £9,492.*

*Frank then winds up Hadden Lettings Limited and his net proceeds of £330,508 (£350,000 LESS £9,492 CT and £10,000 SDLT) give him a capital gain of £80,508. As Hadden Lettings Limited was not a trading company, Frank will not be eligible for entrepreneurs' relief on this occasion, but the non-residential CGT rate of 20% will apply (subject to the 'Wealth Warning' in Section 12.6).*

*After deducting Frank's 2022/23 annual exemption of, say, £13,000, his taxable gain is reduced to £67,508, leaving him with a CGT bill, at 20%, of £13,502.*

*Frank's total tax costs on the property are thus:*

*£18,870 (CGT) + £10,000 (SDLT) + £9,492 (CT) + £13,502 (CGT) = £51,864*

*If Frank had still held the property personally at the time of sale, he would have had an overall capital gain of £300,000. As the property had been used for long-term lettings for the previous eight years, no entrepreneurs' relief would have been available.*

*After deducting his 2022/23 annual exemption of, say, £13,000, Frank would therefore have had a taxable gain of £287,000 and a CGT liability at 28% of £80,360.*

*Hence, by transferring the property into a company in 2018, Frank has ultimately reduced his overall tax bill by £28,496, or **over 35%!***

This example shows that an incorporation of a business that qualifies for entrepreneurs' relief on the transfer may ultimately be beneficial when a change in use of the property (or properties) has occurred, or is anticipated in the future.

This will, however, depend on the relative length of time and growth in value of the property in private ownership and qualifying business use, as compared with the length of time and growth in value of the property in company ownership and non-qualifying use. In practice, it will be necessary to prepare forecasts of the expected final sale position in order to decide if this route is beneficial.

## 15.11 'TRADING' BUSINESSES

If your business is regarded as 'trading' for tax purposes (see Chapter 3), then both the relief for 'gifts of business assets' and incorporation relief should be available to deal with the problem of capital gains arising on the transfer of assets into your company.

**Wealth Warning**

When considering the transfer of a property trade, it is important to remember that there will also be other tax issues involved.

Such a transfer will be regarded as a cessation of trade for Income Tax purposes. It will also be necessary to make appropriate elections relating to trading stock, development work-in-progress and capital allowances, in order to prevent unwanted and unnecessary tax liabilities from arising.

The transfer will probably also give rise to SDLT or LBTT liabilities, as explained in Section 15.2.

Transfers of trades will also mean a change in the 'taxable person' for VAT purposes and this will lead to a few formalities which will need to be observed (see Section 15.16).

Each of the two key CGT reliefs should readily be available to a property development or property management business, although, in the latter case, there may not be many assets to transfer.

As for a property dealing, or property trading, business (see Section 3.4), the CGT reliefs are theoretically available but:

- Will be of little benefit, as the properties held by the business represent trading stock and not capital assets,
- Could potentially be denied by HMRC who may argue that the business is actually one of property investment

In most cases, it will make more sense to simply start up a new property dealing business within a company, rather than attempt to transfer the existing business.

## 15.12 FURNISHED HOLIDAY LETTINGS

As usual, furnished holiday letting businesses (see Section 4.6) have a special status and transfers of such businesses are eligible both for the relief for 'gifts of business assets' and for incorporation relief.

As explained in Section 15.9, where both reliefs are available, the best choice will depend on future plans and expectations and the choice will generally be made through the structure used for the transfer transactions.

As also explained in Section 15.9, relief for 'gifts of business assets' is usually preferable where entrepreneurs' relief is available.

Whilst qualifying furnished holiday letting properties do enjoy a number of advantages for CGT and Income Tax purposes, they are unfortunately still classed as residential properties for SDLT or LBTT purposes, and are subject to these charges in the usual way on a transfer into a company (see Section 15.2).

Where a furnished holiday letting business is registered for VAT (see Section 9.3), the transfer of the business to a company will again mean a change in the 'taxable person' for VAT purposes. We will look at some of the formalities which need to be dealt with in this situation in Section 15.16.

When transferring a furnished holiday letting business, it may also be necessary to make appropriate capital allowances elections, in order to prevent any balancing charges from arising.


## 15.13 TURNING INVESTMENT PROPERTY INTO 'TRADING' PROPERTY

In previous sections of this chapter, we have seen the benefits of the two CGT 'hold over' reliefs when transferring qualifying trading properties or furnished holiday lettings into a company.

Unfortunately, the relief for 'gifts of business assets' is strictly restricted to businesses which also qualify as 'trading' for entrepreneurs' relief purposes (see Chapter 3 and Section 7.3).

On the face of it, therefore, it would appear that a property investment business could never be eligible for relief for 'gifts of business assets'.

Partial relief may, however, be available where the business qualifies as a 'trade' at the point of the transfer. One way to qualify as a 'trade' for this purpose would be to use the property as qualifying furnished holiday accommodation (see Section 4.6).

***Example***

*Anne has a house in Edinburgh which she has held as an investment property since buying it for £500,000 in April 2015. In April 2018, she starts to let the property out as qualifying furnished holiday accommodation.*

*In April 2021, Anne transfers the property into her company, Patron SRU Limited. The property's value at this point is £700,000.*

*Anne is deemed to have made a capital gain of £200,000. However, as she has used the property for a qualifying purpose for three years out of a total period of ownership of six years, Anne may claim to 'hold over' 3/6ths of her capital gain, i.e. £100,000.*

As can be seen from the example, changing an existing property's use provides some scope to reduce the CGT liability arising on a transfer into a company by claiming relief for 'gifts of business assets', but the relief is only partial.

Incorporation relief may provide a better solution under these circumstances since, as explained in Section 15.8, there is no reduction in the amount of gain which may be 'held over' when the property has not always been used in a qualifying business.

All that is required in order to claim incorporation relief without restriction is that the property is used in a qualifying business at the point of transfer. (Although, in practice, qualification for a reasonable period both before and after the point of transfer is probably necessary, for the reasons explained in Section 15.6.)

In the next section, we will look at whether a property investment business may itself be a qualifying business for incorporation relief purposes, without any need to change the nature of the business.

What is more certain, however, is that if we can change the use of investment property so that it qualifies as furnished holiday letting property (as defined in Section 4.6) or as other qualifying trading property, then it will be eligible for incorporation relief, or for partial relief for 'gifts of business assets', on a transfer to a company.

Unfortunately, not every property is suitable for the 'commercial letting of furnished holiday accommodation' – a term which must be met in order for it to qualify as a furnished holiday letting for the purposes of the two CGT 'hold over' reliefs.

So, can other investment properties ever become trading assets?

To achieve this will require the landlord to provide a significant level of additional services to tenants.

Generally speaking, merely ancillary services, such as cleaning the common stairwell of a block of flats, will not usually be regarded as sufficient to give the landlord trading status.

What is usually required is some form of services to individual rooms or tenants, such as the provision of meals, cleaning bedrooms or making up beds. Where a range of services are provided to individual tenants or their rooms, trading status should be assured and, in these cases, the landlord need not carry out the work personally, but may employ others to do it.

In the middle ground, there are those who provide an intermediate level of services to their tenants, such as window-cleaning and small property repairs. Where the landlord is engaged virtually full-time in managing properties and is providing many of these services personally, HMRC may sometimes accept that he or she is trading, although the position is far from certain.

Another useful indicator of trading status is the average length of a tenant's stay in the premises. The shorter the better from this point of view and average stays measured in days are more likely to indicate a trade than those measured in months.

In short, to achieve trading status generally requires the landlord to be running their property more like a guest house or a hostel than a normal letting business.

If this can be achieved, however, then either incorporation relief or partial relief for 'gifts of business assets' should be available on a transfer of property into a company.

At a later date (say a year or two after the transfer), the company could then cease providing the additional services and revert to a pure property investment business.

### Wealth Warning

It must be remembered that running the business as a trade prior to the transfer will lead to Class 4 NI liabilities (see Section 11.10).

Significant levels of ancillary services will also lead to a requirement for the business to be registered for VAT. Holiday accommodation businesses will also need to be registered for VAT if total annual sales exceed the VAT registration threshold.

## 15.14   PROPERTY INVESTMENT BUSINESSES & INCORPORATION RELIEF

Theoretically, the requirements for incorporation relief are not as strict as for relief for 'gifts of business assets' and only require a 'business' rather than a 'trade'. However, some of the case law on the subject states that the "mere passive holding of investments and collection of rent does not amount to a business" for this purpose.

There is other case law, however, which holds that a 'business' need not be an active one and that such a thing as a 'passive business' might exist.

### The Ramsay Case

The case of 'Elisabeth Moyne Ramsay v Revenue and Customs Commissioners', which was decided in favour of the taxpayer (Mrs Ramsay), has finally given us some legal authority for when a property investment business might qualify as a 'business' for the purposes of incorporation relief.

It is important to understand that this decision does not necessarily mean that all property investment businesses will qualify for incorporation relief; it only gives us an indication of which businesses might qualify.

Furthermore, whilst it was decided that Mrs Ramsay did indeed have a qualifying business, the case does not even draw an accurate 'borderline' which the rest of us can use to decide whether a qualifying business exists in other cases. This is because the judge made it very clear that he accepted Mrs Ramsay had a qualifying business based on all the facts 'taken overall' rather than because of any single factor alone.

Hence, in other cases, where only some of the same factors are present as in the Ramsay case, it will still be unclear as to whether a qualifying business exists for the purposes of incorporation relief.

Nonetheless, it is worth listing some of the factors which may have acted in Mrs Ramsay's favour:

- Her property business consisted of a joint interest in a single property which was divided into ten self-contained flats
- The property had extensive communal areas, as well as a garden, a car park and some garages
- Substantial repairs and maintenance work was carried out on the communal areas, garden, car park and garages

238

- Mrs Ramsay carried out some of this work personally
- Additional assistance was provided to one elderly tenant
- Prior to the transfer of the property to a company, Mr & Mrs Ramsay carried out some preparatory work regarding a proposed project to refurbish and redevelop the property
- Mrs Ramsay and her husband each spent approximately 20 hours per week on activities related to the property
- Neither of them had any other occupation during the relevant period

Based on these facts, the judge concluded:

"that the activity undertaken in respect of the property, again taken overall, was sufficient in nature and extent to amount to a business for the purpose of [incorporation relief]. Although each of the activities could equally well have been undertaken by someone who was a mere property investor, where the degree of activity outweighs what might normally be expected to be carried out by a mere passive investor, even a diligent and conscientious one, that will in my judgment amount to a business."

So, Mrs Ramsay qualified but the judge also made the point that other owners of investment property might only be a 'passive investor' who would not qualify and there was no single factor which determined this distinction: it was down to the degree of activity undertaken by the investor.

## Where Does The Ramsay Case Leave Us?

The Ramsay case has certainly improved the chances of some property investors qualifying for incorporation relief.

Those who can demonstrate that their business activities are equal in scope to Mrs Ramsay's (or greater) should now be able to claim incorporation relief.

This is in addition to those whose businesses can be adapted to achieve trading status in the manner described in Section 15.13 and those with qualifying furnished holiday lettings (who automatically qualify).

Nonetheless, despite the helpful result in the Ramsay case, the question of whether incorporation relief might be available for the vast majority of other property investment businesses still remains uncertain.

The danger in many cases is that the business could be regarded as a 'passive investment'.

HMRC takes the stance that the mere holding of investment property and collection of rent does not constitute a business for incorporation relief purposes. (Whilst happily continuing to collect Income Tax on the profits generated from this 'non-business' activity!)

One of the major problems, of course, is that to get the relief, one must transfer the entire business to the company. If relief is not then forthcoming, there could well be a substantial CGT bill. Furthermore, whether relief is obtained or not, SDLT or LBTT will usually be payable on the total value of all the properties transferred.

So, the stakes are high and the outcome will often be uncertain!

Before even considering whether to attempt an incorporation relief claim, it would be necessary to take a very detailed look at the particular circumstances of the property business in question and establish whether it amounts to more than 'the mere passive holding of investments'.

The Ramsay case will be helpful in carrying out this exercise, but it will be pretty rare for the property owner's circumstances to be exactly the same as Mrs Ramsay's!

So, the question remains: just how much more than passive investment does the business need to be in order to qualify?

As much as Mrs Ramsay, or more, is enough: we know that now. But how much less than Mrs Ramsay might suffice: we still do not know!

Some of the key points which need to be considered after the Ramsay case are whether it is necessary for:

- The property to contain substantial communal areas
- The owner to carry out repairs and maintenance work personally
- The property business to be the owner's only occupation
- The owner to be actively looking at ways to improve the capital value or rental yield of their property

Mrs Ramsay satisfied all of these points. The position where only some of these points are satisfied remains uncertain and I would not like to rely on a claim for incorporation relief for any property investment business other than one which meets all the same criteria as Mrs Ramsay's, or which qualifies as a furnished holiday letting business.

## But What If You Can Get The Relief?

Anyone who does successfully obtain incorporation relief will achieve a tax-free uplift in the base cost of all their properties to current market value.

Well, not exactly 'tax-free', there is either SDLT or LBTT to worry about, and this can be pretty substantial, as we saw in Section 15.3. Nonetheless, this could be a price worth paying in some cases.

As investment properties would be subject to CGT at up to 28% in the transferor's own hands, the uplift in base costs could provide the potential to make massive savings.

Once in the company, properties could generally be sold with a CT exposure of just 17% (for accounting periods commencing after 31st March 2020) of the future increase in their value above the rate of retail price inflation. The company could then reinvest the vast majority of the sales proceeds, having suffered only a minimal level of tax exposure.

Yes, the stakes are high indeed!

### Example

*Jim has a large property investment portfolio with a total current market value of £2.5m. Jim has built the portfolio up over many years and several of the older properties stand at significant capital gains. Jim has a substantial and well-established property business and is actively involved in running his business on a day-to-day basis. We will assume, therefore, that he can successfully argue that he does indeed have a 'business' for the purposes of incorporation relief.*

*Jim's portfolio consists of 20 residential properties, including ten houses in Leeds which he purchased for just £15,000 each and which are now worth £100,000 each. This will give Jim a gain of £85,000 on the sale of each house.*

*Jim is a higher rate taxpayer and has already used his annual CGT exemption, so a sale of the ten houses in Leeds would leave him with a CGT bill of £238,000 (10 x £85,000 x 28%).*

*Jim would like to sell off his old houses and reinvest the money in some new properties which, he anticipates, will yield higher rental returns. He is not, however, happy at the prospect of losing almost £240,000 of his proceeds in CGT.*

*Instead, therefore, Jim transfers his entire property investment business to a new company, Telfer Limited, in exchange for shares. Jim then holds over his capital gains under incorporation relief.*

*Whilst Telfer Limited will have to pay SDLT on the transfer, it will be able to claim multiple dwellings relief (see Section 8.6) to reduce the applicable rate to 3%, thus giving rise to a charge of £75,000.*

*The old houses in Leeds can now be sold with no CT liability arising, leaving a net sum of £925,000 available for Jim to reinvest, or £163,000 more than he would have had if he had simply sold the houses in Leeds himself.*

*Furthermore, the company will probably have capital losses of around £30,000 to carry forward (equivalent to the SDLT paid on the houses which have been sold) and all of Jim's remaining properties will now have a base cost equal to 103% of their current market value, thus significantly reducing any exposure to tax on future sales.*

## 15.15 OTHER INVESTMENT PROPERTIES

So, what happens if we transfer investment properties to a company and cannot claim either of the two CGT reliefs which we have already explored?

Without the availability of any special CGT relief, the owner of investment properties faces the problem of separate capital gains calculations on the transfer of each individual property and a CGT bill based on a 'deemed' sale at market value. SDLT or LBTT liabilities will also still arise in the usual way.

Sometimes, with careful timing and the use of annual exemptions, it is, however, still possible to make the transfers at little or no CGT cost, especially where a couple own properties jointly.

The possible availability of principal private residence relief on some properties should also be borne in mind when considering this type of strategy. (But see Section 16.2 regarding the pitfalls of private use after putting property into a company.)

### Tax Tip

A former principal private residence may usually be transferred into a property investment company at any time up until at least eighteen months after it ceased to be your main residence (and possibly much later in some circumstances) without incurring any CGT liability.

Be careful, however: if the property was not always your main residence throughout the period from purchase up until when you finally moved out of it, there might be some exposure to CGT.

Remember also that SDLT or LBTT will be payable as usual (including the additional 3% charge) based on the property's market value.

Nevertheless, generally speaking, if you do not feel confident about attempting an incorporation relief claim, it remains difficult to get an existing property investment business into a company without running the risk of incurring a large CGT bill.

In many cases, therefore, it is safer to look to the company as a vehicle only for your future investments and to keep your existing properties in your own hands.

### The 'Backdoor Route'

Borrowings secured on your existing personal property portfolio could be invested in the company to enable it to acquire new property. You, in turn, would be eligible for Income Tax relief on the interest on such borrowings, as the funds are being invested in a 'Close Company' (see Section 16.1). This would minimise your personal tax exposure on your own personal portfolio whilst enabling you to build up a new portfolio within your company.

Note, however, that the Income Tax relief on your interest costs would be subject to the limitations discussed in Section 13.9 (but not the much harsher restrictions applying to individual landlords discussed in Section 13.10).

### Other Possibilities

Another possibility which might be worth exploring in these circumstances is the use of a property management company (see Section 17.1).

Or maybe think about leasing your properties to your own company?

This is far from simple and, like any other tax planning, will require detailed professional advice.

## 15.16 VAT AND BUSINESS TRANSFERS

### Whole Businesses

If the whole business is transferred and is registered for VAT, this will mean that there is a change in the 'taxable person' for VAT purposes.

The transferor will need to cancel their VAT registration or apply to transfer it to the company. The transferee company will need to register for VAT.

It is important that the business is transferred as a going concern or there may be VAT charges arising on the assets transferred.

Where some assets are retained, VAT charges may also arise on these. VAT charges may also arise if the transferee company does not register for VAT.

### Partial Transfers

If only part of the business is transferred, the transferor may need to charge the company VAT on the assets transferred if any of the transfers amounts to a taxable supply (see Chapter 9).

The transfer will not represent a taxable supply, however, if the part of the business transferred amounts to a 'going concern' in its own right (e.g. ten furnished holiday letting properties, together with an office and staff, out of a total portfolio of twelve properties) **and** the transferee company registers for VAT.

If the transferor is not left with a taxable business after the transfer then they will need to cancel their VAT registration and this may lead to VAT charges on the assets retained.

### Commercial Properties

If a commercial property on which the option to tax has been exercised (see Section 9.4) is transferred, a VAT charge will arise unless:

i) The transfer is part of the transfer of a business as a 'going concern', and

ii) The transferee company notifies HMRC **on or before the date of the transfer** that it also opts to tax the property.

# Chapter 16

# Some Other Important Tax Issues

## 16.1 CLOSE COMPANIES AND CLOSE INVESTMENT HOLDING COMPANIES

Broadly speaking, a company is a 'Close Company' if it is under the control of five people or less. The vast majority of private property companies will therefore be Close Companies.

This is good news since additional reliefs are available in respect of shares and other investments in Close Companies, including interest relief, as discussed in Chapter 13.

### Close Investment Holding Companies

Any close company which does not exist wholly or mainly for a 'qualifying purpose' is a Close Investment Holding Company. Fortunately, 'qualifying purposes' include carrying on a trade and renting property to unconnected persons.

Hence, a property business will generally represent a qualifying purpose and a property company will not, therefore, usually be a Close Investment Holding Company.

This is very important because investors are not eligible for interest relief on investments in Close Investment Holding Companies.

## 16.2 THE DANGERS OF PRIVATE USE

It is generally not advisable to hold properties through a company where there is some private use. For these purposes, 'private use' would include:

- Using it as your own private residence (whether or not your main residence)

- Allowing your spouse, partner or any other member of your family to use it as a private residence

- Letting the property to any 'connected' person (see Appendix D)

Private use of a property held through a company could result in:

- The company becoming a Close Investment Holding Company and therefore losing many important tax reliefs
- Loss of interest relief on sums invested in the company
- Loss of entrepreneurs' relief on company shares (where they might otherwise qualify)
- Income Tax Benefit-in-Kind charges on the company's directors
- Class 1A NI liabilities for the company
- Deemed distributions of income which are taxable on the shareholders as if they were dividends

Plus, for property worth in excess of £500,000:

- SDLT at 15% on purchases or transfers (see Section 8.4)
- The Annual Tax on Enveloped Dwellings (see Section 16.7)
- Capital gains being subject to CGT at 28% instead of CT at between 17% and 19% (see Section 16.7)

Furthermore, where a property with private use is owned personally, there is scope to make use of the principal private residence exemption, private letting relief and rent-a-room relief. The scope to use these reliefs is lost if the property is held in a company.

Certainly therefore, as far as UK property is concerned, any private use of property held by a company is best avoided.

The position for foreign property is somewhat different since there are often good reasons for holding a second home abroad through a company.

Furthermore, HMRC has confirmed that the owners of a company which exists solely to hold a private residence overseas will be exempt from any Benefit-in-Kind charges in the UK in respect of their personal use of the property.

The exemption only applies, however, if the company exists solely to hold foreign property. If the company has any other activities, the Benefit-in-Kind charge for personal use by the company owners will continue to apply under normal principles.

The company must also be held directly by individuals. The exemption is not available, for example, where a company is held by a trust or another company.

Hence, whilst this exemption may be useful in some cases, it will generally make sense to ensure that any company formed to hold a second home abroad is kept entirely separate from any other company owned by the same person or persons.

## 16.3 SELLING THE COMPANY

Very often a property company will continue in the same ownership (or at least the same family) until its usefulness has expired, when it will be wound up. We looked at this in Section 12.6. Sometimes, however, a property company may be sold with its existing business intact. This is particularly likely in the case of a property development company, as we saw in Section 12.15.

Another time when a property company may be sold with its existing business intact is when the purchaser wishes to acquire a ready-made portfolio held by a property investment company.

The sale of the company represents a capital disposal and the individual investor making the sale will therefore have a CGT liability in much the same way as that arising on a winding up (except, of course, that the 'anti-phoenixing' rules described in Section 7.7 cannot apply).

### *Example*

*Morgan started her property investment company, Angel Limited, in 1985 with an investment of just £10,000 share capital.*

*In December 2017, Morgan decides to sell Angel Limited to Big Properties PLC for £1m. Her capital gain on the sale is therefore £990,000. After deducting her annual exemption of £11,300, she is left with a taxable gain of £978,700. She is a higher rate taxpayer, so she will pay CGT at 20%, i.e. £195,740.*

### Stamp Duty

A huge advantage for the purchaser of a property company is the ability to make large Stamp Duty savings, as only 0.5% will need to be paid on the purchase price of the shares. Not only is this considerably less than the SDLT or LBTT rates applying to property purchases, but also the actual amount of consideration to which the duty applies will often be reduced.

### *Example*

*Di Rollo Properties Limited owns a portfolio of residential properties in Scotland with a total value of £5m (and an average value of £250,000). The company also has borrowings and other liabilities totalling £2m, giving it a net value of £3m.*

*Marcus is interested in acquiring the Di Rollo Properties Limited portfolio. If he buys the property portfolio from the company, he will have to pay LBTT of £192,000 (even after multiple dwellings relief – see Section 8.6).*

*Alternatively, if Marcus buys the company, he will only have to pay Stamp Duty at 0.5% on £3m, i.e. £15,000 – a saving of £177,000!*

(If Di Rollo Properties Limited's portfolio had been in England, Wales or Northern Ireland, Marcus would have had to pay SDLT of £200,000 on a direct purchase and would therefore save £185,000 by buying the company instead.)

Given the commercial advantages of acquiring an existing, well-run property portfolio and the potential Stamp Duty savings, a well-packaged property company can be a very attractive target for potential purchasers. Naturally, one can expect this to be reflected in the sale price!

## 16.4   BENEFITS AND DANGERS OF MULTIPLE COMPANIES

Investors sometimes consider making their property investments through an existing trading company.

Here though, great care needs to be exercised. If your company is carrying on a business which is regarded as a 'trade' within the UK tax system, your shares in that company will be eligible for entrepreneurs' relief and holdover relief for CGT purposes (see Chapter 7) and also for business property relief for IHT purposes.

Putting non-qualifying property investments into such a company could jeopardise the 'business asset' status of your shares in that company and could eventually cost you dearly in CGT or IHT (see Section 3.6 for further details).

Furthermore, there is often increased resistance from lenders to financing property investments within an existing trading company: they generally prefer a 'clean' company with no other activity in it (also sometimes known as a 'special purpose vehicle').

Given that the existence of any associated companies no longer has any impact on CT liabilities, the long-term savings provided by retaining the 'business asset' status of an existing company generally mean that it will be preferable to make your property investments through a different company.

On the other hand, however, where property investments form an integral part of a 'mixed' property business, there can sometimes be advantages to running the whole business through a single company. This idea is examined further in Section 3.6 and in the Taxcafe.co.uk guide 'How to Save Inheritance Tax'.

## 16.5   SHORT AND LONG ACCOUNTING PERIODS

For a variety of reasons, companies sometimes prepare accounts covering periods other than a year. This often occurs at the beginning or end of a company's life, although it will also occur in the event of a change of accounting date. (We saw one reason why you might wish to consider changing your company's accounting date in Section 2.7.)

As shorter or longer accounting periods will often occur at the beginning of a company's life, it is worth us spending a little time on the CT implications of such periods.

### Longer Accounting Periods

For CT purposes, periods of over one year must be divided up into two periods:

- The first twelve months, and
- The remainder

Trading profits may be divided between the two periods on a pro-rata basis, although a strict 'actual' basis may be used if there is reasonable justification for doing so.

Rental income should strictly be allocated on an 'actual' basis, although a pro-rata basis will often be acceptable.

Other investment income and capital gains should be allocated to the period in which they arose.

Each of the two periods is then taxed separately in its own right. The first period is taxed under the normal principles applying to a period of a year. The second period is dealt with as a short accounting period.

## Short Accounting Periods

Where a company has a short accounting period, some key tax reliefs and limits must be reduced accordingly, on a pro rata basis. These include:

- The amount of annual investment allowance available (see Section 4.4)
- The rate of writing down allowances (see Section 4.4)
- The £2m threshold for interest relief restrictions (see Section 4.7)
- The £5m limit for loss relief restrictions (see Section 4.8)

In the case of a very short period, some of these restrictions might even affect quite small companies.

## Starting Business

It is also important to understand that a new accounting period for CT purposes starts when the company starts business. This will generally be some time after the date of incorporation.

### Example

*Webster Limited is a property investment company. The company was incorporated on 12th May 2017 but does not rent out its first property until 15th September 2017.*

*Webster Limited changes its accounting date to 30th June and prepares its first set of accounts for the period from 12th May 2017 to 30th June 2018.*

*For CT purposes, however, the company is regarded as having one accounting period as a dormant company, from 12th May to 14th September 2017, and then a second accounting period, as a property investment company, from 15th September 2017 to 30th June 2018.*

If Webster Limited prepared its first set of accounts to a date more than twelve months after it commenced business, it would have three accounting periods for CT purposes.

## Ceasing Business

For CT purposes, an accounting period is also deemed to come to an end when the company ceases business.

## Tax Returns & Tax Payments

In any case where a company's accounting period must be divided up into more than one period for CT purposes each period will require its own Corporation Tax Return.

The filing deadline for each Return will usually remain twelve months from the company's accounting date, except in the case of periods in excess of 18 months, when returns are due within 30 months of the beginning of the accounting period.

The due date for payment of CT (except for large companies under the instalment system – see Section 2.6) is always nine months and one day after the end of each period.

### *Example*

*Hastings Limited draws up accounts for the fifteen months ending 31st December 2017.*

*The company will need to prepare a tax return for the year ending 30th September 2017 and pay the CT due for that period by 1st July 2018.*

*The company will also need to prepare a tax return for the three-month period ending 31st December 2017 and pay the CT due for that period by 1st October 2018.*

*The filing deadline for both tax returns will be 31st December 2018.*

As a general rule, I would advise all company owners to keep HMRC informed of any changes which affect their company's tax return periods, including any changes of accounting date, the setting up of new companies and commencement of business.

Most important of all is to advise HMRC if the company ceases all business activity and becomes inactive.

In this way, one hopes that HMRC will issue notices requiring the company to deliver tax returns for the right periods.

There are detailed rules governing the position where notices are issued requiring the company to deliver a Corporation Tax Return for a period which does not correspond to one of its actual accounting periods.

In most cases, such notices will result in a requirement to submit at least one CT Return and penalties (as detailed in Section 2.9) will arise for failure to do so.

The important point to note is that you cannot afford to ignore a notice to deliver a CT Return just because it has been issued for the wrong period!


## 16.6   BECOMING NON-RESIDENT

Throughout this guide, we have been looking at the implications for UK resident property investors using a UK resident property company. Space does not permit a detailed examination of the position for non-residents, but it is worth making a few brief observations.


### Tax Residence for Companies

Subject to any applicable Double Tax Treaty, a company is treated as UK resident if:
  i)   It is UK registered, or
  ii)   It has its place of central management and control in the UK

A detailed examination of (ii) would take too long to fit in here, but it is fair to say that if you are UK resident, it is very difficult for any property company which you run not to be regarded as UK resident also.


### Emigration for Companies

Generally speaking, a UK registered company cannot 'emigrate' – i.e. it cannot cease to be UK resident. This may, however, in some cases, be overridden by the terms of a Double Tax Treaty between the UK and another country.

If a UK resident company does succeed in 'emigrating', i.e. becoming non-UK resident, then, unless it does so with the specific consent of Her Majesty's Treasury, it must pay an 'exit charge'. The 'exit charge' is basically a sum equal to the CT which would arise if the company were to sell all of its assets at their market value.

In view of these points, any UK resident individual who ultimately intends to emigrate should think very carefully before using a property company.

## Non-Resident Companies

In the same way as for non-resident individuals, a non-UK resident company is generally liable for UK tax on income from UK property, but is exempt from tax on capital gains except:

- Gains on assets connected with trading activities in the UK
- Gains on UK residential property arising after 5th April 2015 (only the increase in value after 5th April 2015 is subject to UK tax in this case)

However, if a non-UK resident company is under the control of a UK resident individual, then the individual is personally liable for CGT on all the capital gains made by that company.

Hence, overseas (non-resident) companies are generally of little use to UK resident individual investors buying UK property.

### Wealth Warning

If attempting to run a UK property portfolio through an overseas company, it is essential to ensure that the company's 'place of central management and control' is outwith the UK. Otherwise, the company will be deemed to be UK resident, thus bringing all of its properties into the UK tax net for capital gains purposes, etc.

This can be very difficult (and costly) to achieve in practice and detailed professional advice should always be sought before attempting to rely on this strategy.

At present, a non-UK resident company generally pays UK tax as follows:

- Income Tax at basic rate on rental income from UK property
- CGT – but computed at normal UK CT rates (including indexation relief) on gains on UK residential property arising after 5th April 2015
- CT at normal rates on trading profits arising on UK land and property

The CGT charge at normal CT rates is overridden by the higher charge discussed in Section 16.7 when it applies.

The Government is currently considering proposals to change the way in which non-UK resident companies with UK-source rental income or capital gains on UK residential property are taxed, so that all of these items will be subject to CT instead of Income Tax or CGT. As yet, there is no date for the introduction of these changes.

**Non-UK Resident Individuals**

Non-UK resident individuals are subject to UK CGT on:

- UK residential property, including furnished holiday lettings (but only on the element of the gain arising after 5th April 2015)
- Any assets connected with a UK trading activity which they carry on

Non-UK residents are exempt from UK CGT on:

- Commercial property in the UK (except where connected to a trading activity which they carry out in the UK)
- The element of any gains on UK residential property arising due to increases in value prior to 6th April 2015
- Overseas property

**Investment in UK Residential Property**

For new investments made from 6th April 2015 onwards, non-UK residents will be in a similar position to UK residents, as they will be subject to both UK Income Tax and UK CGT on these investments.

For UK tax purposes, the use of a UK company to hold UK residential investment property will therefore be subject to the same benefits and pitfalls for these individuals as for UK resident individuals. This, however, is subject to the terms of any applicable Double Tax Treaty.

Furthermore, the tax issues arising in the individual's own country of residence must also be considered. Detailed professional advice in both the UK and the individual's own country is therefore essential.

## Investment in UK Commercial Property and Overseas Property

Subject to the further comments below, it would generally not make any sense for a non-UK resident individual to put any of these types of property into a UK resident company, as this would be bringing these properties fully into the UK tax net.


## Trading (or Potential Trading) in UK Property

Non-UK resident individuals are subject to UK Income Tax on any trading profits derived from UK land and property. This includes any 'deemed' trading profits under the principles discussed in Section 3.7.

Furthermore, as discussed in Section 3.4, where a non-UK resident is investing substantially in UK property, there is often a risk that HMRC will argue that the individual has a taxable UK trading activity rather than falling under the capital gains regime and therefore being exempt on some or all of their UK property gains.

A UK property company may be useful in such a case, as there is less difference in the amount of tax payable *within* a company between a property 'trading' business and a property 'investment' business. Although this does mean that the business will be fully taxable in the UK, it is nevertheless a case of 'damage limitation', as the CT rates applying will generally be lower than the Income Tax which is potentially at stake.

Furthermore, since the income from UK properties is always taxable in any case, the use of a UK company may often remain advantageous.

Nevertheless, the major drawback for a non-resident in using a UK company remains the fact that the company will be subject to UK CT on all of its capital gains, whereas the individual could be exempt from UK tax on some or all of those gains.

The only way to avoid any tax on the properties' capital growth in the company would be for the non-resident individual to sell the company itself, rather than the properties held within it. Nevertheless, even then, one might reasonably expect the purchaser to take the potential CT liability on capital gains in the company into account when negotiating a purchase price! (Although, against this, there are also Stamp Duty advantages to be considered, as explained in Section 16.3.)

**More Information for Non-Residents**

For more information on the UK tax treatment of non-UK resident individuals and companies, including many tax-saving opportunities, see the Taxcafe.co.uk guide *'Tax Free Capital Gains'*.

## 16.7    MANSION TAXES

The Government has introduced a series of additional tax charges aimed at UK residential property owned by 'non-natural persons'. The definition of 'non-natural persons' includes companies, partnerships where a company is a partner, and collective investment schemes. Most commonly, the charges apply to companies. They do not apply to property investors operating purely as individuals.

Three charges are involved:

- The 15% rate of SDLT (see Section 8.4)
- The Annual Tax on Enveloped Dwellings ('ATED')
- CGT at 28% on the disposal of the property

These charges are sometimes collectively known as 'mansion taxes' and they apply regardless of where the company or other 'non-natural person' is resident for tax purposes.

However, the charges only apply to single dwellings worth in excess of the specified threshold. They do not only apply by reference to the total value of the property portfolio.

The specified threshold for all three charges is now £500,000.

**Business Exemption**

The good news for most property investors operating through a company (or any other 'non-natural person') is that properties are exempt from these charges if they are being used in a business: including a property rental business.

Hence, in most cases, property investment companies should be exempt from the three 'mansion taxes'; although it will be essential to ensure that properties are being acquired for use in the business, and continue to be held for business purposes thereafter.

The bad news, however, is that any company or other 'non-natural person' which is eligible for this exemption will need to claim it – whenever they buy property worth more than £500,000 for SDLT purposes; and on an annual basis when they own any property worth more than £500,000 for the purposes of ATED.

Hence, even if there is no extra tax, there will still be plenty of extra administration to deal with!

## The Annual Tax on Enveloped Dwellings

The ATED charges applying for 2017/18 are:

| Property Value | Charge |
|---|---|
| Over £500,000, but not more than £1m | £3,500 |
| Over £1m, but not more than £2m | £7,050 |
| Over £2m, but not more than £5m | £23,550 |
| Over £5m, but not more than £10m | £54,950 |
| Over £10m, but not more than £20m | £110,100 |
| Over £20m | £220,350 |

ATED charges are increased annually in line with the Consumer Prices Index.

## Capital Gains Tax Charges

The 28% CGT charge applies to gains on properties worth over £2m accruing after 5th April 2013; gains on properties worth over £1m, but no more than £2m, accruing after 5th April 2015; and gains on properties worth over £500,000, but no more than £1m, accruing after 5th April 2016.

In each case, the CGT charge only applies to the increase in the property's value between the specified date and the date of disposal.

A UK company which is caught by this charge would also still pay CT in the usual way on the gain arising up to the specified date.

### *Example*

*On 31st March 2014, Threequarter Investments Ltd bought two properties for £750,000 each: numbers 10 and 11 Dingnow Street.*

*No. 10 Dingnow Street is used as a rental property and is rented out to unconnected tenants.*

*No. 11 Dingnow Street is used as a private residence by Mr Dnommah, the company's owner.*

*Both properties are sold on 31st March 2018 at a price of £1m each.*

The SDLT arising on the purchase of No. 10 (the rental property) will be at the usual rates set out in Section 8.3 and will therefore be £50,000. Threequarter Investments Ltd will be subject to CT on the gain arising on the sale of this property: £200,000 (£1m - £750,000 - £50,000). The company may, however, claim indexation relief (see Section 6.4). Let's say this amounts to 8%, giving relief of £64,000 (£800,000 x 8%).

The company thus pays CT at 19% on £136,000 (£200,000 - £64,000), which is just £25,840.

This property will be exempt from ATED, but the company has to claim exemption from the charge on annual returns for 2016/17 and 2017/18. (The charge only applies to property worth more than £500,000, but no more than £1m, from 2016/17 onwards.)

The SDLT arising on the purchase of No. 11 (the private residence) will be at 15%: i.e. £112,500. The company will also be subject to ATED at £3,500 for both 2016/17 and 2017/18.

When the company sells the property, it will be subject to CT in the usual way on the part of the gain arising up to 5th April 2016. Let's say the property was worth £875,000 at that date, so this part of the gain amounts to £12,500 (£875,000 - £750,000 - £112,500).

The indexation relief for this period amounts to 2.6%, giving relief of £22,425 (£862,500 x 2.6%). This exceeds the amount of the gain, so no CT is due. This may sound like a good outcome, but it only happens because of the huge amount of SDLT paid on the purchase of the property. Furthermore, the company is unable to claim any loss in respect of the excess indexation relief.

The remaining £125,000 of the gain on this property (i.e. the part of the gain arising between 6th April 2016 and 31st March 2018) is subject to CGT at a flat rate of 28%, i.e. £35,000.

In total, the tax paid on the private residence amounts to £154,500 (£112,500 + £3,500 x 2 + £35,000), compared with £75,840 (£50,000 + £25,840) on the rental property. Mr Dnommah might also be subject to Income Tax charges in respect of his private use of No. 11. If so, the company would be subject to Class 1A NI on this too.

In short, holding private residences through a company has become a very expensive business!

For more details on both ATED and the CGT charges described above, see the Taxcafe.co.uk guide 'Tax Free Capital Gains'.

## 16.8 THE GENERAL ANTI-ABUSE RULE

The general anti-abuse rule (or 'GAAR' for short) was introduced with effect from July 2013. The GAAR is targeted at 'artificial' and 'abusive' or 'aggressive' tax avoidance schemes which go beyond the scope of normal tax planning and which use loopholes in the tax legislation in a way that was not intended by Parliament.

So far, we are being told that 'normal' tax planning is not affected by the GAAR.

Where the GAAR applies, any tax advantage gained through the use of the 'abusive' scheme will be reversed.

Personally, I would not regard any tax planning strategies discussed in this guide as particularly 'abusive' and I believe that most professional tax advisors would agree with me. I would thus hope that none of the techniques discussed in this guide will be affected by the GAAR.

Nonetheless, at present, it is way too early to tell just exactly how HMRC will apply the GAAR in practice. It is therefore possible that some more advanced planning strategies could be at risk of being targeted under the GAAR: perhaps including the one which we will be looking at in the next chapter.

## 16.9 SCOTTISH TAXPAYERS

From 2017/18 onwards, the Scottish Parliament is able to set separate Income Tax rates and thresholds for Scottish taxpayers. Generally, you will be a Scottish taxpayer if you live in Scotland (but see the Taxcafe.co.uk guide *'How to Save Property Tax'* for further details).

The Scottish Parliament cannot, however, alter:

- The personal allowance (although it can effectively extend it by introducing a zero-rate tax band – as noted below)
- The High Income Child Benefit Charge
- The withdrawal of personal allowances where income exceeds £100,000
- UK tax rates on dividends, interest, savings income, etc. (see below)
- Capital allowances

Similarly, it has no power over other taxes, such as NI, VAT, CGT, CT and IHT.

The amount of income on which a Scottish taxpayer is liable for tax continues to be computed in exactly the same way as for other UK resident taxpayers: it is only the rates of tax which are different. Hence, the vast majority of the advice in this guide remains equally valid for Scottish taxpayers – it is only the amount of tax which might be saved by using a company which may vary.

Scottish Income Tax rates apply to all of a Scottish taxpayer's income except:

- Dividends
- Interest and other savings income
- Income from Real Estate Investment Trusts or Property Authorised Investment Funds

Hence, Scottish Income Tax rates apply to all of a Scottish taxpayer's property rental or trading income, regardless of where their properties are located.

In other words, a Scottish taxpayer pays Scottish Income Tax rates on income derived from property both within and outwith Scotland. Other UK resident taxpayers continue to pay Income Tax at normal UK rates on all of their income, even if it is derived from property in Scotland.

**Scottish Tax Rates**

The higher rate tax threshold for Scottish taxpayers has been frozen at £43,000 for 2017/18 (the same level as in 2016/17). The Scottish Government has also announced that the threshold will only rise by inflation until at least 2021/22. (Whereas the UK Government has 'promised' an increase to £50,000 by 2020/21)

Estimating annual inflation at 2.5% would produce a Scottish higher rate tax threshold of around £46,000 by 2020/21, costing Scottish higher rate taxpayers an additional £800 per year: including those forced into higher rate tax by the restrictions on interest relief examined in Section 13.10.

The tiny silver lining is that the Scottish Government proposes to introduce a small zero-rate band by 2021/22 which will ensure that at least the first £12,750 of Scottish taxpayers' income is free from Income Tax.

No changes to the 45% additional rate have been announced for Scottish taxpayers so far; although we may see changes in a few years' time.

## Impact for Scottish Property Investors

Given that Scottish Income Tax rates apply to rental or trading income received by a Scottish taxpayer, but UK Income Tax rates continue to apply to dividend income, and CT rates are the same for Scottish companies, the potential savings available to a Scottish higher rate taxpayer by using a property company are greater by:

- £400 in 2017/18, rising to
- An estimated £800 by 2020/21

## 16.10  NORTHERN IRELAND

If and when the proposals for a separate CT rate for companies operating in Northern Ireland come to fruition (see Section 2.3), nearly all taxpayers investing in property in the province may be able to save an additional 4.5% of all rental or trading profits derived from Northern Irish property by using a company.

# Chapter 17

# Specialised Property Companies

## 17.1 PROPERTY MANAGEMENT COMPANIES

We have looked at the taxation status of property management companies a few times throughout this guide and it is now worth taking a look at how these companies might be used as a planning tool.

The objective of this type of planning is to reduce the tax burden on the income from your properties without having the problems inherent in putting the properties themselves into a company.

### *Example*

*Jonah has a large property portfolio generating annual gross rents of £500,000 and a taxable profit before interest of £350,000. He is therefore an additional rate taxpayer paying Income Tax at 45%.*

*He decides to sub-contract the management of his properties to a new property management company, Lomu Property Services Limited.*

*Lomu Property Services Limited charges Jonah 15% of the gross annual rents on the properties (£75,000) as a service charge for managing the portfolio. Naturally, the company also ends up bearing some of the expenses in running the property portfolio and these amount to £10,000.*

*Jonah will now have £65,000 less taxable income, thus reducing his annual Income Tax bill by £29,250.*

*Meanwhile, Lomu Property Services Limited will have an annual profit of £65,000 (the £75,000 service charge less £10,000 expenses), giving it a CT bill, at 17%, of £11,050 (for periods commencing after 31st March 2020).*

*The overall net tax saving for Jonah and Lomu Property Services Limited taken together is thus £18,200 (£29,250 - £11,050).*

*As usual, however, it doesn't work quite so well if the company's profits are extracted. If Jonah takes out the company's after-tax profit of £53,950 as a dividend, he will have additional Income Tax of £18,182.50 to pay (based on our forecast rates per Appendix B), leaving him almost exactly back where he started!*

### Wealth Warning 1

This type of arrangement is likely to attract close HMRC scrutiny and it is essential to ensure that the commercial reality of the situation matches up to the tax planning.

Firstly, the amount of service charge levied by the company must not exceed a normal commercial rate for those services.

Secondly, for Jonah to be able to claim a valid Income Tax deduction for these charges, he must be able to show that they were incurred wholly and exclusively for the benefit of his property rental business. In other words, there must be a genuine provision of services by the company.

### Wealth Warning 2

If the total level of service charges (and other fees, commission, or sales) being charged by the company exceeds the VAT registration threshold, it will need to register for VAT and charge VAT at the standard rate of 20%.

If, as will often be the case, the individual landlord is unable to recover this VAT, it will completely undo the whole purpose of the exercise and could turn it into a costly mess!

The arrangement will work best if there is a full-blown property management business, managing properties for a number of unconnected landlords on a fully commercial arm's length basis.

Despite this, the company's total gross income will need to be kept below the VAT registration threshold unless the individual landlord who owns the company is fully taxable for VAT purposes. Generally, this would mean that they only hold commercial property which they have opted to tax or holiday accommodation.

The service charges levied on the owner's property business from the company should be on the same basis as those for other landlords using the same services.

### Tax Tip

Subject to the points set out above, even greater tax savings may be possible if the property management company is owned by and/or employs the investor's spouse, partner or other family members.

# Chapter 18

# In Conclusion

## 18.1 WEIGHING IT ALL UP

Now that we have carried out a detailed examination of the tax implications of using a property company, what conclusions can we draw?

* A property company is generally of little or no use to basic rate taxpayers

* In the absence of any interest on residential lettings, property companies are only of any benefit to higher rate taxpayers if they are prepared to retain a significant proportion of profits within the company

* Where there are interest costs on residential lettings, the benefit of using a property company is greatly increased for higher rate taxpayers, including those who will become higher rate taxpayers due to the restrictions on interest relief currently being phased in for individual landlords

* The benefits of using a company where there are interest costs on residential lettings may be great enough to compensate for higher interest charges paid by the company

* Some benefit may still remain for a higher rate taxpayer, even when all of the profits are extracted from the company each year, *if* there are interest costs on residential lettings

* The greatest savings are achieved when the company's profits are continually reinvested. This, in turn, may lead to a significant growth in pre-tax income and the total capital value of the company

* A company provides greater scope to obtain tax relief for rental losses, interest and finance costs

* Additional savings are available to:
    i) Scottish taxpayers,
    ii) Investors over state pension age,
    iii) Many investors with young children, and
    iv) (In future) taxpayers investing in property in Northern Ireland

- Greater tax liabilities will arise on property disposals if the investor wishes to extract the proceeds from the company

- Capital growth retained in the company, however, may ultimately be sold at a lesser tax cost

- A successful property company is attractive to purchasers

- Properties held in companies should not generally be used privately (although exceptions sometimes arise for foreign holiday homes)

- Transferring existing investment properties into a company is extremely hazardous to your wealth!

- On the other hand, companies may sometimes be used as a means to save CGT on future property disposals

- Making property investments through existing trading companies is generally unwise, although there are some circumstances in which it may be beneficial

- Property management companies may be considered as an alternative to property investment companies in the right circumstances

- To be certain about the benefits of a property company requires a crystal ball

- The decision whether to use a company is dependent on a great many factors and each property investor's position is unique

In short, though, the greatest benefits of using a property company arise in the case of higher rate taxpayers who wish to use the company as a long-term investment vehicle.


## 18.2    FUTURE TAX CHANGES

In the fourteen years since I wrote the first edition of this guide, we have seen enormous changes to the UK tax system. In fact, if there is one thing which the last fourteen years have taught us, it must surely be to take nothing for granted!

One might expect, therefore, that the changes we have seen over the last fourteen years would have made an enormous difference to the question of whether it is beneficial to use a property company or not.

Not so! My main conclusion fourteen years ago was that a property investment company was of only marginal benefit unless the investor was prepared to reinvest their profits within the company over a long period of time.

Fourteen years later, we still see that a property company is at its most beneficial when profits are reinvested within the company.

Admittedly, there is now little or no benefit for basic rate taxpayers in using a company: but there never was much benefit for them anyway.

On the other hand, the impact of the interest relief restrictions now applying to individual landlords means that some benefit often remains for higher rate taxpayers even when all profits are being extracted from the company.

Nevertheless, despite all of the changes over the last fourteen years, higher rate taxpayers remain in the same fundamental position: there are massive savings to be made by using a company as a long-term investment vehicle.

The question for us now is this: if the tax changes made over the last fourteen years have not altered the basic rationale behind using a property company, what is the likelihood that future changes will?

The Government always seems to be unhappy with the tax advantages enjoyed by private 'owner-managed' companies and appears to be constantly on the lookout for ways to curtail those advantages.

But they are also hampered in this pursuit by their need to keep the UK's corporate tax regime competitive at an international level. Not to mention the need to stimulate the UK economy!

As a result, many previous proposals and rumoured 'crackdowns' have often come to nothing.

The most effective measure introduced to date has been the increase in tax rates applying to dividends. We have already anticipated further increases in these rates within this guide, but our fundamental conclusion has remained unaltered.

The Government did commission a review (by the Office for Tax Simplification) of the possibility of introducing 'look through' taxation for small private companies. The idea was that the owners of the company would be taxed directly on the company profits, in a similar way to how partners in a partnership are taxed. Thankfully, this project has now been abandoned!

In summary, most of the pressure to reform the taxation of small companies seems to be focused on the extraction of profits by company owners.

Generally speaking, what the Government seems most intent on attacking is not small companies themselves, but rather small company owners who simply use their company as a means to save tax on what, in reality, is effectively just personal income.

Hence, whilst we cannot be certain what the future may hold, it nevertheless seems to me that any further changes which we may see in the near future are likely to simply reinforce the conclusion that a property company is only at its most beneficial when a significant proportion of its profits are being retained and reinvested each year.

Whilst the Treasury can be expected to eat into your tax savings to some extent, my feeling is that, whatever changes we may see, property companies are still likely to remain beneficial to higher rate taxpayers who wish to make long-term property investments and build up a property business over a number of years.

And long may it continue!

# Appendix A

## UK Tax Rates and Allowances: 2016/17 to 2018/19

| | Rates | 2016/17 £ | 2017/18 £ | 2018/19 £ |
|---|---|---|---|---|
| **Income Tax** | | | | |
| Personal allowance | | 11,000 | 11,500 | 11,800(2) |
| Basic rate band (3) | 20% | 32,000 | 33,500 | 34,800(2) |
| Higher rate/Threshold (3) | 40% | 43,000 | 45,000 | 46,600(2) |
| Personal allowance withdrawal | | | | |
| Effective rate/From | 60% | 100,000 | 100,000 | 100,000(2) |
| To | | 122,000 | 123,000 | 123,600(2) |
| Additional rate/Thresh. | 45% | 150,000 | 150,000 | 150,000(2) |
| | | | | |
| Starting rate band (4) | 0% | 5,000 | 5,000 | 5,000(2) |
| Personal savings allowance (5) | | 1,000 | 1,000 | 1,000(2) |
| Dividend allowance | | 5,000 | 5,000 | 2,000 |
| Marriage allowance (6) | | 1,100 | 1,150 | 1,180(2) |
| | | | | |
| **National Insurance** | | | | |
| Primary threshold | 9%/12% | 8,060 | 8,164 | 8,372(1) |
| Upper earnings limit | 2% | 43,000 | 45,000 | 46,600(2) |
| Secondary threshold | 13.8% | 8,112 | 8,164 | 8,372(1) |
| Employment allowance | | 3,000 | 3,000 | 3,000(2) |
| Class 2 – per week | | 2.80 | 2.85 | n/a |
| Small profits threshold | | 5,965 | 6,025 | n/a |
| | | | | |
| **Pension Contributions** | | | | |
| Annual allowance | | 40,000 | 40,000 | 40,000(2) |
| Lifetime allowance | | 1m | 1m | 1.025m(1) |
| | | | | |
| **Capital Gains Tax** | | | | |
| Annual exemption | | 11,100 | 11,300 | 11,600(1) |
| | | | | |
| **Inheritance Tax** | | | | |
| Nil rate band | | 325,000 | 325,000 | 325,000 |
| Main residence nil rate band | | n/a | 100,000 | 125,000 |
| Annual Exemption | | 3,000 | 3,000 | 3,000 |
| | | | | |
| **Corporation Tax** | | | | |
| Rates: year commencing 1 April | 20% | | 19% | 19% |

**Notes**
1. Estimated, based on CPI inflation at 2.5%
2. Assumed/estimated based on announcements to date
3. Reduced for Scottish taxpayers from 2017/18 onwards
4. Applies to interest and savings income only
5. Higher-rate taxpayers £500, not available to additional rate taxpayers
6. For married couples and civil partners if neither pays higher rate tax

## Appendix B

# Forecast Future Tax Rates and Allowances

The use of these forecast future rates and allowances within this guide is explained in the Foreword. Further details are also given in Section 11.2.

|  | Rates | Bands, Allowances, Etc. £ |
|---|---|---|
| **Income Tax** | | |
| Personal allowance | | 12,500 |
| Basic rate band | 20% | 37,500 |
| Higher rate/Threshold | 40% | 50,000 |
| | | |
| Personal allowance withdrawal | | |
| Effective rate/From | 60% | 100,000 |
| To | | 125,000 |
| | | |
| Additional rate/Thresh | 45% | 150,000 |
| | | |
| Dividend tax rates | | |
| Basic rate | 10% | |
| Higher rate | 35% | |
| Additional rate | 40% | |
| Dividend allowance | | 2,000 |
| | | |
| **National Insurance** | | |
| Class 1 – Primary | 12% | |
| Class 4 | 11% | |
| Primary threshold | | 9,000 |
| Upper earnings limit | | 50,000 |
| Additional Rate | 2% | |
| Class 1 – Secondary | 13.8% | |
| | | |
| **Corporation Tax** | | |
| Rate | 17% | |

# Corporation Tax Rates
# 2016 to 2021

| Year Ending: | CT Rate |
|---|---|
| 31-Mar-2016 to | |
| 31-Mar-2017 | 20.000% |
| 30-Apr-2017 | 19.918% |
| 31-May-2017 | 19.833% |
| 30-Jun-2017 | 19.751% |
| 31-Jul-2017 | 19.666% |
| 31-Aug-2017 | 19.581% |
| 30-Sep-2017 | 19.499% |
| 31-Oct-2017 | 19.414% |
| 30-Nov-2017 | 19.332% |
| 31-Dec-2017 | 19.247% |
| 31-Jan-2018 | 19.162% |
| 28-Feb-2018 | 19.085% |
| 31-Mar-2018 to | |
| 31-Mar-2020 | 19.000% |
| 30-Apr-2020 | 18.836% |
| 31-May-2020 | 18.667% |
| 30-Jun-2020 | 18.503% |
| 31-Jul-2020 | 18.333% |
| 31-Aug-2020 | 18.164% |
| 30-Sep-2020 | 18.000% |
| 31-Oct-2020 | 17.831% |
| 30-Nov-2020 | 17.667% |
| 31-Dec-2020 | 17.497% |
| 31-Jan-2021 | 17.328% |
| 28-Feb-2021 | 17.170% |
| 31-Mar-2021 | 17.000% |

# Appendix D

# Connected Persons

The definition of 'connected persons' differs slightly from one area of UK tax law to another. Generally, however, an individual's connected persons include the following:

i) Their husband, wife or civil partner
ii) The following relatives:
  - o  Mother, father or remoter ancestor
  - o  Son, daughter or remoter descendant
  - o  Brother or sister

iii) Relatives under (ii) above of the individual's spouse or civil partner
iv) Spouses or civil partners of the individual's relatives under (ii) above
v) The individual's business partners
vi) Companies under the control of the individual or of any of their relatives under (i) to (iv) above
vii) Trusts where the individual, or any of their relatives under (i) to (iv) above, is a beneficiary

# Retail Prices Index

| | 1982 | 1983 | 1984 | 1985 | 1986 | 1987 | 1988 | 1989 |
|-----|-------|-------|-------|-------|-------|-------|-------|-------|
| Jan | | 82.61 | 86.84 | 91.20 | 96.25 | 100.0 | 103.3 | 111.0 |
| Feb | | 82.97 | 87.20 | 91.94 | 96.60 | 100.4 | 103.7 | 111.8 |
| Mar | 79.44 | 83.12 | 87.48 | 92.80 | 96.73 | 100.6 | 104.1 | 112.3 |
| Apr | 81.04 | 84.28 | 88.64 | 94.78 | 97.67 | 101.8 | 105.8 | 114.3 |
| May | 81.62 | 84.64 | 88.97 | 95.21 | 97.85 | 101.9 | 106.2 | 115.0 |
| Jun | 81.85 | 84.84 | 89.20 | 95.41 | 97.79 | 101.9 | 106.6 | 115.4 |
| Jul | 81.88 | 85.30 | 89.10 | 95.23 | 97.52 | 101.8 | 106.7 | 115.5 |
| Aug | 81.90 | 85.68 | 89.94 | 95.49 | 97.82 | 102.1 | 107.9 | 115.8 |
| Sep | 81.85 | 86.06 | 90.11 | 95.44 | 98.30 | 102.4 | 108.4 | 116.6 |
| Oct | 82.26 | 86.36 | 90.67 | 95.59 | 98.45 | 102.9 | 109.5 | 117.5 |
| Nov | 82.66 | 86.67 | 90.95 | 95.92 | 99.29 | 103.4 | 110.0 | 118.5 |
| Dec | 82.51 | 86.89 | 90.87 | 96.05 | 99.62 | 103.3 | 110.3 | 118.8 |

| | 1990 | 1991 | 1992 | 1993 | 1994 | 1995 | 1996 | 1997 |
|-----|-------|-------|-------|-------|-------|-------|-------|-------|
| Jan | 119.5 | 130.2 | 135.6 | 137.9 | 141.3 | 146.0 | 150.2 | 154.4 |
| Feb | 120.2 | 130.9 | 136.3 | 138.8 | 142.1 | 146.9 | 150.9 | 155.0 |
| Mar | 121.4 | 131.4 | 136.7 | 139.3 | 142.5 | 147.5 | 151.5 | 155.4 |
| Apr | 125.1 | 133.1 | 138.8 | 140.6 | 144.2 | 149.0 | 152.6 | 156.3 |
| May | 126.2 | 133.5 | 139.3 | 141.1 | 144.7 | 149.6 | 152.9 | 156.9 |
| Jun | 126.7 | 134.1 | 139.3 | 141.0 | 144.7 | 149.8 | 153.0 | 157.5 |
| Jul | 126.8 | 133.8 | 138.8 | 140.7 | 144.0 | 149.1 | 152.4 | 157.5 |
| Aug | 128.1 | 134.1 | 138.9 | 141.3 | 144.7 | 149.9 | 153.1 | 158.5 |
| Sep | 129.3 | 134.6 | 139.4 | 141.9 | 145.0 | 150.6 | 153.8 | 159.3 |
| Oct | 130.3 | 135.1 | 139.9 | 141.8 | 145.2 | 149.8 | 153.8 | 159.5 |
| Nov | 130.0 | 135.6 | 139.7 | 141.6 | 145.3 | 149.8 | 153.9 | 159.6 |
| Dec | 129.9 | 135.7 | 139.2 | 141.9 | 146.0 | 150.7 | 154.4 | 160.0 |

| | 1998 | 1999 | 2000 | 2001 | 2002 | 2003 | 2004 | 2005 |
|-----|-------|-------|-------|-------|-------|-------|-------|-------|
| Jan | 159.5 | 163.4 | 166.6 | 171.1 | 173.3 | 178.4 | 183.1 | 188.9 |
| Feb | 160.3 | 163.7 | 167.5 | 172.0 | 173.8 | 179.3 | 183.8 | 189.6 |
| Mar | 160.8 | 164.1 | 168.4 | 172.2 | 174.5 | 179.9 | 184.6 | 190.5 |
| Apr | 162.6 | 165.2 | 170.1 | 173.1 | 175.7 | 181.2 | 185.7 | 191.6 |
| May | 163.5 | 165.6 | 170.7 | 174.2 | 176.2 | 181.5 | 186.5 | 192.0 |
| Jun | 163.4 | 165.6 | 171.1 | 174.4 | 176.2 | 181.3 | 186.8 | 192.2 |
| Jul | 163.0 | 165.1 | 170.5 | 173.3 | 175.9 | 181.3 | 186.8 | 192.2 |
| Aug | 163.7 | 165.5 | 170.5 | 174.0 | 176.4 | 181.6 | 187.4 | 192.6 |
| Sep | 164.4 | 166.2 | 171.7 | 174.6 | 177.6 | 182.5 | 188.1 | 193.1 |
| Oct | 164.5 | 166.5 | 171.6 | 174.3 | 177.9 | 182.6 | 188.6 | 193.3 |
| Nov | 164.4 | 166.7 | 172.1 | 173.6 | 178.2 | 182.7 | 189.0 | 193.6 |
| Dec | 164.4 | 167.3 | 172.2 | 173.4 | 178.5 | 183.5 | 189.9 | 194.1 |

|      | 2006  | 2007  | 2008  | 2009  | 2010  | 2011  | 2012  | 2013  |
|------|-------|-------|-------|-------|-------|-------|-------|-------|
| Jan  | 193.4 | 201.6 | 209.8 | 210.1 | 217.9 | 229.0 | 238.0 | 245.8 |
| Feb  | 194.2 | 203.1 | 211.4 | 211.4 | 219.2 | 231.3 | 239.9 | 247.6 |
| Mar  | 195.0 | 204.4 | 212.1 | 211.3 | 220.7 | 232.5 | 240.8 | 248.7 |
| Apr  | 196.5 | 205.4 | 214.0 | 211.5 | 222.8 | 234.4 | 242.5 | 249.5 |
| May  | 197.7 | 206.2 | 215.1 | 212.8 | 223.6 | 235.2 | 242.4 | 250.0 |
| Jun  | 198.5 | 207.3 | 216.8 | 213.4 | 224.1 | 235.2 | 241.8 | 249.7 |
| Jul  | 198.5 | 206.1 | 216.5 | 213.4 | 223.6 | 234.7 | 242.1 | 249.7 |
| Aug  | 199.2 | 207.3 | 217.2 | 214.4 | 224.5 | 236.1 | 243.0 | 251.0 |
| Sep  | 200.1 | 208.0 | 218.4 | 215.3 | 225.3 | 237.9 | 244.2 | 251.9 |
| Oct  | 200.4 | 208.9 | 217.7 | 216.0 | 225.8 | 238.0 | 245.6 | 251.9 |
| Nov  | 201.1 | 209.7 | 216.0 | 216.6 | 226.8 | 238.5 | 245.6 | 252.1 |
| Dec  | 202.7 | 210.9 | 212.9 | 218.0 | 228.4 | 239.4 | 246.8 | 253.4 |

|      | 2014  | 2015  | 2016  | 2017  |
|------|-------|-------|-------|-------|
| Jan  | 252.6 | 255.4 | 258.8 | 265.5 |
| Feb  | 254.2 | 256.7 | 260.0 | 268.4 |
| Mar  | 254.8 | 257.1 | 261.1 | 269.3 |
| Apr  | 255.7 | 258.0 | 261.4 |       |
| May  | 255.9 | 258.5 | 262.1 |       |
| Jun  | 256.3 | 258.9 | 263.1 |       |
| Jul  | 256.0 | 258.6 | 263.4 |       |
| Aug  | 257.0 | 259.8 | 264.4 |       |
| Sep  | 257.6 | 259.6 | 264.9 |       |
| Oct  | 257.7 | 259.5 | 264.8 |       |
| Nov  | 257.1 | 259.8 | 265.5 |       |
| Dec  | 257.5 | 260.6 | 267.1 |       |

# Short Leases

(See Section 4.10)

Proportion of the original cost of a lease of 50 or more years' duration allowed as a deduction for capital gains purposes on a disposal of that lease.

| Years Remaining | % | Years Remaining | % |
|---|---|---|---|
| 50 | 100 | 25 | 81.100 |
| 49 | 99.657 | 24 | 79.622 |
| 48 | 99.289 | 23 | 78.055 |
| 47 | 98.902 | 22 | 76.399 |
| 46 | 98.490 | 21 | 74.635 |
| 45 | 98.059 | 20 | 72.770 |
| 44 | 97.595 | 19 | 70.791 |
| 43 | 97.107 | 18 | 68.697 |
| 42 | 96.593 | 17 | 66.470 |
| 41 | 96.041 | 16 | 64.116 |
| 40 | 95.457 | 15 | 61.617 |
| 39 | 94.842 | 14 | 58.971 |
| 38 | 94.189 | 13 | 56.167 |
| 37 | 93.497 | 12 | 53.191 |
| 36 | 92.761 | 11 | 50.038 |
| 35 | 91.981 | 10 | 46.695 |
| 34 | 91.156 | 9 | 43.154 |
| 33 | 90.280 | 8 | 39.399 |
| 32 | 89.354 | 7 | 35.414 |
| 31 | 88.371 | 6 | 31.195 |
| 30 | 87.330 | 5 | 26.722 |
| 29 | 86.226 | 4 | 21.983 |
| 28 | 85.053 | 3 | 16.959 |
| 27 | 83.816 | 2 | 11.629 |
| 26 | 82.496 | 1 | 5.983 |

# The European Union &
# The European Economic Area

### The European Union

The 28 member states of the European Union are:

| | |
|---|---|
| Austria | admitted January 1995 |
| Belgium | founding member |
| Bulgaria | admitted January 2007 |
| Croatia | admitted July 2013 |
| Cyprus | admitted May 2004 |
| Czech Republic | admitted May 2004 |
| Denmark | admitted January 1973 |
| Estonia | admitted May 2004 |
| Finland | admitted January 1995 |
| France | founding member |
| Germany | founding member |
| Greece | admitted January 1981 |
| Hungary | admitted May 2004 |
| Irish Republic | admitted January 1973 |
| Italy | founding member |
| Latvia | admitted May 2004 |
| Lithuania | admitted May 2004 |
| Luxembourg | founding member |
| Malta | admitted May 2004 |
| Netherlands | founding member |
| Poland | admitted May 2004 |
| Portugal | admitted January 1986 |
| Romania | admitted January 2007 |
| Slovakia | admitted May 2004 |
| Slovenia | admitted May 2004 |
| Spain | admitted January 1986 |
| Sweden | admitted January 1995 |
| United Kingdom | admitted January 1973 |

The European Economic Area comprises the 28 member states of the European Union plus Iceland, Liechtenstein and Norway.

# Abbreviations Used in this Guide

| | |
|---|---|
| ADS | Additional Dwelling Supplement |
| ATED | Annual Tax on Enveloped Dwellings |
| CGT | Capital Gains Tax |
| CT | Corporation Tax |
| CTSA | Corporation Tax Self Assessment |
| FRSs | Financial Reporting Standards |
| GAAP | Generally Accepted Accounting Principles |
| GAAR | General Anti-Abuse Rule |
| HMRC | HM Revenue and Customs |
| IFRS | International Financial Reporting Standards |
| IHT | Inheritance Tax |
| LBTT | Land and Buildings Transaction Tax |
| LLP | Limited Liability Partnership |
| MTD | Making Tax Digital |
| NI | National Insurance |
| PAYE | Pay As You Earn |
| SDLT | Stamp Duty Land Tax |
| SE | Societas Europaea |
| UK | United Kingdom |
| VAT | Value Added Tax |

Lightning Source UK Ltd.
Milton Keynes UK
UKOW01f0743110517
300967UK00005B/76/P